The Twins players and myself have always trusted
and respected Sid for being the hardest working member
of the Twin Cities media. Sid is always there. We've always
felt comfortable with him, and we never had to worry about
him eavesdropping on a conversation and publishing it or
announcing it on the radio. I am proud to call myself
one of Sid's close personal friends.
—Kirby Puckett

I first met Sid when I was playing in Minneapolis in 1938,
on my way to the big leagues. We were both young men with
big dreams back then. And we both succeeded in fulfilling
those dreams. Sid has quite a story to tell in how he did it.
—Ted Williams

I grew up on Sid Hartman columns about my
Midwestern sports heroes—and I still think of him as a
Hall of Fame newspaperman.
—Tom Brokaw

When Sid starts talking about his friends, you start to
wonder if it's possible that anyone knows this many people.
You know what? He does. The stories here cover one of the
largest clubs in America: Sid's close personal friends.
—Lou Holtz

I've made a number of visits to Minnesota, a great golf state, through the years. I've discovered that you never get too far into a conversation with a Minnesotan without hearing the name "Sid." You never have to ask, "Sid who?" These intriguing tales from the life of a Minnesota legend are long overdue.
—Arnold Palmer

Sid and I have been friends since 1947, when he helped sign me to a contract with the Minneapolis Lakers. I think he is still the best sportswriter in the Twin Cities. If anyone ever had a book to write, it's Sid.
—George Mikan

When you love something, it's easy to keep going. Sid loves sports, and that's why he's still going. Thankfully, he slowed down long enough to write this long overdue book.
—Don Shula

In my days with the Vikings, we played a lot of practical jokes on Sid. He would always say, "Wait until I write my book, Tarkenton. I'll get you then." Finally, Sid has written that book. It was worth the wait.
—Fran Tarkenton

The last few years in the National Hockey League have not been the same . . . without the North Stars in Minnesota, and without Sid sticking a microphone in front of you in the locker room after a game. It's about time the legend of Minnesota's press boxes wrote his book.
—Wayne Gretzky

The New York tabloids spend a lot of time congratulating themselves for digging up information. The truth is, all the New York reporters could take a lesson from my friend Sid Hartman in Minneapolis. Finally, we get the behind-the-scenes look at how Sid came up with all those scoops—real scoops—through the years.
—George Steinbrenner

Sid Hartman has not thrived as a reporter for over five decades by settling for hearsay. Sid talks to the people involved, asks questions, and writes with genuine knowledge. More than anything, this is the story of a great reporter.
—Bob Knight

There is only one sports institution in Minnesota that pre-dates the Vikings and Twins, and that's Sid Hartman. For half a century, Sid has been the lighthouse illuminating the world of sports in the Twin Cities. He is one thing all Minnesota sports fans have in common. The rule of thumb for anyone in sports needing to know what's going on in Minnesota is this: call Sid. His knowledge, contacts, reporting skills, and style have made his column and radio show fixtures on the Minnesota sports scene for decades. He's been a great friend to sports and a best friend to sports fans. His story is the complete story of Minnesota sports in the second half of the twentieth century, and it's a fascinating one. What kind of guy is he? Sid's the type of person that if he called and asked you to join him for chicken dinner at a sports banquet in the basement of a church, you would immediately reach for the airline guide. I know. I did it in 1993.

—NFL Commissioner Paul Tagliabue

Sid is more than a sportswriter. He is a passionate advocate for the Twin Cities and Minnesota. Sid helped build a solid foundation for the NBA as an executive with the Minneapolis Lakers, the Chicago Zephyrs, and the Baltimore Bullets. Today, he remains an ardent chronicler for the home state and all of its teams—the Timberwolves, Twins, Vikings, and Gophers.

—NBA Commissioner David Stern

Sid Hartman and Patrick Reusse. (Photo © Brian Peterson)

Sid!

The Sports Legends,

the Inside Scoops, *and the*

Close Personal Friends

By Sid Hartman
with Patrick Reusse

Forewords by Bud Grant *and* Bob Knight

Voyageur Press

To my mother and father, Celia and Jack Hartman

First published in 1997 by Voyageur Press. This edition published in 2007 by
Voyageur Press, an imprint of MBI Publishing Company LLC, Galtier Plaza,
Suite 200, 380 Jackson Street, St. Paul, MN 55101 USA

The information in this book is true and complete to the best of our knowledge.
All recommendations are made without any guarantee on the part of the author
or Publisher, who also disclaim any liability incurred in connection with the use of
this data or specific details.

We recognize, further, that some words, model names, and designations mentioned
herein are the property of the trademark holder. We use them for identification
purposes only. This is not an official publication.

Voyageur Press titles are also available at discounts in bulk quantity for industrial or
sales-promotional use. For details write to Special Sales Manager at MBI Publishing
Company, Galtier Plaza, Suite 200, 380 Jackson Street, St. Paul, MN 55101 USA.

To find out more about our books, join us online at www.voyageurpress.com.

Library of Congress Cataloging-in-Publication Data

Hartman, Sid, 1920-
 Sid! / By Sid Hartman and Patrick Reusse.
   p. cm.
 Includes index.
 ISBN-13: 978-0-7603-3190-3 (softbound)
 ISBN-10: 0-7603-3190-1 (softbound)
 1. Hartman, Sid, 1920- 2. Sportswriters--Minnesota--Biography. 3.
Sportscasters--Minnesota--Biography. I. Reusse, Patrick. II. Title.
 GV742.42.H37A3 2007
 070.4'40796092--dc22
 [B]

                    2007006356

Printed in the United States of America

Acknowledgments

It was Steve Cannon who coined the term about me and my "close personal friends." This all started when I had a radio show on WCCO called *Sports Hero*, and through my various contacts, I was able to locate people like Muhammad Ali, Joe Frazier, Jack Nicklaus, Arnold Palmer, Joe DiMaggio, Mickey Mantle, Roger Maris, Wayne Gretzky, and many other big names. One thing I learned many years ago from my close personal friend at the Minneapolis *Tribune*, Mark Cox, was that if someone does you a favor and goes out of their way to be interviewed, you show your appreciation by writing a letter of thanks, and I have done this all of my life. This acknowledgments is my letter of thanks to the people who have helped make this book possible.

I want to thank everybody mentioned in this book for being a friend and allowing me to do a job that I love and look forward to doing every single day of the year. I remember my third-grade teacher at Minneapolis's Harrison Grade School at Fifth and Irving who told the class one day, "I wish you guys would quit looking at the clock all the time and not be so anxious to have the school day end. Your ambition in life should be to get a job where the time you spend working is not a factor, one that you enjoy so much that hours you put in don't mean a thing."

I can't help but to think how lucky I was to get downtown at age nine to sell newspapers and get the opportunity to meet Dick Cullum and Charlie Johnson who gave me the chance to be a sports writer.

There have been three editors at the newspaper who have been very important to me: David Silverman, who played a big part in getting me hired at the *Tribune* when the *Star* and *Tribune* merged; and current Publisher Joel Kramer and current Editor Tim McGuire who have tolerated me and provided me with many opportunities.

I also want to thank Larry Haeg and Phil Lewis for giving me the opportunity to do all the pregame shows and other shows on WCCO Radio.

I want to thank Mrs. Julie Michaelson, the Minneapolis Lincoln Junior High English teacher who gave me a chance to write on the *Lincoln Life* school newspaper and got me started on my career.

Thanks to Harvey Mackay for his input and chance to use his know-how and experience in book publishing.

I have always said that Patrick Reusse is as good a columnist as there is in the entire USA, and I can't thank him enough for the great job he did in putting this book together. Without him, it would not have happened.

Thanks also to *Star Tribune* photographer Brian Peterson for all of his photography work on the book.

Finally, thanks to Michael Dregni as well as Dave Hohman, Tom Lebovsky, and all the others at Voyageur Press who have made this book a success.

—Sid Hartman

My thanks to: Judd Zulgad, a sports copy editor at the Minneapolis Star Tribune, who contributed research and suggestions to this book. My wife, Kathleen Dillon, who read the chapters of this book in their raw form, offering many helpful suggestions. I would also like to thank Bernice Shafer, Sid's sister; Al Rubinger, Sid's business partner; and Bud Grant, Sid's longtime friend, for the insights that provided much assistance in writing this book.

—Patrick Reusse

Contents

Bud Grant's Hall of Fame induction, 1993

I had the great honor of presenting Bud Grant at his induction into the Pro Football Hall of Fame in Canton, Ohio. We have been friends since his days as a Gopher football and baseball player, as a Lakers player, coaching Canadian football, and through his years coaching the Minnesota Vikings.

Bud Grant

After graduating from Central High in Superior, Wisconsin, I joined the Navy. I was assigned to the Great Lakes Naval Base in Chicago, where I played football for coach Paul Brown and basketball for coach Weeb Ewbank.

I went to the University of Minnesota after World War II. At the time, Sid Hartman was a young reporter covering the Gophers for the Minneapolis *Times*. Sid was such a presence around Bernie Bierman's postwar football team that the players composed a ditty that went like this: "Bernie loves us, yes we know, 'cause Sid Hartman tells us so." The players would sing that when Sid appeared in the locker room. I don't know what Bierman thought, but we had fun with it.

Sid was a young reporter, and most of us were older college athletes because we had been in the service. The age difference was not great, and Sid was more a friend to the players than he was a reporter.

Sid became one of my closest friends at that time and that has not changed. As an athlete, a coach, and a friend, I have observed the man doing his job for more than fifty years. Several times during our lives, I have said, "Sid, do you want to triple your salary at the newspaper?"

He would look at me quizzically and say, "Sure."

I would tell him, "Then, you have to quit your job. Once you do that, the editors will call you in and say, 'We can't lose you, Sid. What do we have to do to keep you?' That's when you say, 'The only way I'm coming back is if you triple my salary.' The newspaper would have no choice but to agree because it has to have you. The editors know that."

Sid would look at me like I was crazy and say, "I can't do that."

Most of us who were young men going to college and playing sports in the 1940s have gone through our working lives and are retired. We are hunting and fishing, or we have moved to Arizona to play golf. And that's why it's amazing that Sid's presence is greater than ever in the Twin Cities, in Minnesota, and in the Upper Midwest. His column is still the first thing people turn to four days a week in the *Star Tribune*. His standing as a radio personality is greater than ever. And now you see him on television all the time.

I don't know how a book about Sid Hartman could be written. If you start all the way back when he was a nine-year-old kid delivering newspapers and go to the present day, the life story of Sid would contain more volumes than the Winston Churchill memoirs.

A remarkable fact about Sid is that he has gotten where he is without much support. He did not inherit anything. He was not handed anything. He had a serious relationship with a woman when he was in his late thirties and it ended tragically with her death. It was a difficult portion of Sid's life.

When Sid did get married, it was only for several years. It has only been in recent times that Sid has had a family circle for support. That family includes his two kids, Chris and Chad, Chad's wife, Kathleen, and four grandkids. When he was climbing the ladder of success, Sid was on his own.

I really haven't seen that many changes in Sid in our decades of friendship. That's what happens when you grow up with somebody. They never age and you never age. You have a background of experiences that make you ageless to one another. To this day, the conversation, the banter, is similar to what it was when I was an athlete at Minnesota and we were going out to dinner after I was finished with football or basketball practice.

If there has been a change, it is that in the forties and fifties, Sid did not have varied interests. He had the newspaper, the Gophers, and his involvement with the Minneapolis Lakers. Now, he is involved in everything—newspaper, radio, television, all the professional teams, business, family.

For many years, Sid's column was strictly notes. Little opinion would make its way into the column. I was privy to his opinions from seeing him every day, and he would express those opinions forcefully at dinner, when he came into my Vikings office, when we talked on the phone.

Now, the whole world is privy to Sid's opinions. He puts more of those opinions in his newspaper column. A huge number of people hear those opinions daily on radio and television. Sid hasn't really changed; it's just that the audience for his opinions has increased from his close personal friends to most everyone who reads a newspaper or turns on a radio or television.

All of us are interested in promoting our friends and in promoting what we think is best for the area of the country where we live. Most people are reserved about it. They prefer to work behind the scenes to promote the things that are important to their friends and community. Even if we are public with our opinions, there is a tendency to express those things quietly—to attempt to sway the other side through rational discussion.

Not Sid. His opinions are strong and so are his emotions. He is a town crier. He shouts from the roof tops. He is brash and boisterous and, invariably, that will offend people. Sid's motive is not to be nasty. He expresses his opinions so emphatically out of a sense that he is doing right, out of a sense of loyalty to his friends, to his cause, to his university.

There is no better example of Sid's loyalty than his love for the University of Minnesota. His formal education ended when he dropped out of Minneapolis's North High as a junior, but Minnesota is still Sid's university. No one wants that university to be great more than Sid.

And it is not just sports. It sickened Sid when the university fired Dr. John Najarian as its chief of surgery. It sickened Sid when the university—and his newspaper, the *Star Tribune*—dragged Dr. Najarian, a man he has looked at as a hero, a saver of lives, through the mud.

I coached the Vikings for eighteen seasons. Jerry Burns, another of Sid's closest friends, coached the Vikings for six seasons. I know that Sid lived and died with our teams—partly because he wants every Minnesota team to win, but more because the success and well-being of friends and family are the two most important things in the world to Sid.

As strong as that attachment has been to the Vikings, the source of unquestioned loyalty and eternal hope for Sid is Gophers football. He celebrated when the Twins won two World Series. He suffered with our Super Bowl losses. Yet nothing would cause more celebration with Sid than a return to the Rose Bowl or a national championship for the Gophers, and nothing on his sports beat has caused more suffering with Sid than the university's long struggle to re-establish a winning football program.

Every coach the Gophers have brought in was sure to be the person to get the job done. Cal Stoll. Joe Salem. Lou Holtz. John Gutekunst. Jim Wacker. Sid believed fully in all of them, that they would take the team to the top. And now Sid is 100 percent sure that Glen Mason, hired before the 1997 season, is going to be the man to do it. I hope Mason is the person who will take the Gophers back to the Rose Bowl—not so much because I'm an old Gopher, but because of the reward it would be to my friend Sid after all the years of faith and suffering.

Coming on as strong as he does with his opinions is also an example of Sid's competitiveness. That word is used in sports more than in any endeavor. That is because competitiveness manifests itself so clearly on an athletic field. Most people do not have an outlet to display their competitiveness as do athletes and coaches.

The truth is, after all my years of being involved with athletes, I believe Sid might have as competitive a nature as anyone I have met. There is no doubt if Sid had the body and the coordination, he would have been one of the all-time greats as an athlete. Sid did not have those things. All he had was the nature—and heart—of a competitor. And he took that with him to the newspaper business.

After I would finish basketball practice at the university or with the Lakers, Sid would wait around and we would go out to dinner. By the time that was over, it would be 9:30 or 10 P.M. We then would have to drive to the newspaper and get an early edition. His eyes would race through the sports section to make sure no one had scooped him on a story or a note. Sid did not want to be scooped, even if it was by a reporter from his own paper.

Sid had the toughest job of anyone at the paper. Other sportswriters could get one topic, one idea, and turn it into that day's column or that day's article. Sid did not have that ability. Sid was not a writer—he was a reporter, a collector of information. Every day, he had to come up with fifteen or twenty stories, not just one.

Sid's goal has not changed from the first day I met him: Every time he writes a column, he wants to have something in there that nobody else has. And when someone else has a scoop or a story, he is devastated. Sid reacts to that the same way a great coach or great athlete reacts to defeat. That's why I describe Sid as one of the top competitors I have known.

Relaxation has always been something that Sid can only take in limited doses. When I was at the university, Sid got to know my folks well. Sid and my dad, Harry, became buddies. If Sid and I both had a day off, we would often drive to Superior to see my folks. For Sid, that trip was a lot of fun. But it was only fun for a limited time. After a few hours, Sid would start getting nervous that something might be going on in the Twin Cities—that another reporter might be getting a scoop—and we would have to get back, usually the same night.

A number of years ago, Sid bought a house on the St. Croix River. This was perfect for Sid: A place to relax that was conveniently located so he could get back to town and be involved in the turmoil of the sports scene the next morning.

Sid bought the house to enjoy. It became a passion for him. Rather than relaxing, Sid undertook constant improvements—adding rooms, remodeling, building a crow's nest that would give him a better view of the river than any of his neighbors. Sid's relaxation home has become non-stop haggling—haggling with the groundskeepers, haggling with the contractors, haggling with local government over ordinances. Sid could not stand the idea of being out there with nothing to do but relax. The fact that he has had to haggle to get this showplace on the river is what gives Sid the satisfaction in having it. When he gets sports, political, and community leaders out there for one of his famous summer parties, Sid always wants to have a new room, a new something, to show them.

I have spent a lot of time with Sid in cars, on those rides to Superior, driving around the Twin Cities. It has been an amazing experience. I don't think Sid has any idea how these machines work. He knows that they require gas, but I doubt he knows why.

We were in Superior on New Year's Eve many years ago. At Sid's insistence, we started back to the Twin Cities after midnight. The freeway was not yet through to Duluth, so we were on the old highway, skirting Moose Lake, Askov, and all those small towns. It was 2 A.M. and there was not another car on the road. And then we had a flat tire. It was 15 or 20 below that night. Sid went into an absolute panic. He was certain we were going to die—that our bodies would be found frozen the next morning.

I said, "This is not a problem, Sid. I can change a flat tire."

We opened the trunk. Of course, there was no spare. Sid had loaned his car to a friend who had a flat, used the spare, and neglected to tell Sid to get another one. Either that, or the friend told him and Sid did not know what he was talking about.

Sid was in a real panic now. He saw a light in the distance and started charging toward it. He stepped into a snow-covered ditch and was up to his arms in snow.

There was a small town off on a side road. We walked to the town. It was 3 A.M. and there was no sign of life. We found the town cop and he took us to the house where the service station owner lived. He was not going to get up. Finally, Sid had to give the guy $100 to come out and change the tire.

More than anything, that's what Sid remembers about the story—the guy holding him up for the 100 bucks. That was one haggle Sid lost.

An amazing number of people in the sports business—the biggest names in baseball, football, basketball, and hockey over the past fifty years—share a loyal friendship with Sid. It's a phenomenon, really, because sportswriters and coaches and athletes are rivals in many ways. A reporter's job is to try to find out things that, often, you do not necessarily want the reporter to know.

No sportswriter in history has broken as many big stories in his lifetime as Sid Hartman. Yet Sid never broke one of those stories after giving someone his word that it was off the record. Many reporters will be told something off the record, report it anyway, and then offer the excuse to the source: "Well, I heard it from someone else."

Coaches, athletes, and team officials see through that. They soon discover if a reporter can be trusted. Sid always could be trusted. If you said to him, "This is off the record," there were no games played. With Sid, it was always important to know what was going to happen, even if he knew he could not write it.

When I'm with other sports people, the conversation often turns to Sid. I've asked people, "I know why I'm close to Sid. We go back to 1946 at the University of Minnesota. Why do you have a friendship with Sid?"

The answer is always the same: Integrity. They all know that, even though getting the story is more important to Sid than to any reporter in the country, it is not important enough to betray a friend.

In 1993, I was voted into the Pro Football Hall of Fame in Canton, Ohio. It was not something I was counting on, but it was appreciated. One ritual at the Hall of Fame is to have a "presenter" to make a short speech to introduce the individual being inducted. The inductee then follows with his speech. The ceremony takes place on the front steps of the Hall of Fame museum on a Saturday in the middle of summer.

Sid called one day to ask who would be presenting me at the Hall of Fame. There was no ulterior motive in this call, other than he wanted to get the note in his column first.

Sid asked and I said, "It's going to be you, Sid."

He said, "Seriously, who is it going to be?"

And when I said, "You, Sid," there was a pause.

He said, "That would be nice. But you don't have to do that, Bud."

You never know if an honor is going to come. But if it did, I knew Sid was going to be the presenter. All along, I told my wife, Pat, that Sid would be the guy. She was the only one I mentioned it to, because you don't talk about something like the Hall of Fame before it happens.

Sid was concerned. He was nervous that the speech might not contain all that he wanted it to contain. He wanted to make mention of Jim Finks, our mutual friend from the Vikings, who had died from lung cancer.

I thought Sid did a good job. That was the most important thing to him, although not to me. I chose Sid because of a lifetime friendship and respect. And I chose Sid because I knew he would enjoy being part of that weekend—being around all those people, riding in the convertible with us during the parade—more than anyone else who had been important in my life.

I enjoyed that weekend immensely. My family was there, obviously. My kids have all grown up with Sid around. For the Grant family, it was important to have Sid there. I enjoyed that weekend as much for the happiness I saw in Sid as I enjoyed it for myself.

Bob Knight

When I think of Sid Hartman, there are two distinct impressions: First, Sid as a news reporter, and second, Sid as a friend and a person I've known for a long time.

In sports, we always use the term "professional" to describe somebody who has ascended to the top of a particular sport—he's a professional ballplayer, she's a professional golfer. This indicates that an athlete has risen above the vast majority of people who take part in a particular sport, somebody who has risen considerably above the norm.

If you apply that word to sports reporting, there are only a handful of sports writers in history who could be thought of as professionals. Sid Hartman is one. There is nobody I've known in the thirtysome years that I've been involved with college basketball who has worked harder, put in more effort, and has been more concerned about bringing sports news to his community than Sid.

Sid's coverage of sports for the Minneapolis community has involved a wider range of events to discuss and analyze than any sportswriter in the country. What has impressed me the most about Sid and his ability to report on so many different sports has been the honesty, integrity, and concern that he has shown to the people that he is discussing, analyzing, or interviewing.

Sid is able to pick up the telephone and call more people in sports than any writer in the country. The reason is simple: Any sports figure who has dealt with Sid looks on him as being the epitome of honesty and accuracy in a field where those two ingredients are not particularly prevalent. I know Sid to be able to get ahold of people from Vince Lombardi to Roger Maris when they would not accept calls from anyone else. This to me is the greatest example of the way the sports world feels about the man.

By dealing with people in such a professional manner, Sid has been able to provide more information to readers of one of his columns or listeners to a thirty-minute radio show than most sports reporters can provide in a month.

That is the type of professional relationship I have with Sid as a sports reporter—one based on honesty and accuracy.

Sid's concern for others shows up in our personal friendship. He has given much of his time, effort, and money to help people in and out of the sports world.

It has been a special privilege to have Sid Hartman as a friend for most of my career as a college basketball coach. His concern in difficult times over the years has been something that I have appreciated greatly. No one I have known—in or out of sports—understands the meaning of friendship more than Sid.

The people of Minnesota have been extremely fortunate in having a man like Sid in the forefront of sports reporting in their state for more than fifty years. Sid has always felt that his main responsibility has been to provide readers and listeners with an honest and accurate accounting of what is going on in the world of sports.

I'm much more fortunate than Sid's readers and listeners because, for over thirty of those years, I've had him as a friend. The friendship we have maintained is all the more remarkable because of Sid's chosen field of endeavor.

Patrick Reusse

My father, Richard Reusse, was both the undertaker and a booster of town-team baseball in Fulda, Minnesota. Through the baseball hobby, Richard was able to meet Ted Peterson, the grand gentleman who covered outstate Minnesota sports—high schools and amateur baseball—for the Minneapolis *Tribune*.

Years passed, and late in the summer of 1963, Richard was able to use his familiarity with Ted to get me a job as a copy boy in the sports department. I started by answering phones on the nights of heavy high school action and soon was working three or four nights per week. I still was able to find those two hours per week to dedicate to studying for freshman classes at the University of Minnesota. It was a young man's beer-drinking time that was being reduced by this increased workload.

Sid Hartman was the boss of the *Tribune* sports department. His column—"Hartman's Roundup"—would appear six mornings per week, and yet he had time to serve as sports editor on a hands-on, daily basis. Sid would do this by making his reporting rounds during the day, then entering the *Tribune* newsroom as would a tornado at around 4:30 P.M. every day. Sid would consult with either Louie Greene or Bob Sorenson, the people who ran the sports copy desk and made up the paper, and decide what would be in the next morning's *Tribune* and how it would be displayed.

The fact he was involved in this whirlwind existence—reporting, writing a column, running the department, doing the coaches shows and other duties for WCCO Radio—did not prevent Sid from monitoring the work habits of the most lowly mammals in the newsroom, the copy boys.

I was scheduled to work on a Sunday in the summer of '64. The morning broke blue and warm, and the lure of this beautiful day became too strong to resist. On summer days such as this, the raucous youth of Prior Lake would invariably get custody of a keg of beer, take it to the pasture of a tolerant area farmer, then spend several hours slurping tepid, sudsy brew and talking smart.

Such a pasture party was scheduled on this beautiful Sunday, and I made the only decision that seemed logical to a nineteen-year-old: I called the *Tribune* early in the afternoon, leaving a message that I was sick and would not be able to report for my shift that was scheduled to start at 5 P.M.

A couple of hours later, the farmer and owner of the pasture where the beer drinking was taking place came driving up the dirt road. He stopped near the keg and said: "Is Pat Reusse here?"

Figuring a calamity might have occurred in my immediate family, I confessed to being there. "Sid Hartman wants you to call him at the *Tribune* sports department," the farmer said. "And he also is going to call me back, to verify that you have received this message."

I reported for work within fifteen minutes of my scheduled starting time. I never again called in sick—not even if I was sick—during my remaining months as a *Tribune* copy boy. And, from the spectacular summer day in 1964 when the farmer's vehicle came charging up the path in a cloud of dust, I have never doubted Mr. Hartman when he says: "I can find anyone on the telephone. If I don't know where someone is, I know someone who will know where he is."

Getting sources on the phone—digging up information, getting the story—was always a quality more admired by Sid than the ability to write grand prose. During my copy-boy days, Sid hired a young fellow named Ira Berkow fresh from journalism school. Berkow was such a great admirer of Walter W. ("Red") Smith, the wordsmith of New York sportswriting, that later in life he wrote an autobiography of Red. Berkow is now a sports columnist at the *New York Times* and is known for writing wonderful tales, rich with descriptive phrases and human drama. But he was just a kid when he arrived at the

Minneapolis *Tribune*, working on the sports desk, covering high school games, being told by Sid to forget all those flowery paragraphs at the top of his stories and to get to the point.

Berkow had occasion to cover a game in which a team kept making comeback after comeback, only to fall short. Berkow's story compared the losing team's effort to Sisyphus's attempt to push a heavy stone up a slope. Sid saw that lead and bellowed across the newsroom: "Sisyphus? Who is he writing about now? I never heard of Sisyphus. What team does he play for?"

Berkow kept going to Sid and complaining about the lack of opportunity he was being given to write truly inspiring sports stories. Finally, Sid decided to give the kid a break. He stretched the *Tribune*'s sports travel budget and sent Berkow to Louisville for the Kentucky Derby.

This was the mid-sixties, when out-of-town copy still was transmitted directly to the sports desk by Western Union machines. The transmitting operator would bang the key that sounded like a bell jangling a few times to let the people in a newsroom know that a story was starting. Sid had been waiting nervously to see what young Berkow was going to transmit on his first day in Louisville—spending all that *Tribune* money, twenty-five bucks for a hotel, six bucks for dinner, a few bucks for cabs, as he was.

The Western Union machine jangled and Sid raced across the room. As it turned out, Berkow had gone to see the famous race horse Citation, retired at a thoroughbred farm in the rolling hills of Kentucky. Not only did Berkow see Citation, but he had engaged in a mythical conversation with the great, four-legged champion.

Sid watched as the story came in, line by line. First, he looked puzzled. Then, he turned ashen, as the realization of what Berkow had done with this first great opportunity to write, struck him.

"I knew this was a terrible mistake," Sid said. "The son of a bitch interviewed a horse."

At age twenty, I ended a faltering academic career at the university and went off to try my hand at creating prose as a sportswriter for the *Duluth News Tribune*. I went from there to the *St. Cloud Times*, then landed at the *St. Paul Pioneer Press* in September 1968. After nearly twenty years in that wonderfully chaotic, underdog newsroom, I returned to the *Tribune*—by then, *Star Tribune*: Newspaper of the Twin Cities—in June 1988.

This has been the surprise: Basically, my relationship with Sid was not much different during those two decades working for the across-the-river rival than it has been since returning to the newspaper of my youth.

Five times per month when I was writing in St. Paul, Sid would say, "Patrick, I love you, but you are 100 percent wrong on this." And, five times per month since I have been back in Minneapolis, Sid has said, "Patrick, I love you, but you are 100 percent wrong on this."

We have had some lively battles. I was an opponent of building the Metrodome, although not nearly as vociferous in print about it as was Joe Soucheray, then Sid's fellow sports columnist in Minneapolis. And, I took to calling Lou Holtz, Sid's man if there ever was one, the "Music Man" in print during Lou's tenure at Minnesota.

Sid's presence on issues such as the Dome and Coach Holtz was so high profile that he gained an identity in my St. Paul sports column as "the Minneapolis media celebrity."

Sid commented with full-blown platitudes on Holtz, Billy Martin, Bob Knight, George Steinbrenner, Fran Tarkenton, Carl Pohlad. I took printed shots at all of them.

And yet, as we hardly agreed on an issue or on the character of a sports personality, there was a friendship—Sid's based on the fact he had started me in the business and felt somewhat fatherly about my career, and mine based on our shared love for the newspaper business.

I was employed in St. Paul when Sid first mentioned that, some day, we would work together on "his book." A year would pass and the book would be discussed again, but always in the abstract. Finally, in the summer of '96, we got to it.

One motive for being involved in this project was to find the answer to a fascinating question: What drives this man?

Sid started off at age nine selling newspapers at two cents apiece. Through a real-estate partnership with lifelong friend Al Rubinger, Sid is now financially secure. His wealth is an issue Sid does not choose to discuss at length, even for his autobiography.

But it is intriguing in this sense: He is a man in his seventies, a man who has been busting his hump since the Depression, a man who has secured his financial future, a man who has meant enough to be a one-name celebrity—"Sid"—in his home state, and yet there remains insecurity.

Sid still needs to know the story first. As Bud Grant points out in his insightful foreword to this autobiography, Sid needs to have known it first, even if he is unable to print it because the source gave him the information "off the record."

Ninety-nine percent of us would be living somewhere warm, watching the blue-green water of the Atlantic slap across white sand, if we had worked as hard, done as well in our occupations, done as well in our financial lives.

Not Sid.

Relaxation such as that could never be an option for Sid. He lives life on a treadmill. The treadmill will spin for Sid as long as there are friends and causes to fight for. There is also an ego to be fed—an ego the existence of which Sid chooses to deny. More than anything, there is the drumbeat of the news business that still fills Sid's soul.

Soucheray, my friend, radio partner, and Sid's former colleague, has said the goal with this autobiography should be to solve the ulti-mate paradox of Mr. Hartman's career: Sid comes from a background that made him the ultimate underdog, yet rarely has he sided with an underdog.

According to Sid, Carl Pohlad, the billionaire Twins owner, deserves to have his ballpark paid for by the public. According to Sid, Norm Green, the Canadian dandy who owned the North Stars, should have been handed developmental rights to public land in Bloomington.

Always, Sid, the ultimate working stiff growing up in north Min-neapolis, seems to align himself with the powerful over the working stiff. Why, Sid?

You will be lucky to get more than a shrug out of Sid when you ask a question that would require so much introspection. The pace at which Sid has attacked his life has been far too hectic to permit moments of self-analysis.

Besides, Sid will say, the NHL was a good thing for Minnesota, major league baseball is a critical thing for Minnesota. Sid merely is trying to get the politicians and the public to do what is best for Minnesota. Save hockey. Save baseball. Not permit the Twin Cities to become a "cold Omaha."

Take all the shots you want at Sid, but there can be no question of his affection for this frozen wasteland that he has called home for an entire life.

The Gophers, the Vikings, the Twins, the Timberwolves, the Dome, the Ordway, the Mayo Clinic, Dr. John Najarian, Northwest Airlines . . . Sid roots for, lobbies for and, if necessary, shouts for all things Minnesotan.

After sixty-three years on the sports pages of a Minneapolis newspaper, after fifty years of that self-admitted "terrible" voice on 'CCO, maybe we should ignore the paradoxes—soft-pedal those differences of opinion we have with Sid —and enjoy this:

Another amazing character, a uniquely Minnesota treasure, has traveled through our time. Hubert. Halsey. Calvin. Bud. Kirby. Sid. First-name celebrities. They have belonged to our generations. They have belonged to Minnesotans and no one else.

Without Sid, would Minnesota have had anyone to get on the most highly rated Sunday radio show in the United States and lament the lung cancer of his friend, Jim Finks, by saying, "He smokes like a fish"?

I think not.

After all these decades, Sid still leaves debris in his path as he rumbles into the *Star Tribune* newsroom at 4:30 P.M. He still will notice the obituary writer and shout, "Mr. Mortuary. I'll bet you are working hard again today." He still will notice a Chicago Bears fan and shout, "George Halas, Jr."

You will hear grumbling from Sid's coworkers in the sports department. You will hear grumbling from every corner of this newsroom—a place that now employs more than 300 people. Many of these 300-plus will question whether we still need Sid.

And then this happens:

The University of Minnesota, in the process of selecting a new president, cuts the list to three finalists. The editors want the names for the next morning's *Star Tribune*. The education reporters and political reporters—the combined reporting forces of this massive newsroom—cannot come up with the names.

What are the editors going to do now? They are going to do exactly what newspaper editors in Minneapolis have been doing for more than five decades. They are going to find Sid Hartman and ask for help.

Fifteen minutes later, the editors have the three names.

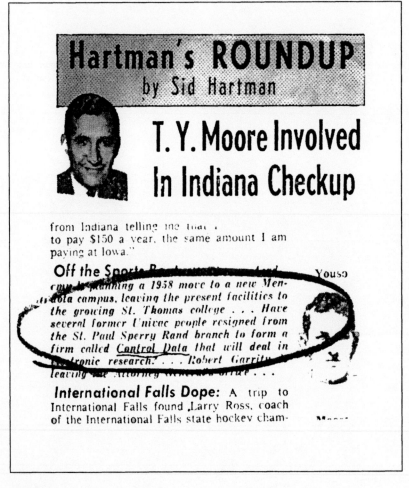

Hartman's ROUNDUP
by Sid Hartman

T. Y. Moore Involved In Indiana Checkup

from Indiana telling me that to pay $150 a year, the same amount I am paying at Iowa."

Off the Sports Youso

planning a 1958 move to a new Mendota campus, leaving the present facilities to the growing St. Thomas college . . . Have several former Univac people resigned from the St. Paul Sperry Rand branch to form a firm called *Control Data* that will deal in electronic research." . . . Robert Garrity leaving the Attorney General's office . . .

International Falls Dope: A trip to International Falls found Larry Ross, coach of the International Falls state hockey cham-

Moore

Scoop!
On July 30, 1957, my column in the Minneapolis Tribune *reported on a scoop I wasn't supposed to get as it was outside of my sports beat. I noted that several former Univac people were leaving the St. Paul Sperry Rand branch to form a new company to be called Control Data.*

Chapter 1

Getting the Scoop

Dick Cullum loved to write. As the sports editor and columnist at the Minneapolis *Times*, he was the best writer we had in the Twin Cities in the old days. He was probably the best writer we've had, period. Cullum would only go to the things he liked. He wouldn't go to a basketball game to save his life. Boxing. Football. That was it for him.

Cullum was mostly a positive writer, although he could cut a guy up and make him laugh at the same time. The Minneapolis Millers were the Triple A farm club for the New York Giants. One summer, the Giants had recalled all of the Millers' good players and left Minneapolis with nothing. Cullum was upset at the Giants. The owner, Horace Stoneham, happened to be visiting Minneapolis, along with Carl Hubbell and Dutch Reuther, his two guys in charge of the minor leagues. Cullum referred to the three of them being at the Millers game the previous night, writing the game had been observed by "a wink, a blink and a nod." That was about as mean as Cullum would get.

By his admission, Cullum was a terrible reporter. He didn't care. He had me.

Cullum was my first boss in a sports department. He couldn't report. I couldn't write. I knew it and Cullum knew it. I would go to him and say: "Dick, I appreciate the opportunity, but I don't know if I want to stay here. I'm not a writer. I'm not capable of working on the desk. My spelling is bad and my grammar is worse."

Cullum would say, "Don't worry about writing. Give us the news. Writers are a dime a dozen. Reporters are impossible to find."

When I started for Cullum at the Minneapolis *Times* in 1944, most of the sportswriters in town were sitting on their rear ends. They would write something off the top of their heads or something the coaches fed them.

I started hanging around at the University of Minnesota every day, getting news, getting notes, breaking stories. Not to blow smoke, but a lot of other guys had to wake up and start covering their beats because of me.

Cullum got the biggest kick out of it. He would brag to the *Times* editors and people from the other newspapers about the way I worked. He always said, "This kid has the greatest 'legs' of any reporter I've seen."

Cullum always told people that the only reason I started writing a column was because he was stuck in a snowstorm. "I was snowed in one morning and couldn't get to the office," Cullum would say. "The *Times* came out that afternoon and there was Sid Hartman's column."

That might not be the whole truth, but it's a good story, so we might as well stick with it.

At one time I was covering the Gophers, writing my column in the Minneapolis *Tribune* seven days a week, and operating as the behind-the-scenes general manager for the Minneapolis Lakers.

We now have six sports editors—yes, six—running the *Star Tribune* sports department. There was a period of more than ten years when I ran the *Tribune* sports department and also wrote a column six or seven days a week.

Work has never scared me. All it takes is a great pair of legs and a lot of contacts.

During the forties and fifties, most of my time was spent at the university. Gophers football was No. 1. There was no No. 2. The situation became more complicated in 1961, when we became a true big league area. We had the Twins, the Vikings, and then the North Stars, to go with the Gophers. Now, we have the Wild and we have the Timberwolves, so there are now five big-time outfits to check on every day.

I'm a great believer that you can't do everything on the telephone. If you get around and see the main people on the sports scene all the time, you're going to get the stories. I call it "making the rounds."

IM A CLOSE PERSONAL FRIEND OF SID HARTMAN

Every day my routine has been to go to the team offices and go to the practices. Then, I go back to the newspaper and start making calls. I have the phone numbers of more important sports people than anyone in the country. One reason for this is that I am always fair with people and write letters of thanks to them after we've had a phone conversation or an in-person interview. I've always written letters—to anyone who did something to help me out on a story, anyone I met for the first time, and people I know who had a celebration or a sad event in their lives.

I've had a long relationship with football coach Dan Devine going back to his days when he lived in Duluth. The relationship with Devine allowed me to get what was my most infamous scoop—first for the ridicule it received, then for the attention it received when it turned out to be a huge national story.

I stayed in close contact with Devine when he coached at Arizona State and Missouri. When he was at "Mizzou," his teams played the Gophers regularly, and they were big games.

Devine originally wanted to go from Mizzou to the St. Louis Cardinals. He asked me to call NFL Commissioner Pete Rozelle to ask what he thought about the possibility of the Cardinals hiring Devine.

Rozelle said, "Tell Devine the Cardinals are having enough trouble drawing people. The last thing they should do is hire away a popular coach from Missouri."

Devine still wanted to go to the NFL. The Packers fired Phil Bengtson after the 1970 season. Devine called and said, "Who do you know in Green Bay?"

I called Tony Canadeo, a former great player and then a broadcaster. He was on the board of directors. Canadeo thought hiring Devine would be a good move. He told me to call Packers President Dominic Olejniczak. Olejniczak got all excited, and the Packers brought in Devine for an interview.

Devine told the Packers, "I think I want the job, but I have to go back home and think about it."

Devine went back to Missouri, and the Packers didn't hear from him for a week. Finally, Olejniczak called me and asked, "What's going on with your man? We have to hire a coach here."

I called Joy Devine, and she said her husband was in Kansas City. "He's making a speech and doing a lot of praying," she said. "He doesn't know whether to take the job or not."

I tracked down Devine and said, "Forget praying and make up your mind. You have to get off the pot on this deal, Dan. Do you want this job or don't you?"

Devine paused for a few seconds, then said, "I just decided. I want it." So he called Olejniczak from the hotel room in Kansas City and got the job.

Green Bay didn't turn out for him. He was there from 1971 through 1974 and his record was 25-28-4. The Green Bay people were still hung up on Lombardi and that Titletown USA stuff, so Devine was getting severe heat at the end of the 1974 season. Some genius Packers fans even shot his dog.

I was in Minnesota on a Saturday afternoon, writing a column for the Sunday *Tribune*. If I didn't have anything great, I would keep making calls, looking for some news—some "dope," as Cullum used to call it—that would give the readers something to talk about when they picked up the *Tribune* the next morning.

The Vikings were playing in Kansas City in the last regular-season game. It was not an important game, because the Vikings had another Central Division title wrapped up. So, I didn't make the trip.

I called Devine to see how things were going in Green Bay. I was looking for a note or a quote, not a great story. But Devine said, "Off the record, don't quote me, but I'm going to be coaching at Notre Dame."

Ara Parseghian still was coaching at Notre Dame. He was the biggest name in college football, along with Bear Bryant at Alabama. And Parseghian's team was going to be playing Bryant's team in the Orange Bowl in a couple of weeks. Ara was fifty years old. It did not make any sense that he would be leaving Notre Dame, but if Devine was saying this, I knew it was the gospel.

I went crazy knowing I had this story, but I didn't want to scare off Dan. So I calmly said, "What's happening at Notre Dame?"

Devine said, "Ara is quitting. Father [Edmund] Joyce was in Green Bay this week. I've agreed to replace Parseghian, but they want to wait and announce it next week."

I knew Father Joyce and Father Theodore Hesburgh well. They ran Notre Dame. They were the greatest administrators a school ever had. Father Joyce loved Devine. He tried to hire him when Devine was at Missouri, but Dan turned him down that time. Now, with Ara retiring, Father Joyce had another chance. He went to Green Bay and made the deal with Devine.

If I was going to write this in Sunday's *Tribune*, Devine did not want it to be traced to him in any way. He said, "You can write that Parseghian is probably going to quit, but you can't mention me as the replacement."

I didn't know whether to splash it across the front sports page—"Parseghian expected to quit"—or to go with it as a column lead. For Devine's sake, I decided to go with the softer approach. On December 15, 1974, my column lead was: "It's a good bet that the Orange Bowl against Alabama will be the last game Ara Parseghian coaches at Notre Dame." I suggested a couple of pro jobs that might interest Parseghian—the Baltimore Colts and the Chicago Bears—and then added: "It is also possible Parseghian may quit coaching."

The way it works in the newspaper business is if you see something and think it's accurate, you use it yourself. If you don't think it's accurate, then you give the other reporter credit. There was a Chicago sportswriter in town, covering a basketball game at Williams Arena. He saw our early edition and called his office. The story on Sunday morning in Chicago was: "According to Minneapolis *Tribune* columnist Sid Hartman, Ara Parseghian is expected to coach his last game for Notre Dame in the Orange Bowl."

The Chicago media also had denials from Father Joyce and Parseghian. I don't know why they chose to deny it, but I wasn't worried. I had as solid a source as you can get—the next coach, Devine.

Notre Dame football is big everywhere, and especially in Chicago. I had reporters from the Chicago papers calling me on Sunday morning to say what a dumb ass I was for writing that Parseghian was going to retire at the peak of his career.

Then, later that day, Notre Dame made the announcement that Parseghian would step down as the Irish coach after the Orange Bowl. Nothing was said about Devine being the replacement. Parseghian still was trying to talk Notre Dame into hiring someone from his staff as the replacement.

I called Devine on Sunday to check when the announcement on him going to Notre Dame would be made. Devine said he would be in South Bend the next day for a press conference. That was my story in Monday's *Tribune*—another Notre Dame scoop, this time that Devine would be named coach. As soon as I got home Sunday night, there was a call from Devine.

"You better not write that I'm going to get the job Monday," he said. "Father Joyce is mad and embarrassed by your Ara story. If you write I'm getting the job, he might decide I was the source and tell me to take a walk."

I drove back to the paper to make sure they took out the Devine story. My reasoning was, with Devine there, I was going to have a fantastic contact at Notre Dame. But if I ran the story and Father Joyce got so mad he changed his mind on Devine, I would be stuck with a bum scoop and would have lost a good friend in the process. It wasn't worth going with the story.

Going to Notre Dame turned Devine's stomach into a giant ulcer. He had gone from the toughest job in pro football, being the second coach to follow Vince Lombardi in Green Bay, to the toughest job in the world, being the football coach at Notre Dame.

"I Sat in Sid's Section," 1996
The Minneapolis Star Tribune *sponsors an annual "Sit With Sid" day at a Minnesota Twins game. Here was our section during the 1996 game.*

After a few years, Devine wasn't feeling well, nor was his wife. He went to the Mayo Clinic in Rochester for an examination. I bumped into the doctor a week later and asked him, "What's wrong with Devine?"

The doctor said, "I can't give you any details, but Devine has a rare disease."

"What's that?"

"Notre Dame–itis," the doctor said.

Parseghian had it. Frank Leahy had it before him. Devine had it after him. Gerry Faust suffered from it. My friend Lou Holtz battled it for eleven years before resigning near the end of the 1996 season. There is pressure in most any coaching job. There is only one job that can give a coach Notre Dame–itis.

After he went to the Mayo Clinic, Devine was talking to another friend, a Detroit TV reporter, and told him he had turned in his resignation, effective after the upcoming 1980 season. Devine told the Detroit guy off the record, but the story wound up leaking.

Notre Dame and Devine denied he had already resigned, although I knew it was true and wrote it a couple of times that season. The Irish wound up having a heck of a season, and Devine started to feel like he wanted to stay.

There really was no chance of that happening. Father Joyce was infatuated with the idea of hiring Gerry Faust, who had been getting a lot of attention as an ultra-motivated high school coach in Cincinnati.

Faust turned out to be a disaster for Notre Dame, of course. His idea of coaching was to tell the players on the sidelines to say a "Hail Mary" while Notre Dame was trying to make a goal-line stand.

Parseghian and I had gotten along well, going back to his pre-Notre Dame days at Northwestern. I helped him get an interview for the Vikings job before Norm Van Brocklin was hired. At that time, Parseghian said, "Sid, if you ever need a favor, give me a call." A few years later, Notre Dame won the national title, and people in the Twin Cities—mostly, the Catholics who loved Notre Dame and Notre Dame football—wanted to get him up here for a big banquet. Everyone took a shot at him and couldn't get Ara to say yes. Finally, Phil Lewis from WCCO Radio asked me to give Parseghian a try. I called and said, "Remember how you said I should call if I needed a favor? This is it." Parseghian came to town, they had a huge turnout, and he did a great job as the speaker, as always.

After he quit coaching, Parseghian was doing the analysis for national TV games. I was in Iowa City for a game, and Ara was there to do the telecast. Parseghian cornered me and said, "After all these years, I want you to tell me: How did you get the story?"

I told him, "Ara, through the years, how many times did you tell me stuff that you didn't want your name attached to? It's no different with this story. I can't tell you."

I never did give up the source for that scoop—until now.

Chapter 2

The North Side
and Newspaper Alley

My father had a habit of drinking too much and then passing out on a platform at a soda pop company that was located in north Minneapolis. It would be early evening, and my mother would say, "Go find him."

The first place I would look was in back of that pop company between Fifth and Sixth Avenues North, less than a block from our house. If he wasn't on that platform, there were a couple of other places where I could check and find him.

My father's name was Jack Hechtman, and he came to the United States from Russia on a boat when he was sixteen. He changed his name to Hartman when he got here.

My mother's name was Celia Weinberg, and she came over from Latvia when she was nine. She had a tough life with my father because of the drinking. My mom left him a few times and later divorced him.

I was born at Maternity Hospital on Glenwood Avenue North, the oldest of four kids. Bernice is two years younger, Harold is four years younger, and Saul is seven years younger.

My father was a transfer guy, meaning he moved furniture and other heavy loads. My mother did all the bookkeeping for him because he didn't have an education—couldn't read, couldn't write. He could sign his name and that was about it. He would park his truck over by the Milwaukee Road Depot and hope, just like a cabdriver today, that someone would hire him to make a delivery. On occasion, he would bring me along to help with the load. I was with him a few times when he got into fights with other drivers trying to take his accounts. My old man made twelve bucks a week if he was lucky, and he would drink most of that away.

My mom ran a women's apparel shop. She worked hard to keep the family going. Her dress shop was on the North side, and it was broken into many times. It was sad for her when that happened, but she kept trying.

When my mom was young, she had rheumatic fever. Later in life, there were aftereffects, and she had rough going—she was sickly, had little money, four kids, and an alcoholic for a husband. We had nothing. We ate chicken every night. My mother would go down to the Jewish butcher and buy two chickens for a buck. She would make chicken soup, chicken this, chicken that. To this day, I hate chicken.

The sad thing is that she would make dinner, and my old man would come home loaded and start raising hell. I still remember the night he took the tablecloth and pulled it off the table, knocking my mother's dinner all over the kitchen. Then he went to the garage to sleep it off.

Throughout my childhood, we lived in four houses on the North side—on Aldrich, then Humboldt, and finally on Irving Avenue, first at 711, then across the street at 726. There were four of us kids in the house, and we slept in the same bedroom in two twin beds.

My father's biggest thrill was when he put a foundation under the house on Humboldt. Then, he was able to have a full basement with a furnace, rather than stove heat. But his drinking kept getting worse, and my mother left him and moved us to Irving Avenue.

Another big moment for him was my bar mitzvah. I always get a smile when I attend one of the lavish bar mitzvahs that are in vogue now. The rich Jewish guys are all trying to outdo one another for opulence. Do you know what my old man did? He saved some money and went out and bought two boxes of Snickers bars for seventy-five cents a box. He was proud of himself. And, man, the chance to get a free Snickers bar—all of my buddies showed up for that.

I attended Talmud Torah, the Hebrew school on the North

side, from age ten to fourteen. I had a busy schedule. I would go to school, then pedal downtown to get newspapers to sell, then pedal back home for dinner, then pedal to Hebrew school, which lasted from 6:45 P.M. to 8 P.M.

The boys in that class were devoted to one idea: To try to cut it short and get out early. There was always a kid assigned to get there early, before the rabbi, and move the clock in the room a few minutes ahead. If that didn't work, someone would sneak out in the hall and clang the ball, so we would be dismissed early. Eddie Litin, who later became the chief psychiatrist at Mayo Clinic, and I were the two kids who did that most of the time. Sam the Janitor caught me clanging the bell once and brought me to the rabbi. He said, "This is the boy causing all the trouble." I almost got thrown out of Hebrew school, which would not have gone over well with my father or mother.

The North side was mostly Jews and blacks when I was a kid. For the most part, we got along. On Sunday mornings, we would have softball games at Sumner Field—Jews against blacks. We didn't have enough players for nine-on-nine, so everyone had to bat left-handed. We would have a pitcher, catcher, first baseman, second baseman, right fielder, and maybe a center fielder. We would play for whatever money we had in our pockets.

I was never a great athlete, but I loved sports from day one. I never cared much for school. I had a friend named Jerry Goodman. We would ride our bikes to Lincoln Junior High, and he would say, "Let's go on the lam today." So, we would take off and skip school.

One part of school I did enjoy was working for the school newspaper—the *Lincoln Life*. My use of the king's English wasn't the greatest, and still isn't, but I enjoyed laying out the paper and writing notes.

There was a gym teacher there named John Deno. He sort of adopted me. He was a wonderful guy. He saw what I did in the school newspaper and kept saying, "This is what you should do for a living."

Mr. Deno used to give me the keys to the gym, and we would go in there and play "21," shooting baskets. We didn't have much money, but whatever we had, we would bet on those "21" games.

I kept in touch with John Deno for years. He would call me at the paper and we would chat. He was proud of what I had accomplished. I always enjoyed that, because he had been an inspiration for me as a kid.

I started selling newspapers when I was nine years old. As soon as school was over, I would ride downtown to Newspaper Alley and pick up papers.

Anybody could sell newspapers. There were three papers in Minneapolis—the *Tribune* had A.M. and P.M. editions, and the *Journal* and the *Star* were afternoon papers. You could get all three papers in Newspaper Alley. You could buy a hundred papers for $1.10 and sell them for two cents. So, if you sold all one hundred, you made ninety cents, plus tips.

You wanted to be first in line to buy papers, so you could start pedaling your bike and beat the other sellers to the best corners. You could find any corner and sell papers, except where there were established news stands.

I got a lucky break. There was a guy by the name of Joe Katzman who was the street circulation manager for the *Tribune*. He took a liking to me, this little kid down there hustling papers with all these older guys.

My favorite stop was at Jack Doyle's restaurant on Hennepin Avenue between Fourth and Fifth Streets. Before Hubert Humphrey closed down the town as mayor in the late forties, Doyle had one of the big gambling operations in Minneapolis. The restaurant was downstairs and the upstairs was the gambling joint. You could bet on horse racing, baseball games, football, and basketball. They had chalkboards with the races from around the country, and the gamblers hanging out there would get a radio call of the race.

I was ten or eleven when Katzman took me to Doyle's upstairs and introduced me to all the characters. I was a kid with dark hair and a dark complexion so they started calling me Blackie. I first got the nickname from a guy named Goggles. There were a lot of mysterious nicknames in a thirties-era gambling joint.

Doyle's was where all the people who were called "racketeers" hung out—Isadore Blumenfeld, Tommy Banks, Chickie Berman. I would walk in with my papers and get a half-buck, maybe a buck, for a paper. I was selling two-cent newspapers and would walk out of there with ten bucks.

The trouble was, I then would go back to Newspaper Alley and the older newspaper carriers would get me in a craps game and I'd lose the ten bucks. Eleven, twelve years old, and I had a terrible gambling problem. The problem was that I always lost.

The other carriers knew that Joe Katzman and Sam Brody, the circulation manager for the *Journal*, were taking care of me with good locations. So, when they had a chance to get me in a craps game, they really took advantage.

The city law required you to have a street badge to sell newspapers. You had to be twelve to get a badge. That was a child-labor law. Nathaniel Johnson was employed by the city to keep kids without street badges from selling papers. Johnson used to chase me all over town. One time he caught me, but Sam Brody talked Johnson out of doing anything about it. Brody said: "Leave the kid alone. He's taking money home."

I always tried to do that, to help my mother, because we lived in poverty. I could have helped her a lot more if it wasn't for those craps games.

To sell newspapers, it was important to get to the good spots first. Even if you got there first, some of the older hawkers might decide they wanted the corner and threaten to kick the crap out of you. I was the smallest kid out there selling newspapers. I was chased off a few corners, but I also knew the downtown cops. They took a liking to me and protected me.

I remember the summer night in 1936 that Floyd B. Olson died. He was only forty-five and had cancer. Olson was probably the most beloved politician Minnesota has ever had, Hubert Humphrey included. Olson died on a Saturday night. A buddy and I worked Hennepin and Lake that night and sold 1,500 Minneapolis *Stars*.

Katzman was a big guy in town for reasons beyond running street circulation for the *Tribune*. He was a genius when it came to sports betting.

There was a place called Gorham Press that was a publisher of gambling sheets among other things. Leo Hirschfield owned it. At one time, Minneapolis was the odds-making capital of the country because of Gorham Press. Hirschfield and Katzman basically invented points spreads and odds on games. It was amazing how close they came to hitting the number on a high percentage of games. It's hard to figure out how the oddsmakers in Las Vegas are so good today. But with all the sophisticated ways to get information that they have now, the Vegas guys are no better than Hirschfield and Katzman were sixty years ago.

I don't know why Katzman did so much for me. He had one girl, no boys, so I became his son. When I was twelve, I was driving his brand-new car around town. My mom would get so mad at Joe she wanted to kill him. He used to bring me home at eleven at night, after I had been hanging out at Doyle's with the "racketeers."

The most notorious man in the group was Isadore Blumenfeld. The newspapers and the cops always referred to him as Kid Cann. His friends called him Fergie. He was involved in bootlegging during Prohibition. After booze was legal again, Kid Cann's family had all the big liquor stores—East Hennepin, Loring Liquors, and Lake Street. They monopolized the liquor business, and that's why they had so many enemies.

There was also anti-Semitism involved. It was OK for the Kennedy family in Boston and for some of the families that are now among the wealthiest in the Twin Cities—families living off trust funds in Wayzata—to have made their money in bootlegging. But it drove a lot of people nuts that the Jews were running Minneapolis and were still making all the money in the liquor business.

The government spent years trying to pin something on Kid Cann. There were three U.S. attorneys after him. They tried him for kidnapping in 1933. They tried him for murder in 1935, after Walter Liggett was machine-gunned to death. Liggett published a little newspaper in town—a scandal sheet printed on pink paper. Liggett was rough on Kid Cann in his sheet. The cops simply assumed Kid Cann was responsible for Liggett's death. He was tried and acquitted again. The Liggett murder was never solved. Finally, the Feds were able to pin a white slavery charge—transporting a woman over state lines for a sexual purpose—and then a jury tampering charge. Kid Cann served half of a seven-year sentence, then moved to Miami in 1965, and lived there until his death in 1981.

Fergie Blumenfeld. Tommy Banks. Chickie Berman. I stayed loyal to those guys—and to some childhood pals—through the years, and it did get me in trouble a few times. Half of my grade school buddies ended up in reform school and turned into small-time criminals. I would go to court and tell the judges they were wonderful people. More than once, I had cops say to me, "Sid, why do you want to get involved with this guy? He's a bum." If someone was my friend, I could never believe that about him.

Kid Cann would bring in Sophie Tucker, Cab Calloway—entertainers like that—to appear at his club. Then, after hours, they would close the doors and the real show would begin. One time, the cops came barging in at 4 A.M., took us all out, and put everyone in the paddy wagon. If they had booked me with the rest of the people, I probably would have made the newspaper and lost my job at the *Tribune*. I did some begging and the cops let me go.

Chickie and Dave Berman wound up having one of the first gambling spots in Vegas. I used to send guys out there all the time, and they had a tough time paying for anything in Chickie's place.

The thing about those guys is they weren't looking for anything from me. They saw me grow up, and all of a sudden, I'm in the paper. They were proud of me.

One fellow was an exception to this: Willie Alderman. He was a guy in his fifties and had a girlfriend who was my age—maybe twenty-one. Willie caught us together one night in a room at the Hotel Buckingham. He said, "Kid, if I ever see you with her again, you'll have a couple of broken arms."

I stayed as far away from Willie's girlfriend as I could get after that.

For all the grief he caused our family with his drinking, my father was a hard worker. He was an intelligent man. He could read Yiddish and Russian, but he had no formal education and could not read English. He was an underdog all his life. He was a fierce competitor. He would fight for customers if he had to when he was waiting to get a load of furniture at the railroad depot.

I think that's one thing I picked up from my old man—that competitiveness. I had nothing going for me as a kid. I've always fought, always have been relentless, in trying to get the story first. I don't think it has been an ego thing. It's more that, like my old man, I felt like an underdog who had to fight for everything.

After awhile, the booze started to take my father's health. I got a call one day from General Hospital. My Dad had suffered a minor stroke. I went over there, and he was just laying there. He had been at the hospital for a couple of hours and nobody had looked at him. I went to the head of the hospital and yelled, "Why don't you do something?" I was never so mad in my life.

My father died in 1972. My mother died the same year. She went through so much. I could have helped her more, if it wasn't for those craps games. I felt guilty about that for a long time. That's why I haven't gambled in over forty years.

Chapter 3

Breaking into the Business

I went to school until my junior year at North High. Then a plum job opened at the *Tribune* called a news run. The *Tribune* split the North side news run, and I was given everything from Twenty-sixth Avenue to the end of the city.

You would pick up a large load of papers and take them to stores and drop points for delivery in your area. I was the first guy to start newspaper boxes. You could trust people back then. I would leave a load of papers in the boxes and the money would have been left for most every paper that was gone. I would drop the papers in bulk and collect for them. You would get a cut from every paper sold in your area. You could make fifty dollars a week—big money in the late thirties.

I started making the news run in a 1929 Oldsmobile that I bought for $50. Then, I bought a 1939 Chevrolet from Max Grossman for $640. My mom helped me come up with $100 for the down payment and I financed the rest.

I had started hanging out at the *Tribune* newsroom when I was eleven or twelve. I would be with Joe Katzman. He was gambling on games, so he would go upstairs to the sports department to get the scores. I developed a great relationship with the fellows who were on the copy desk at the old *Tribune*. Emil Krieg. Earl Wheeler. Ed Franey. I became their go-fer. I was around, so they would put me to work clipping articles from papers. Horsey Taylor had a cigar store on Fourth and Marquette. Those *Tribune* guys would say, "Blackie, go get us a couple of sodas and sandwiches at Horsey's."

There was a pool hall called Kirk's right next to the *Journal*. That's where I met the greatest newspaper character of all, Halsey Hall, and Dick Cullum, who was then sports editor at the *Journal*. You could gamble on the baseball games in Kirk's. You could bet any amount, with a quarter as the minimum. Halsey was the cheapest son of a gun of all time. He would get someone to split a twenty-five-cent ticket with him and sit in Kirk's all day, worrying about his twelve cents.

At Kirk's they would keep the scores from the ballgames up to date on a chalkboard. A man named Adolph updated the scores. Adolph would stick the chalk in a nostril while he went through the Western Union ticket, looking for updates.

I was way underage to be in there. Kirk would run me out all the time. Finally he said, "What good does it do to run you out? You sneak right back in. So stay in the back where people can't see you, because I don't want to chase you anymore."

The big shakeup in the newspaper business in Minneapolis came in 1935, when John Cowles, Sr. came in from Des Moines and bought the afternoon *Star*. The *Journal* was the biggest of the afternoon papers at the time. The Murphy family published the *Morning Tribune* and the *Evening Tribune*. The *Star* had been the nothing paper. Then, Cowles moved in and went crazy promoting. The slogan you saw every place was, "Don't say paper, say *Star*." The *Star* went from 80,000 a day to 155,000 and was killing the *Journal*.

The Jones family, local people, owned the *Journal*. Jones sold out to Cowles in 1939, and the name of the newspaper was changed to the *Star-Journal*. The Murphys wanted to give a separate identity to their afternoon paper to compete with Cowles, so they changed it from *Evening Tribune* to *Times-Tribune*.

Charlie Johnson had been the *Star*'s sports editor. The *Star* always had been the underdog paper, and because of that, Charlie didn't like Dick Cullum, who had been the *Journal* sports editor. Charlie had the power after Cowles bought the *Journal*, and he didn't want Cullum. So, Cullum went to the Murphys and got a job as the sports editor of the *Times-Tribune*.

Then, in 1941, Cowles bought the Tribune Company from the Murphy family. Cowles changed the name of the *Times-Tribune* to the *Times* and kept it in its own building as competition for the afternoon *Star-Journal*. The *Times* was competition for news, but not for advertising dollars. Cowles's idea for keeping the *Times* as a P.M. paper was to discourage a competitor from coming in. There were three papers left, all owned by Cowles: The *Tribune* was the morning paper, the *Star-Journal* and the *Times* were afternoon papers.

When the old *Tribune* company went down in the merger in '41, I lost my news run. I was out of work. I started selling vacuum cleaners and had a chance to be the world's worst vacuum cleaner salesman. Fortunately, Louie Mohs saved me. Mohs wound up as the circulation manager at the *Times*. There was only one *Times* news run, in the downtown area, and Mohs gave it to me.

In 1944, Cullum told Mohs that he needed an intern on the sports desk. Louie said, "I got the guy for you," and mentioned my name. Cullum knew me from Kirk's pool hall and said, "Why not? Let's give the kid a shot." Cullum hired me for $11.50 a week. I was making more than that on the news run. So, I did both—worked in the sports department and kept my news run.

Cullum put me in the slot, laying out the sports pages, about the second day I worked for him. Can you imagine that today—taking a guy off the street and putting him in the slot, in charge of laying out a section? But Cullum was no dummy. I had been brought up by Krieg, Wheeler, and Franey, and now those old-timers were on the *Times* copy desk. Cullum knew they would take care of me, even if the only newspaper experience I had was at the *Lincoln Life*, my junior high paper.

I would go into the office at ten o'clock at night and do some preliminary work on the next afternoon's paper. I would stay until maybe 1 A.M., then come back at 6 A.M. and put the paper together. Then, at noon, I would pick up my papers and make the news run.

I was laying out the paper, delivering the paper, and in between, I was reporting. I wasn't a good reader or student in school because I had to work all the time. My only hope to be successful in this business was to be an exceptional reporter.

When I started reading out-of-town newspapers, one guy I admired was John Carmichael of the Chicago *Daily News*. He was big on getting interesting notes in the paper.

Cullum hired me with the idea of covering the state colleges. He was covering the Gophers, but it was only because the *Times* staff was so small. Cullum had not covered a beat—other than boxing—when he was running the *Journal*. I always had loved the Gophers, so I started going over to the University of Minnesota, talking to the athletes and the coaches. Soon, I was getting all the stories. Cullum thought that was great. It meant he could write the analysis in his column and not have to worry about reporting.

Lloyd ("Snapper") Stein, the university trainer, helped me a lot when I was a novice reporter. Bernie Bierman was coaching football, and he didn't want newspapermen snooping around, but Stein didn't see the problem with it. Snapper knew everything that was going on and tipped me off on many stories. Stein was at the university for another thirty-five years after I first started covering the Gophers, and he became one of the greatest friends I had. Snapper did me a lot of good with Frank McCormick, who was the Minnesota athletic director when I first started.

McCormick did not approve of how tough Bierman tried to make it for the newspaper reporters. McCormick helped me with quite a few stories, including his search for a basketball coach in 1948.

Gopher basketball coach Dave MacMillan had a bad season in 1947–1948. He had been around since 1927, and the university decided it was time for him to step aside. But MacMillan was such a wonderful fellow that McCormick wanted the new coach to keep him as an assistant.

The coach McCormick wanted to hire was John Wooden, then at Indiana State. Wooden was going to take the job, but he wanted to bring an assistant coach with him. McCormick had to check with the administration and was supposed to get back to Wooden on a Monday to let him know. McCormick had a number of independent investments, and he was in South Dakota over the weekend, checking on one of his businesses. He got snowed in and was not able to get back to Wooden with an answer. By the time McCormick reached him, Wooden already had taken a job at UCLA, where he eventually won ten national championships.

Thanks to McCormick I had that story from start to finish, when they lost Wooden and wound up hiring Ozzie Cowles, the Michigan coach.

After the war, most of the athletes at the University of Minnesota were armed services veterans. (I had tried to enlist three times but was always rejected because of my bad asthma.) The veterans started coming back to play football and basketball in 1946. I was about the same age as many of the athletes. We chased around together. We became buddies, and I knew everything that was going on with those teams.

I started writing a column in 1946. Cullum said my column started when he couldn't make it to the office because of a snowstorm, and I stuck a Sid Hartman column in the paper instead. Cullum got a lot of laughs out of that story through the years.

Actually, what happened was Cullum said, "You have all these notes that we can't get in the paper anywhere else. Start rounding them up and we'll run a column." For years, that was the name of the column—"Hartman's Roundup." Cullum did not want any opinion from me, just notes. He did not want anything that would hurt Gophers football.

Cullum liked Bernie Bierman. *Star* Sports Editor Charlie Johnson never was a fan of Bierman's, especially after Bernie came back from the war and couldn't win big. The different views on Bierman were part of the Cullum-Johnson rivalry that went back to the thirties when Dick ran the more-powerful *Journal* and Charlie ran the smaller *Star*. Cullum was a cheerleader. If you read the *Times* sports section, there was no question we wanted the Gophers to win.

In 1947, Cowles dropped the *Journal* part of the *Star-Journal* title. So, in the building on Portland Avenue, Cowles had the *Morning Tribune* and the afternoon *Star*. The *Star* was entrenched now. There was no longer a fear of competition.

In May 1948, Cowles announced he was folding the *Times*. We were all out of work. My *Times* news run was gone. My *Times* sports-writing job was gone. I was worried sick. But right away, Charlie Johnson called and offered me a job at the *Tribune*.

Charlie was the executive sports editor of the *Star* and the *Tribune*. Joe Hendrickson was Charlie's sports editor for the *Tribune*. Dave Silverman was the managing editor. Hendrickson's plan was to put me on the desk and to have a fellow named Glen Gaff cover the Gophers. Silverman went to Charlie and said, "You're bringing in the best reporter in town and putting him on the desk. What sense does that make?"

The next day, I was assigned the Gophers beat.

I would never have had the job if Louie Mohs, the circulation manager for the *Times*, had not come clean with Charlie after an incident a few months earlier.

The Gophers were getting ready for a game, and I found out that star center Jim McIntyre was hurt and would not be playing that night. I had the story in the afternoon *Times*: "McIntyre Won't Play Tonight."

Before the *Times* hit the streets, a bookie named Petey Cohen called Charlie and said, "Do you know what's going on with this Gophers game? Minnesota was a ten-and-a-half-point favorite this morning and now so much money has come in on the other side that the game is even."

When Charlie saw the *Times* and my McIntyre story a few minutes later, he went crazy. He called the *Times* and accused me of working with the gamblers. I knew those guys, but I didn't pass them information.

It had happened this way: Mohs, a big gambler, had been walking through the *Times* composing room that morning and saw the headline. He called in a huge bet, a couple of his pals called in huge bets, and that's where all the money came from. Mohs talked to Charlie and got me off the hook.

One thing I learned quickly was that the most important thing a reporter could have was someone's phone number. I would ask everyone I bumped into, everyone I interviewed, for a phone number. If a guy hesitated, I would keep on him until he gave me the number. The numbers all went into my phone book. I always have had a great book. My motto is: "I can always get a hold of anybody. If I don't know him, I know somebody who knows him."

We had a copy boy at the *Tribune* twenty-some years ago named Charley Walters. He now writes a notes column at the St. Paul newspaper. One of the things Walters learned from me was to always get a phone number.

Legend has it that Walters, in his copy-boy days, saw my book on a desk one night while I was at dinner. He ran to the Xerox machine and photocopied the numbers. Some day, I'll have to ask Walters if that is true.

Dick Cullum and I had a fantastic relationship. He was twenty years older than me. He had five daughters. He used to tell people, "I have five daughters and one son—Sid." He's the guy who gave me my first opportunity. If not for him, I would have had a career selling vacuum cleaners.

Cullum lived out on Willow Lane in the country. He had thirty acres on a farm. Many a big meeting was held out there with the leading sports people in town.

After the *Times* folded, Charlie Johnson didn't want Cullum at the *Star* and *Tribune*. The editor, Gideon Seymour, finally told Charlie, "Listen, get Cullum over here. He's the best writer in town."

Dick became the *Tribune*'s columnist, and we worked together for another thirty years. Dick Cullum was a beautiful man.

When the *Star* was struggling, Charlie Johnson took his salary in stock rather than money. Later, Cowles bought the *Star*, turned it into a success, bought out the *Journal*, bought out the *Tribune*, and all that stock Charlie owned made him a rich man.

When the *Times* folded, Charlie called me the first night and said, "Come on down tomorrow. You're working for the *Star* and *Tribune*. We'll take care of you."

Every day when I came in from making the rounds, Charlie would be writing his column for the next day. We would sit down and talk about what was going on with the Gophers, with the other teams. He would give his opinion and I would give mine.

Charlie gave me a chance to resume writing a column within a year after I started at the *Tribune*. He sent me to the Rose Bowl, the College Football All-Star Game, and other events, where I made contacts that have lasted my whole career. He made me the *Tribune* sports editor in 1957.

Charlie Johnson was behind most of the great opportunities I've had in the newspaper business.

Chapter 4

A Reporter's First Love

The Gophers were the kings of college football in the 1930s. There was money to be made on those Saturday afternoons at Memorial Stadium. I started going over there at age eleven or twelve. We would take over a parking lot and charge fifty cents to park. The Gophers did not have game programs, so the *Tribune*, the *Star*, and the *Journal* all put out stadium editions with the lineups. I was in charge of selling the *Tribune*s at Gophers games.

The Gophers were the heroes, but you could not get close to them. Bernie Bierman kept everybody away from the players. This worked in the thirties, but when he came back after the war, things had changed. The players were older, the newspapers were promoting Gophers football more than ever, and Bierman could not control everything and everybody. That was part of his downfall.

The boosters broke a few rules to get players for Bierman after the war. There was a fellow named Lyle Strandlen in Chicago, and he sent Bierman the great tackle, Leo Nomellini. Local millionaire Alget Johnson had the Touchdown Club that was also getting players. The Touchdown Club would create jobs for the players. If you were a good football player, you did not have to show up at the job to get paid. Bud Grant worked for IDS in Minneapolis, and he showed up once a month to get his paycheck.

Bierman did not know what was going on. He was like John Wooden when he was winning the basketball championships at UCLA. Wooden thought those All-Americans from the East Coast went to UCLA because they wanted to play for him.

I was the first reporter to hang around the team every day and the players came up with this song: "Bernie loves us, yes we know, 'cause Sid Hartman tells us so." Running back Billy Bye was the instigator. He would get the whole team to sing in the locker room at Cooke Hall. I was a young reporter and Bierman was the biggest name in the state. I was scared to death of him. They would start singing that song and I would run for cover.

Bert Baston, Bernie's No. 1 assistant, used to say this about Bierman: "Don't worry about that old son of a bitch. He likes you. He just doesn't want anyone to know it."

Years later, after he was done coaching, I asked Bierman what he thought when Bye and the players started singing the "Sid Hartman" song. "We would be in the coaches room, laughing like hell," he said.

Bierman won his last national championship in 1941. He coached the service team, the Iowa Seahawks, for three years and then came back in 1945. The Gophers had mediocre teams during the war, but then all these tremendous players started getting out of the service and showing up at Minnesota.

They can talk all they want about Bierman's 1934, 1935, 1936, 1940, and 1941 teams that were national champions, but the teams he had from 1946 through 1949 had more talent. Amazing talent. They were more than the first team I covered on an everyday basis. They were my buddies.

Bud Grant and Gordie Soltau were the best ends in the country. Leo Nomellini and Floyd Jaszewski were the tackles, Harry Hendrickson and John Lundin were the guards, and Clayton Tonnemaker was the center. Verne Gagne was another end. Larry Olsonoski, a terrific guard, was with that group for a couple of years. Nomellini and Tonnemaker were the two best linemen in the country. Jaszewski was a great tackle. No team in history had a line like that. And, if it was not for faculty representative Henry Rottschaefer, the Gophers would have had a fantastic runner to go with that line.

Frank Aschenbrenner had played for the Great Lakes Naval Base with Grant. He wanted to come to Minnesota. He was all set, and then Rottschaefer decided he would have to sit out a quarter before being eligible to play football at Minnesota. Aschenbrenner wound up going to Northwestern, and he beat the Gophers in 1946 and again in 1948.

Billy Bye was a good back, but not in Aschenbrenner's class. A great running back would have made a difference, since Bierman did not believe in passing. The Gophers' famous play was "27," an off-tackle run.

Minnesota football after the war was bigger than it was from 1934 through 1941, when the Gophers were winning those five Associated Press national championships. The war was over and people had more money. The whole atmosphere in the Twin Cities and the country was electric, and it carried over to Gophers football.

Friday nights before a Gophers game were great in Minneapolis. You couldn't get in the restaurants. You couldn't get a hotel room. There were parties all over town. There would be a big press party with coaches, local reporters, visiting reporters, and university officials. Charlie Johnson, Dick Cullum, Halsey Hall, and a few of the coaches—everyone would get loaded. One night, the press party was over and we couldn't find John Carmichael of the Chicago *Daily News*. The next morning, the people who were cleaning up the room found him sleeping behind the bar.

John Cowles, Sr. used Gophers football to sell newspapers, and the circulation of the Sunday paper soared to more than 600,000. We had six or more photographers at those Gophers games shooting every play with machine-gun cameras from the tops of the stadiums. Television didn't start replay. We started replay in the 1940s in the *Tribune's Peach*, as the Sunday sports section was called since it was printed on peach-colored paper. We would have photo sequences of five, six, and even eight pictures of the biggest plays in the game.

All of this revolved around the fact that, every year from 1946 through 1949, the season started with Minnesotans thinking the Gophers were going to win the national championship. The talent was there.

The legendary Paul Brown was the coach at Great Lakes, and he said Grant was the best eighteen-year-old athlete he had ever seen. Nomellini came out of Chicago. He had not played much football until the service. Nomellini was the strongest man ever to play at Minnesota, with the possible exception of Bronko Nagurski. Nomellini was a big, goofy Italian who would give me the same answer after every game the Gophers won: "We were bigger, we were stronger, and we won the game. How do you like that quote?"

Nomellini would say he had a sore ankle, and trainer Snapper Stein would tape him up for a game. Later, Stein would ask him how the ankle felt, and Nomellini would say, "It felt great." Then, Stein would say, "I taped the other ankle, you dumb son of a bitch. I taped your good ankle. I knew you couldn't tell the difference."

There were a number of tremendous players from Minneapolis, especially from Edison High, at that time. Tonnemaker and Jaszewski were both from Edison. Tonnemaker lived at home and rode the street car to campus.

There were no scholarships. The players would pay for school and their expenses with the jobs that Alget Johnson and the Touchdown Club arranged for them. I helped out Grant, Bye, and a couple of other players by finding clients for their tickets. Art Murray, the owner of Murray's Steakhouse in downtown Minneapolis, would buy most of the tickets from me, then sell them to customers. The players would get four three-dollar tickets and Art would pay ten dollars for them.

Unethical? Hey, it was the 1940s. The newspaper wanted the Gophers to win. We would increase the press run for Sunday by 30,000 if the Gophers won on Saturday.

Plus, the players from that era were my buddies, my all-time favorites. They are the reason that, when it comes to covering sports, Gophers football always has been and always will be my first love.

The Gophers were 5-4, 6-3, and 7-2 from 1946 through 1948. Most of the great players were seniors in 1949 and the last step was going to be the Rose Bowl. The Gophers won the first three games handily—beating Washington, Nebraska, and Northwestern—and then they were going to Ohio State. The Buckeyes were unbeaten and rated No. 1 in the country.

We left early Friday morning on the train ride to Columbus, Ohio. There would be two or three cars for the team, and then there would be a car in the back—with a bar—for the press. Obviously, there was a lot of drinking in the press car. On the train rides back to Minneapolis, the assistant coaches would come back to the press car, and the fun would start.

Charlie Johnson would be among the first to be overserved. The more he drank, the more blunt Charlie became with his opinions. Come about two or three in the morning, Charlie and Bert Baston, Bierman's assistant, would start fighting. They would wrestle each other to the floor. It was a tradition. The night would always end the same way, with Baston saying, "Next week, Charlie, you coach the team and I'll write the column."

On the Ohio State trip in '49, we stayed in Dayton on Friday night, then rode the train in to Columbus on Saturday morning. The train got in late, the players barely had time to get in uniform before kickoff. Bierman was going crazy. The Gophers went out and kicked the stuffing out of Ohio State 27-0.

It was probably the greatest game a Minnesota football team has ever played. It was such a rout that Bierman was letting the players do their own substituting in the second half.

After that game, Bierman screwed up like no coach has ever screwed up. Michigan was next, and Bierman was afraid the Gophers would have a letdown. He put the players through full-contact, three-hour practices every day that week. He killed them.

To top it off, the team stayed in Jackson, Michigan, on Friday night, and Bierman decided he was going to get the players to Michigan Stadium early Saturday. The players sat around the locker room for two hours, then went out and got beat 14-7.

Bud Grant learned a couple of things that week, and they became two "don'ts" in his coaching career: First, don't use up your team in practice; and second, don't get your players to the stadium too early.

After the Michigan loss, Bierman practiced the Gophers hard again and they lost 13-7 to a terrible Purdue team. Bierman was dead after that. We ran the people's column—letters to the sports editor—on Sunday, and the fans were killing him in that column. The only guy in town still defending Bierman was Dick Cullum.

University President Lew Morrill called in Bierman after the Purdue loss and said: "That's enough of this concentration camp approach. We're getting complaints from everyone, including parents of the players." Bierman was upset. He was going to show everyone they were wrong. He didn't have the players do anything in practice the next week.

What happened? They went out and beat Iowa 55-7. They finished with wins over Pittsburgh and Wisconsin. They still had a chance to go to the Rose Bowl, but Michigan screwed up an extra point against Ohio State in the last game, and that sent Ohio State to the Rose Bowl instead.

All of the great players were gone in 1950, and Bierman went 1-7-1. Some of his old players from the national championship teams, guys like Babe LeVoir, went to Bernie and convinced him to quit. This was the equivalent of a guy like Bear Bryant getting run off at Alabama.

Lew Morrill was at Ohio State when Wes Fesler was there. Fesler quit—just walked out—but Morrill still thought he was the right guy for Minnesota.

Fesler was a terrific salesman. He could sell you the Brooklyn Bridge. That was his No. 1 quality, the ability to talk. Fesler never worked on Sundays. Early in the fall, he would play golf on Sundays.

Paul Giel had come up from Winona. Freshmen were no longer eligible, so the fans spent all of 1950 waiting for Giel to become a sophomore. He was called the Winona Flash. He was huge with the public—the all-time golden boy with Minnesota football.

At first the fans loved Fesler, because he had Giel, and compared to Bierman, he played a wide-open offense. But Fesler couldn't win. The Gophers were terrible his first year and around .500 in 1952 and 1953.

Lyle Clark was the line coach. He had been with Fesler at Ohio State. With two games left in the '53 season, Clark came over to me at practice and said, "I've seen this before. The son of a bitch is going to quit. Go write that."

So I wrote it, and Fesler was steaming. He denied it, and the university denied it. A week after the season ended, he quit.

There was a movement to get Bud Wilkinson up here from Oklahoma—first after Bierman was bounced, again after Fesler quit. It would have been tough to get Wilkinson away from the dynasty he had built in Oklahoma, but the Gophers boosters were ready to give him a ton of money.

Wilkinson was from Minneapolis. He played for the Gophers

from 1934 through 1936. Charlie Johnson wanted Wilkinson in the worst way. Charlie and J. P. Wilkinson, Bud's father, lived in the same apartment building—2615 Park Avenue—and they were big buddies.

Wilkinson had gotten into coaching by accident. After getting out of the Navy, he wound up on Jim Tatum's coaching staff at Oklahoma. Bud was getting ready to come back to Minneapolis to run his father's mortgage business. Then Tatum surprised everyone by quitting and going to Maryland, and Oklahoma offered the job to Wilkinson.

Charlie Johnson managed to get Wilkinson to come up here for an interview after Bierman was finished. Morrill was supposed to meet Wilkinson that night. Charlie, Bud Wilkinson, Bud's dad, and I sat in Charlie's apartment, waiting for Morrill to call. He didn't call that night. Morrill called the next morning and had only a brief meeting with Wilkinson.

That was it. Wilkinson went back to Oklahoma and kept his dynasty going. After Wilkinson, the coach everyone wanted was Biggie Munn, another ex-Gopher. Munn was winning at Michigan State.

Ike Armstrong had come in as the athletic director in 1950, Bierman's last season. Armstrong had been the football coach and athletic director at Utah. He worked against hiring Wilkinson and against hiring Munn. Armstrong knew those guys would have had all the power and he would have been a paper tiger.

Another candidate at that time was Sid Gillman, a great friend of mine who also came from the North side of Minneapolis. Gillman was probably the most innovative coach of all time when it came to passing offense. He interviewed for the Gophers job. I'm convinced that Armstrong didn't hire Gillman because he knew he was a friend of mine.

Armstrong was the worst athletic director Minnesota has ever had. He tried to get me fired a dozen times. I was getting news in the paper before he had a chance to announce it—sometimes, before he knew about it.

One day, I was at Charlie's house, and Armstrong came over, mad as hell. Charlie had me hide in the next room before he let Armstrong in the house. I sat there and listened to Armstrong tell Charlie all the reasons he should fire me. Charlie had three or four drinks in him,

Reunion of Gophers football stars

Gophers football was this reporter's first love, and I have keep in contact with many of the players through the years. We gathered for this photograph during a banquet in honor of former University of Minnesota trainer Lloyd Stein. Front row, from left: Bob Bjorklund, Stein, Gene Flick, and two unknown players. Back row: Norm McGrew, Babe LeVoir, Phil Lewis, myself, Bill Bloedel, Bruce Telander, and Fred Carlson.

so it was funny. After Armstrong left, Charlie said to me: "Well, you heard it all. Now you know officially what he thinks of you."

I was in Ann Arbor, Michigan, for a Big Ten meeting. There was a group of reporters waiting for the meeting to end, so we could find out what happened. Armstrong told the other athletic directors, "That Sid Hartman is sitting out there. You have to be careful what you tell him."

Fritz Crisler was the Michigan athletic director. I knew him going back to the thirties when he was the athletic director at Minnesota and I was selling newspapers. Crisler told Armstrong, "I'll tell you what, Ike. I'll trade Sid Hartman for four of our Detroit guys."

Another athletic directors meeting was being held in Alexandria, Minnesota. Biggie Munn was the A.D. at Michigan State. He got up and said, "Look, Ike. There's Sid Hartman in a boat. He's looking up here with binoculars. I'll bet he has a listening device in this room."

Armstrong was paranoid about me. I drove him crazy. I loved doing it. If it wasn't for him, we could have had Bud Wilkinson—maybe the best college coach who ever lived—back at Minnesota in 1951.

When Fesler resigned, it caught Morrill and Armstrong completely by surprise. They had no idea where to look for a coach.

Murray Warmath was at Mississippi State, and he wanted the job. This was almost unheard of—a guy from the South being hired to coach in the Big Ten. Warmath had worked for Army coach Earl Blaik, and Blaik had a tremendous amount of influence in college athletics at that time. Blaik called the university to recommend Warmath. That's how he got the job.

Charlie Johnson ripped Warmath's hiring for a long time. Warmath did not want any newspapermen around. He was more paranoid than Bierman ever had been. But Murray could coach. He was a defensive genius, and he ran an offense with a lot of option plays, something the Big Ten had never seen.

The Gophers were supposed to be great in 1957, with Bobby Cox as the quarterback. They were upset at Illinois when Red Grange came back and gave a motivational speech, and then the team went in the tank. They finished 4-5. Pinky McNamara was on that team, and he said, "Cox thinks he should carry the ball every play. All that's important to him is whether he carries the ball left or carries it right."

By 1959, the public was trying to run Warmath out of town. The students hung him in effigy on a tree outside of Territorial Hall. People were throwing garbage on his lawn. Only the fact he had some promising sophomores—such as quarterback Sandy Stephens—kept Warmath from getting fired.

In December, I was in Colorado Springs, Colorado, covering the winter baseball meetings. A graduate assistant I knew from Arkansas left me a message. I called him and the young coach said: "It's all set. Arkansas is going to name Warmath as its coach this week."

I checked and the kid was right. I started writing that Warmath was going to leave. Morrill was all for it, but Don Knutson—the big construction guy in town—put the pressure on Warmath to stay. Knutson and Herman Lange, the owner of Marquette Manufacturing, had been involved in bringing in players for Warmath. They took care of getting players like Stephens, Judge Dickson, and Bill Munsey from Pennsylvania, and John Mulvena and Tom Hall from Delaware.

The big thing was that, for the first time, Minnesota also went to the South and recruited black players. Segregation was in effect, so the black athletes had to play in the North, and the Gophers brought in the great tackles Bobby Lee Bell and Carl Eller from North Carolina.

Murray needed help recruiting, one reason being this tendency he had when recruits made a campus visit: The kid would be brought into Warmath's office, and Murray would chat for a couple of minutes, then say, "Roll up your pants. I want to see your legs."

Murray did not think a kid could play football if he had skinny legs. He decided not to go after Dale Hackbart because he thought Hackbart had skinny legs. Hackbart went to Wisconsin, played quarterback, and had some great games against the Gophers. After those games, Hackbart would say to me, "Does Warmath thinks my legs are OK now?"

John Hallenbeck was an outstanding player from Rochester. His father George was one of the top surgeons in the world. John Hallenbeck was going to Michigan. I kept calling Dr. Hallenbeck, saying, "At least have him come up and take a look at Minnesota."

As a favor to me, John visited Minnesota. Warmath pulled the let's-see-your-legs stunt. Dr. Hallenbeck was fuming. He called and said, "Sid, it's a good thing you don't have surgery scheduled at the Mayo Clinic this week."

Knutson and Lange were getting the players for Warmath, just as Alget Johnson and Lyle Strandlen had done for Bierman after World War II. They were getting jobs for all of these players. If a player's family needed some help, they would take care of mom and dad, too.

The Gophers were 1-8 in 1958 and 2-7 in 1959. But Knutson said: "We put our necks on the line for you, Murray. You're staying here and taking us to the Rose Bowl." So, Warmath pulled out of the

Old football friends, 1960s

From left: longtime Oklahoma coach Bud Wilkinson; former Gopher football player and assistant coach John Kulbitski; longtime Gopher football assistant coach Butch Nash; former Gopher football player and head coach at Utah State John Roning; myself; former Minneapolis North High and Ohio State football player and coach of the Los Angeles Rams and San Diego Chargers Sid Gillman; St. Louis sporting goods representative Mike Close (standing); and Minnesota Athletic Director Fritz Crisler.

Arkansas job at the last minute. Arkansas hired Frank Broyles away from Missouri, and that's when my friend Dan Devine went from Arizona State to Missouri. I had that story first four times—Warmath's ready to go to Arkansas, Warmath's staying, Broyles is going to Arkansas, and Devine's going to Missouri.

Thanks to Knutson and Lange, Warmath survived. And, to his credit, Warmath's personality had changed a lot. His son Billy was sickly and that became a turning point in Warmath's life. He received a lot of support during Billy's illness, and Murray became a less hard-nosed person. We became good friends.

For all those years, I had been going to the Rose Bowl to cover

Michigan, Ohio State, Iowa, and Wisconsin, and then in 1960, Warmath took us there—finally.

The Gophers had hammered Iowa 27-10 at Memorial Stadium, in the game where Iowa was No. 1 and the Gophers were No. 2. That afternoon belonged to Tom Brown, Minnesota's great senior guard.

The Gophers were upset by Purdue the next week, but they went 8-1, wound up tying for the Big Ten title, and received the Rose Bowl invitation. It was a big, big thrill to be going to the Rose Bowl with the Gophers, even though they were upset 17-7 by Washington.

Fortunately, Ohio State won the title in 1961 and turned down the Rose Bowl invitation, so the Gophers went again. They whipped UCLA 21-3 that day. That's the only Rose Bowl victory for the Gophers.

Along with the result, the big difference between the Gophers' first and second Rose Bowl trips was the bill for the hospitality room at the headquarters hotel.

Roger Rosenblum was one of the reporters sent to Pasadena by the St. Paul paper the first time. He was there a week and never left the hospitality room. They couldn't get enough food and enough whiskey in there to satisfy Roger.

The next year, the St. Paul paper didn't send Roger. The service people at the hotel were shocked. They kept saying, "Why is all this food and whiskey still here? Don't you Minnesota people eat and drink anymore?"

Chapter 5

Running the Lakers

Once the Gophers were done with a football season, things were rather dead on the Twin Cities sports scene. The biggest events in the winter were Gophers basketball in Minneapolis, Hamline and St. Thomas basketball in St. Paul, and the regular boxing cards. There was also minor league hockey in Minneapolis and St. Paul.

The public was in a mood for another sports attraction. Mike Alpert, Ben Berger, and I brought in the professional basketball teams from Oshkosh and Sheboygan, Wisconsin, for an exhibition game at the Minneapolis Auditorium.

When the game drew well, I went to Morris Chalfen and raised the possibility of getting a basketball team. Chalfen and his brother, Carl, owned Lincoln Recreation and the Nankin Cafe.

Morris Chalfen also had hooked up with Emory Gilbert of Toledo, Ohio. Gilbert had a machine that could create a temporary ice sheet in arenas that did not have ice-making equipment. Chalfen started the Holiday on Ice show. With Gilbert's machine, they were able to go to arenas all over the South, where there previously had been no ice shows.

When I went to him about getting a basketball team, Chalfen said: "I'll back it financially, but I don't want to be the front guy. Go check with Berger."

Berger owned Schiek's Cafe and also a number of theaters around town. Berger told Chalfen that we should go for it. Berger didn't know anything about sports—when the Lakers scored a basket, he would say, "Good ball" —but he loved the attention of owning a team and getting his name in the paper.

There were two main leagues in those days: the Basketball Association of America (BAA) and the National Basketball League (NBL). Morris Winston owned the Detroit Gems of the NBL, and he was going broke. We probably could have had the franchise for $5,000, but I was too anxious.

I called Winston and offered him $15,000. Winston jumped at it. Then, I went to Chalfen and got him to write the check. I met Winston at the airport in Detroit, gave him the check, and he signed the purchase agreement. The Minneapolis Lakers were set to join the NBL for the 1947–1948 season.

I was in charge of getting players for Chalfen and Berger, and my No. 1 accomplishment was signing Jim Pollard, a great forward from Stanford. He was out of college and playing for an Oakland team in industrial basketball. There were a number of companies around the country—Phillips 66 in Oklahoma was the most famous—that sponsored basketball teams and hired players in the forties and fifties. Every team in the BAA and NBL wanted Pollard. I signed him.

We were at a meeting in Chicago, and commissioner Doxie Moore was lecturing the owners on the big money teams were starting to pay players. He said, "I know everyone wants Pollard, but we shouldn't be getting into bidding wars and driving up salaries." The same thing—escalating salaries—that commissioners and owners are talking about today is what they were talking about in 1947.

I was a twenty-seven-year-old kid, representing a new team and attending one of my first league meetings. I raised my hand in the middle of the conversation and said: "Commissioner, I would like to announce that the Minneapolis Lakers have signed Jim Pollard."

You could have heard a pin drop in that room.

I also convinced Chalfen and Berger to come up with $15,000 to buy the rights to Tony Jaros and Don Carlson, two Minnesota guys, from the Chicago Stags of the BAA.

Berger wanted me to quit the paper and run the Lakers as the general manager. I considered that, but it was not an either-or situation. This was a time when most of the sportswriters had something else going. Frankie Diamond did the promotion for boxing. Rolf Fjelstad did the promotion for pro wrestling. Halsey Hall wrote releases for the Minneapolis Millers baseball team. Newspapers paid

Minneapolis Lakers celebrate, 1954

The Lakers players and staff celebrate yet another National Basketball Association championship. The Minneapolis pro basketball team won the National Basketball League championship in 1948, followed by five NBA championships in 1949, 1950, 1952, 1953, and 1954. Front row, from left: Max Winter, tall men Jim Pollard and George Mikan (holding the trophy together), coach John Kundla, Bob Harrison, Don Carlson, Slater Martin, and Buddy Hassett (kneeling). Back row: myself, Herman Schaffer, Vern Mikkelsen (just visible behind Schaffer), Bud Grant, Arnie Feerin, and Tony Jaros.

so little back then that the editors had no problem with reporters having another job on the side.

Chalfen and Berger realized that if I was not going to work for the team full-time, they needed someone to run the business side. That is when they brought in Max Winter as general manager, about a month before the start of the 1947–1948 season.

Max owned The 620 Club on Hennepin Avenue, famous as the place "Where Turkey is King." He also managed boxers. He was a buddy of Jack Dempsey and the guys Dempsey was tied in with in New York. The deal was that Max would take care of the business end of the Lakers and I was in charge of the basketball. Max would be the spokesman and promote the team. I remained in charge of getting the players. It worked out well. Max and I became lifetime friends.

Before Max came on board with the Lakers, we had tried to hire Hamline University legend Joe Hutton, Sr. as the coach. I was at Hutton's house in St. Paul and at Hamline every day, pestering him, but Joe would not take the job.

Hamline's big rival was St. Thomas. John Kundla, a standout player with the Gophers in the thirties, was the coach there. After Hutton turned us down, we went to Kundla, and he turned us down, too. Finally, I sat down with Kundla and offered him $9,000, twice what he was making at St. Thomas. He said yes.

The Lakers players loved Kundla as a person. That was the most important thing, since we gave Kundla so much talent that he did not have to be a great coach.

Pollard was the star as we headed into our first season. When it came to the ability to do things while he was in the air, Pollard was the Michael Jordan of his day. He was six foot seven and could do everything in the world on the court. They called him "The Kangaroo Kid," a perfect nickname for the way he played.

You never knew what Pollard's outlook would be from one night to the next. When he wanted to play, there was nobody who could contain him. He could play terrific defense, although many nights he would not bother to do it.

The biggest break of all was that the Detroit Gems had finished last in the NBL during the 1946–1947 season. Since we had bought the franchise, that meant the Lakers had the first rights to a player who was available if another team folded—something that was not unusual in those days.

In Chicago, Maurice White had a team called the Chicago Gears, and he signed the nationally famous big man George Mikan out of DePaul University. White gave Mikan a big contract, and then started his own league. The concept was that Mikan would draw such large crowds that the league would not need other gate attractions. But White was in big financial trouble before the exhibition schedule was over. The Gears folded early in the schedule.

That made Mikan available. There was no argument in our league. Minneapolis had first rights to Mikan. There was an argument in the BAA. Art Morse was running the Chicago Stags. It was his contention that, since Mikan had played at DePaul, he should belong to Chicago. The other owners were disputing this.

We were able to get Mikan to fly into Minneapolis. He wanted $12,000 to sign, which was a ton of money in 1947. Mikan was scheduled to fly back to Chicago that night on the last flight out. Max and I talked it over and figured that if Mikan got on that flight, he was gone for good. We assumed the BAA was going to give the Chicago Stags the right to sign Mikan, rather than lose him to the Lakers and the NBL. So I drove Mikan to the airport, and I made sure to get lost on the way. I drove north toward Anoka, rather than south toward the airport.

After Mikan missed his flight, we put him up in a downtown hotel, then brought him to the Lakers office in the Loeb Arcade the next morning and agreed to give him the $12,000.

Mikan joined the Lakers for the second game of the season. It was the start of a dynasty that lasted through 1954, until Big George retired for the first time.

We always had trouble signing Mikan. He had his mind set on becoming a lawyer and every contract was a hassle. One time, training camp was getting ready to start, and we negotiated with Mikan until midnight at his home until he finally agreed to a deal. I told Max Winter, "I'm going to the office and get a contract for him to sign."

Max said, "Don't worry about it. George can sign in the morning."

The next morning, George came to the office with his wife, Pat, who ran the show in that house. They wanted to negotiate some more. I looked at Max and said, "I told you we should have gotten that contract signed last night."

The deal with Mikan was this: Once we had him signed, he always gave us more than our money's worth.

Rival teams and the NBA did everything they could to stop Mikan. The lane was widened from six feet to twelve feet because they thought it would stop Mikan from camping out next to the basket and shooting his hook shot. They also talked about raising the basket. Teams couldn't believe Big George was that good, but they were wrong. Bud Grant played two seasons with the Lakers, and he has said many times that Mikan was the greatest competitor he has ever been around. I agree with that.

Mikan was also the biggest name in basketball. One night, we went to New York, and the marquee in front of Madison Square Garden read, "Geo. Mikan vs. Knicks." Before the game, the other players were milling around in the visitors locker room. It was getting close to game time, and Mikan was the only player dressed. Finally, he said, "Come on, gentlemen. We have a ballgame to play."

And the other players said: "No, George. You have a ballgame to play. We saw that sign out front. Mikan vs. Knicks. We can't wait to see how you do against them."

Then they all started laughing, got dressed and, I'm sure, went out and kicked the hell out of the New York Knickerbockers.

In 1949, we were playing Red Auerbach's Washington Capitols, a great team, in the finals. Mikan fell down and cracked a bone in his wrist. He went to the Georgetown University hospital, they put a cast on the wrist, and Mikan did not miss a game.

The only time the Lakers lost the championship was in 1951, when Mikan was not able to play because of a broken ankle, and we lost to the Rochester Royals in the Western Division finals.

We had the best big man in basketball in Mikan and the best athlete in Pollard. They led us to the NBL championship in 1948, our first season, and then our league merged with the BAA. That was the real start of the National Basketball Association.

Originally, the BAA was only going to take in the teams from Indianapolis and Fort Wayne, two of the best franchises, and the BAA figured that would kill our league. The merger meeting was held at the Morris Hotel in Chicago. Max Winter stayed there and argued, and finally they let in the rest of the teams.

We had great rivalries in that league—Fort Wayne, Rochester, Syracuse, the New York Knickerbockers. In Fort Wayne, the floor was about forty feet wide. The big men, Mikan and Larry Foust from Fort Wayne, would plug up the whole court, and it would be absolute war around the basket.

Les Harrison was the Rochester coach and a true crazy man. One night, I was watching Rochester play a game in Fort Wayne. Pat Kennedy, one of the best officials of all time, was working the game. Bob

Davies of Rochester made a basket, Kennedy went to blow his whistle, and somehow the ball in the whistle came out and went down his throat. Kennedy collapsed on the floor. He was choking. Harrison ran out and screamed, "Pat, before you die. Did the basket count?"

The Lakers won what was first true, post-merger NBA championship, in 1949, followed by four more NBA titles in 1950, 1952, 1953, and 1954.

Mikan and Pollard were the constants on our six championship teams in seven years starting with the NBL in 1948. For the 1949–1950 season, I drafted Vern Mikkelsen from Hamline in the first round, Slater "Dugie" Martin from Texas in the second round, and Bobby Harrison from Michigan in the third round. They all started as rookies with Mikan and Pollard on a championship team. That has to be the greatest one-season draft in the history of the NBA.

Martin played what is now called point guard. Bob Cousy was the big star with the Boston Celtics starting in 1950, but Martin was so quick that he would wrap up Cousy defensively. Mikkelsen was six foot ten, strong as a horse, and a center. We had Mikan, and no team had tried to play two big men together like that.

Kundla did not think it would work and was reluctant. Max and I told him that was the front line we wanted—Pollard, Mikan, and Mikkelsen. And it changed the game.

Mikkelsen was able to pass the ball inside to Mikan all night long. He also was able to dominate his side of the board in rebounding. What Mikkelsen became was basketball's first power forward.

Harrison was the shooting guard on three championship teams—1950, 1952, and 1953. Pep Saul also played guard for us. So did Whitey Skoog, after we signed him out of the University of Minnesota in 1951.

The last championship club was in the 1953–1954 season. That team was the prototype for the type of lineup NBA teams still try to put together today: Mikan was the center, Mikkelsen was the power forward, Pollard was the quick forward, Martin was the point guard, and Skoog was the shooting guard.

Skoog introduced the jump shot to the Midwest when he was at the University of Minnesota. Kundla was not a big fan of the way Skoog played defense, and it took a while for him to break into the regular lineup.

We were playing the Knicks in the finals in 1953, and Skoog was unhappy with his playing time. Kundla was upset at the way Whitey had reacted to some order he had given him. Kundla was threatening not to take Skoog to New York. Max and I told him, "Skoog's going to New York."

We would bring in DePaul coach Ray Meyer for the playoffs. Meyer had a tremendous relationship with Mikan, from being Big George's college coach, and Meyer also could help Kundla on the bench. We would give Meyer $2,000 to join us in the playoffs.

On this night in New York, Mikan took a jump shot in the first half, and Meyer said to him at halftime, "Take that jump shot and stick it in your ear." Mikan was mad and would not shoot in the second half. He kept passing the ball outside to Skoog, and Skoog started pouring in jump shots. He went crazy and helped us win two games in New York and another championship.

Whitey's last name was pronounced "Skug." The New York writers came to me and said, "We know about Mikan, Mikkelsen, Pollard, and Martin. But who is this 'Skooj?' Where did 'Skooj' come from?"

The biggest games in basketball in the early years of the NBA were not in the championship series. The biggest games were the Lakers against the Harlem Globetrotters. The NBA was not really integrated, so all of the great black players were working for Abe Saperstein and the Globetrotters.

The biggest crowd they ever had at Chicago Stadium was for the Lakers and the Globetrotters—more than 20,000. We would play two games. Saperstein would keep the gate in Chicago, and we would keep the gate in Minneapolis, where we would jam the Auditorium.

It was a great series, until the Lakers beat the Globetrotters a couple of times. Saperstein wanted to advertise his team as the greatest in basketball, so he canceled the series.

We were able to make slick moves to get the Lakers started with Pollard and Mikan. I had the great draft in 1949 with Mikkelsen, Martin, and Harrison. By '52, we had won four titles in five years, the fans were spoiled, and I had to come up with something that would keep this going down the road after Mikan was finished.

When he was at Kansas, Clyde Lovellette was the outstanding big man in the country. After college, he was playing for Phillips 66, which had been signing most of the top players in Kansas, Oklahoma, and Texas for years.

The league draft meeting was held in Milwaukee that year. We had won another title, so we were drafting last. Max Winter kept bugging me, asking who we were going to draft? Max liked to go out in the hall during breaks and talk to his buddies in the league about the choice we were going to make.

I kept telling Max, "Leave me alone. We'll see what happens."

My guess was the other teams would pass on Lovellette because they figured he was locked into the Phillips 66ers. We had our team coming back intact, so I was thinking long-term—post-Mikan.

No one took Lovellette. When our turn came, I said, "The Lakers take Clyde Lovellette."

Ned Irish of the New York Knicks started screaming bloody murder. "The Lakers have Mikan, they have Mikkelsen, they have Pollard," Irish said. "They can't have Lovellette. We won't have a league."

I got up and said: "This is a free country. I read the NBA constitution. I read the U.S. Constitution. There are no rules against the Lakers drafting Lovellette."

We didn't sign Lovellette right away. He played the 1952–1953 season with the Phillips 66ers.

For us, the wear and tear was starting to show on Mikan. He had been elbowed and kneed and punched every night for six years. It was getting more important to sign Lovellette.

I kept challenging Max. I said, "You won't go down to Kansas because you can't make a deal, and you know it." Finally, Winter turned into Minnesota's Mad Max, went to Kansas, gave Lovellette $9,000, came back home, and waved the contract in my face.

As it turned out, I was glad Max made the final deal, because Lovellette turned out to be much less than a great player. He was a goofy guy. He wasn't the answer to continue the Lakers dynasty.

Mikan retired in 1954, then came back for half of the 1955–1956 season. He was not the same. We had a below-average team.

The Celtics were on the rise in Boston, and Auerbach thought

Old basketball friends, 1996

During a banquet at Hamline University in 1996, former Minneapolis Lakers star George Mikan (left), myself, and former UCLA coaching great John Wooden caught up on old times.

they had a chance to win a championship, if he could get a rebounder to go with Cousy, Bill Sharman, and Ed Macauley. Auerbach wanted Mikkelsen, who still had a couple of years left in him. Boston had three Kentucky guys who were in the service—Cliff Hagan, Frank Ramsey, and Lou Tsioropoulos. We agreed to a deal. Auerbach would get Mikkelsen, and we would get the three Kentucky players, who would not be done with the military until well after the season.

Without Mikkelsen, we were almost a cinch to wind up with the worst record in the league. That's what I wanted. That would have given us the No. 1 draft choice. Bill Russell was coming out of San Francisco, and after we finished last, he was going to be the next great center of the Minneapolis Lakers.

Dick Enroth was the Lakers' play-by-play announcer. He loved Mikkelsen. Plus, Enroth did not want to spend the rest of the season describing a team that had no chance to win. Enroth went to lunch with Berger and pleaded with him not to trade Mikkelsen.

Berger came back and said, "Sid, I don't think we should do this trade."

We argued for a few minutes, and I said, "Fine, Bennie, I'll call Walter Brown [the owner of the Celtics] and cancel the deal, and we can regret it for the rest of our lives."

I called Brown and said the Lakers had decided not to trade Mikkelsen. When the season ended, Rochester had the No. 1 draft choice. Rather than Russell, Rochester drafted Sihugo Green, a guard from Duquesne University. St. Louis had the second pick and took Russell, then traded him to Auerbach and the Celtics for Ed Macauley and Cliff Hagan.

In his autobiography, Auerbach denied he had agreed to a trade for Mikkelsen. After Red got Russell, the Celtics won thirteen championships in fifteen years. The trade for Russell is the source of Auerbach's legend. Do you think Red is going to admit he was ready to make a trade that almost certainly would have led to Russell coming to the Lakers?

Our dynasty was over. The NBA belonged to Russell and the Celtics. I got out of the Lakers operation in 1957. Berger made a deal to sell the franchise to Bob Short and a group of local people for $150,000.

Short was not the type of guy to lose money, so he moved the Lakers to Los Angeles after the 1960 season. Louie Mohs, my old circulation boss at the Minneapolis *Times*, ran the Lakers for Short. After starting in Los Angeles, they sold the team for $5.2 million, an unheard of figure for a basketball team.

The NBA was gone from Minneapolis and did not return for twenty-nine years. I've always blamed Dick Enroth for that.

Chapter 6

Becoming Big League

The idea of major league baseball in Minnesota was not worth considering until the 1950s. The American and National Leagues had sixteen teams in eleven cities. It always had been that way. It seemed like it always would be that way.

St. Louis and Chicago were the only places in the Midwest with big league baseball. The rest of us—Minneapolis, St. Paul, Milwaukee, Kansas City, Denver—were American Association towns.

The Millers played in Nicollet Park on Nicollet Avenue and Lake Street. It was so short in right field that fly balls would sail over the wall and bounce off the President Cafe or the Gabberts Furniture Store across the street. Gabberts lost a lot of windows to home run balls.

I started pedaling my bike out to the park as a kid. Mike Kelly was the owner of the Millers. I would drop off three papers with Kelly, and he would let me hang around the ballpark. I also sold peanuts and popcorn at Millers games. Later, when I had the news run, I continued to bring Kelly his newspapers.

Ted Williams played for the Millers in 1938, and I got to know him. While he was in Minneapolis, Williams bought a Buick. We went for a ride on Wayzata Boulevard in that new car. Williams must have been driving 100 miles per hour. I was certain we were going to crash and die.

Years later, I was doing the *Sports Hero* interview show for WCCO Radio. Williams was voted into the Hall of Fame. I wanted him for the radio show, so I called the Red Sox office and found Bill Crowley, the Red Sox public relations director.

Baseball buddy

I have known Ted Williams since his early days with the Minneapolis Millers. Here I am interviewing him while he was managing the Washington Senators.

"Do you know where Williams is?" I asked Crowley.

"Right here," Crowley said. "But he won't talk to you. He won't even talk to the Boston writers, and they are standing in the next room."

I said to Crowley: "Would you please ask him?"

A few seconds later, Williams came on the phone. WCCO was the only station in the country that had an interview with Williams.

When Williams was in town as manager of the Washington Senators, Shirley Hutton from WCCO-TV wanted to do an interview with him. Shirley is a beautiful woman. I arranged the interview with Williams. She brought her cameraman over to the hotel, and Williams answered the questions.

The next year, Shirley wanted another interview with Williams. I called and he said, "I'll do it, but only if she comes alone."

Williams is a beauty—and the type of lifelong contact I was able to make in the days when Minneapolis and St. Paul were in the American Association.

In the fifties, the Yankees had great Triple A ballclubs at Denver. The Denver Bears would stay at the Nicollet Hotel. I would go hang around in the morning and have breakfast with them. I knew Ralph Houk, Tony Kubek, Bobby Richardson, and Clete Boyer very well before they went to the big leagues.

Indianapolis also had outstanding teams, with Al Lopez as the manager and players such as Herb Score and Rocky Colavito. Lopez was a tremendous manager. He always had some trick up his sleeve.

Halsey Hall covered the Millers, first for the *Journal*, then for the *Tribune*. The Nicollet Park press box was attached to the roof, which was made of tarpaper, except for a few planks. Halsey would get full of gin and start walking around on a plank. He would be teetering on the plank above the tarpaper, and we were always convinced he was going to plunge to his death.

Lopez and his Indianapolis team were playing the Millers in the championship series. The winner would go to the Little World Series to play the International League champion. Indianapolis was leading by three runs late in the game.

Dave Barnhill hit a triple that tied the game. He was standing on third, the crowd was cheering, and then Lopez came out of the dugout to talk to the base umpire. It was a cold night, and Lopez had his jacket on in reverse, zipped all the way up, so all you could see was the black lining and some white of his uniform around the neck.

Hall was on the roof, and he shouted, "Here comes that son of a bitch Lopez. He looks like a Catholic priest but he's going to screw us sure as hell."

Halsey was right. Lopez convinced the umpire that a Millers runner had missed a base. The runner was called out, the rally was over, and Indianapolis won the ballgame.

The first major league move came when the Boston Braves went to Milwaukee in 1953. When the Braves got there, the people went crazy. Milwaukee drew over two million people. Minnesotans were flocking to Milwaukee all summer. Every Rotary Club and American Legion Club was organizing bus trips to see a major league ballgame.

The owners of the American and National League teams looked at those crowds in Milwaukee and all they could see were dollar signs. All the financially struggling teams started looking around for other locations.

The St. Louis Browns moved to Baltimore in 1954. The Philadelphia Athletics were the next team that was going to leave. Abe Saperstein, the owner of the Harlem Globetrotters, and baseball promoter Bill Veeck made an offer to buy the Athletics. If they had gotten the team, they were going to move it to the Twin Cities. The Athletics wound up going to Kansas City in 1955.

We had to get organized if we were going to get a baseball team. John Cowles, Sr. felt it was important to get a baseball team. He had built the circulation of the Sunday *Tribune* to more than 600,000. He felt that sports—especially Gophers football—had been the biggest circulation builder. He put the full force of the *Star* and *Tribune* behind the effort to get a ballclub.

The first time we really thought we had a ballclub was with the New York Giants. The Millers were a Giants farm club after World War II and into the mid-fifties. Giants owner Horace Stoneham had seen the day coming when the Giants would have to leave New York and the Polo Grounds. He bought a piece of land out by what was then the Honeywell plant in St. Louis Park. The idea was to build a minor league park there, then expand it when the Giants moved to Minnesota.

Minneapolis and St. Paul always had competed in everything. The feeling was it would take both cities working together to get a big league team. There were a lot of meetings between politicians, civic leaders, and baseball boosters in Minneapolis and St. Paul, and it was decided to build the stadium on the University of Minnesota's agricultural campus, near the State Fairgrounds in St. Paul.

All that was required was for the university's Board of Regents to approve the sale of land. Behind the scenes, university comptroller Bill Middlebrook was working to kill the deal. So were some people in the little suburb of Falcon Heights, who didn't want the traffic that would be connected with a ballpark.

It surprised everyone when the university decided not to sell the land. The next choice was Bloomington, but St. Paul would not go along with that. They thought it was too much of a "Minneapolis" location.

Minneapolis built Metropolitan Stadium in Bloomington. St. Paul—"East Germany," as I've been known to call it—built Midway Stadium. Then, the two cities fought with one another, as well as fighting with other areas, to get a big league team.

Metropolitan Stadium opened with the Millers playing there in 1956. It was all set that the Giants were going to move to Bloomington for the 1957 season. Stoneham sent in his groundskeeper and had him put in the infield so it would be up to big league standards when the Giants arrived.

Walter O'Malley of the Brooklyn Dodgers heard that Stoneham was going to move to the Twin Cities. O'Malley knew that if he was the only National League team left in New York, the other owners would never let him leave. O'Malley went to Stoneham and offered a package deal: The Dodgers and the Giants would leave for California together in 1958. O'Malley was much sharper than Stoneham. O'Malley took Los Angeles, and he gave San Francisco to Stoneham.

When we lost our shot at the Giants, we had to start scrambling. Charlie Johnson was an official spokesman for Minneapolis in the effort to get a team. Gerry Moore from the Minneapolis Chamber of Commerce and local car dealer Bill Boyer, the head of the baseball task force, would also go to the league meetings and lobby with the owners to get us a team.

Our best bet seemed to be the Cleveland Indians. They won 111 games and went to the World Series in 1954, then started to go downhill as a team and at the gate. Nate Dolan was running the Indians, and his partners were Bill Daley and I. A. O'Shaughnessy, who was from St. Paul.

In 1957, I was packing a bag at my apartment on Xerxes Avenue and getting ready to go to the airport to cover the World Series between Milwaukee and the Yankees. The phone rang, and it was Dolan calling from Cleveland. He said, "Where are you going?"

I told him I was headed for the World Series.

Dolan said: "You're going to the airport, but not to go to the World Series. You're going to pick up Daley. Mrs. O'Shaughnessy is very sick in a St. Paul hospital, and Daley is flying in to see her. I'm ready to leave Cleveland. If you people can meet with Daley while he is in the Twin Cities and convince him to go along, then we will announce that the Indians will be moving to Minnesota for the 1958 season."

I picked up Daley, and he agreed to come down to the newspaper building for a meeting. John Cowles, Sr., Joyce Swan, and I were there from the *Star* and *Tribune*, plus Moore, Boyer, and the other people involved in the effort to get baseball. We talked and finally Daley said, "If Dolan wants to move, we can work it out."

And then he told us one more thing: "O'Shaughnessy has a big ego. St. Paul is his hometown. He would be quite the hero if he brought the team to St. Paul. He might decide that we should take the Indians to Midway Stadium, instead of Bloomington."

John Sr. asked for a suggestion, and Daley said: "If you could run a big story on him, it might help."

Immediately, Cowles called the editor of the *Tribune*'s Sunday magazine, and said: "How much advance time do we need to change the layout?"

The editor said, "Two weeks."

Cowles said, "You're wrong. It takes one week. Next week's magazine is going to be devoted to photos and a story on I. A. O'Shaughnessy."

O'Shaughnessy had his cover story, and we figured we had that ballclub. Then a Cleveland newspaper—the *Press*—started fighting back. The editor of the *Press* called in Dolan and said: "We have heard a rumor you have connections to the Mafia. We're going to investigate. I don't know if you're in the Mafia, but when we get done with the investigation, there's a good chance you will be." That made Dolan nervous, although it didn't kill the move.

What killed it was when the lawyers for Cleveland started going over every inch of the Indians' lease and found out this: After the war, the Indians were drawing huge crowds, and Cleveland built Municipal Stadium for the ballclub and for the Cleveland Browns. Before that, the Indians had played in League Park, which was much more of a baseball park than the big place on Lake Erie. The city had financed the stadium, and the politicians were worried that Bill Veeck, who was then running the club, would move back to League Park if it did not work out at Municipal Stadium. Veeck agreed to language in the lease reading that the Indians could play in no other stadium "in

Cleveland." However, Veeck's lawyer forgot to put "in Cleveland" in the official document, so the lease read that the Indians could play in no other stadium, period.

We were dead on another team. We had lost the Giants to San Francisco, and we were not able to get the Indians out of Cleveland. Another owner who was hurting financially was Calvin Griffith with the Washington Senators.

Calvin was willing to move, but the other American League owners were against it. They were scared to death that the politicians would be upset if Washington, D.C. did not have a team and would take away baseball's antitrust exemption.

That was the big problem. There was another problem that the Minneapolis group always had to be aware of: Charlie Johnson.

When Charlie would get frustrated, he had a tendency to lose all tact and say what was on his mind. And, when he had few drinks on top of frustration, he was apt to say anything.

We were in Baltimore for the 1958 All-Star Game. It was starting to look like Calvin and the Senators were the last best hope for a big league team. Charlie was drinking at the All-Star party, and I was there to keep an eye on him—to make sure he did not say the wrong thing to the wrong person.

When we left the party to go to our rooms, Boston Red Sox General Manager Joe Cronin was getting on the elevator at the same time. Cronin was going to replace Will Harridge as the American League president in 1959. Most importantly, Cronin was Calvin Griffith's brother-in-law.

Cronin was a wonderful human being. Behind the scenes, he was on our side, because he wanted to see Calvin get out of Washington and finally make some money owning that ballclub.

We all stepped into the elevator, the door closed, and then Charlie looked over at Cronin and said: "We don't want your brother-in-law. We don't want that cheap S.O.B. We can do a lot better."

I apologized to Cronin and hustled Charlie off to bed. I knew the story would get back to Calvin. I figured we were dead with another ballclub. I hoped the story on Charlie bad-mouthing Calvin to Cronin would not get back to John Cowles, Sr.

When we got back from the All-Star Game, there was a message waiting for me from Joyce Swan, Cowles's right-hand man. He wanted me to come to his office. He asked, "What happened on the trip?"

Charlie was my boss and my friend. I said, "Nothing happened."

Swan said, "I already know what happened." Then Swan showed me a copy of a telegram he had sent to Calvin Griffith that read: "Charlie Johnson no longer speaks for Minneapolis on baseball matters."

It took a couple more years but the deal finally was worked out. Calvin was ready to make the announcement that he was moving to Minnesota at an American League meeting that was held after the 1960 World Series. Charlie Johnson, Bill Boyer, Gerry Moore, and a couple of other people went to New York for the announcement.

I wasn't part of the group. It was a big disappointment that the newspaper did not send me, but it turned out to be fortunate that I was back in Minnesota.

Charlie called me at home in the morning and said: "This thing is starting to get screwed up. The Indians are fighting it, because they want the Twin Cities available if they can figure out a way to get out of Cleveland. And now, the Yankees are backing Cleveland and voting against the move. How well do you know Dan Topping and Del Webb?"

Topping and Webb were the co-owners of the Yankees. The Yankees were the only big draw in the American League. They could do the other teams favors with the schedule and with exhibition games. So, the Yankees called the shots on an issue like this.

I had to say to Charlie, "I know Webb, but not well enough to call him and exert any influence. I can't help you on this one. I guess we're in trouble."

I hung up the phone and tried to think if there was anyone I knew who could get a big favor out of Webb and Topping. The one thing I knew is they had their physical checkups at Mayo Clinic. Dr. Bayrd Horton was a Mayo department head and had taken care of the Yankees for years.

I called Dr. Horton in Rochester and said: "Have you heard from Topping and Webb lately?" He said no, but they were coming in for the annual checkup in a couple of weeks.

I said: "Doc, you can be a hero. There is supposed to be an announcement today that the Washington Senators are moving to

Baseball friend

Bill Veeck and I relax after an interview. Veeck is famous for his baseball promotions during his years as owner and general manager of several major league teams.

Minnesota, but now there are complications. We need the Yankees' vote to get this baseball team. You're the one guy I know who might be able to get this vote for us, if you would ask Webb and Topping to do it as a favor to you."

Dr. Horton became all upset. He said it took a lot of guts for me to ask him to do something that was so obviously unethical.

I said, "If you can't, you can't, Doc. But here's the number of the hotel. I'm sure Webb and Topping would take your call."

I was walking out of my house an hour later and the phone rang. It was Doc Horton. He said, "Listen, you S.O.B. I made that call. You got the vote."

Calvin's request to move had been tabled at the morning session. At the afternoon session, the Yankees backed it, and we had a ball-club. The American League took care of the Washington problem by deciding to put expansion teams in Washington and Los Angeles.

John Cowles, Sr. always felt—and I agreed with him—that an area could not be big league if it did not have a major league ballclub.

We became big league on October 31, 1960, when Calvin Griffith announced he was bringing his team to Minnesota.

The excitement was unbelievable. For Minnesota to get a major league team after all the work we did—it was the greatest feeling in the world. The other sports were nothing compared to baseball at that time. Baseball was what made you big league. And the *Star* and *Tribune* had done more in getting the Twins here than any outfit in town.

The Dodgers had the farm club in St. Paul and the Red Sox were in Minneapolis. Calvin was not going to pay the territorial fees to those teams, so the *Star* and *Tribune* wrote out the checks to the Dodgers and the Red Sox.

The other big thing for Calvin was radio and television money. The Senators were getting next to nothing for those rights in Washington. Larry Haeg at WCCO Radio and Art Lund at the Campbell-Mithun advertising agency were able to line up a big radio and TV package with Hamm's Brewery. It was worth something like $600,000, big money back then.

Calvin came to town and we had big luncheons and banquets for him. After being poor-mouthed in the Washington newspapers, Calvin was a hero. He loved it.

Morris Chalfen and Ben Berger sold the Lakers to Bob Short and his group in 1957. Max Winter and I dropped out of the basketball picture. Max was interested in getting involved in pro football.

The pro football franchise that was in big trouble at the time was the Chicago Cardinals. The owner was a guy named Walter Wolfner. His wife, Vi Bidwill, had inherited the team. Gerry Moore and I went to Chicago to try to convince Wolfner to have the Cardinals play a couple of regular-season games at Met Stadium. We wanted to prove to the National Football League that the Twin Cities would support a team.

Joyce Swan and I helped convince Cowles to guarantee the money to get the games. Wolfner agreed to play two of his home games—one against Philadelphia, the other against the New York Giants—at the Met for $125,000 apiece.

After Wolfner took the money, Swan said, "Sid, if these games don't draw, we're both going to be looking for jobs."

The Minneapolis and St. Paul Minutemen—the group of civic and sports boosters—went out and hustled tickets. The Eagles-Cardinals game was played in late October and drew 20,112. The Giants-Cardinals game was played in late November and drew 26,625. This was before the Met was expanded, so it was jammed for the Giants game.

John Mara, co-owner of the Giants, said, "I didn't think pro football would work here because I thought it was strictly Golden Gopher country. I think I was wrong. If you can draw 26,000 for this game, it shows me there is interest in pro football here."

We thought after the way those games drew and the amount of money we paid that the Cardinals would move to Minnesota. Instead, Wolfner moved the team to St. Louis, which was his hometown.

Those crowds had demonstrated that Minnesota was more than a college state. Max Winter, Bill Boyer, and H. P. Skoglund had formed a partnership to get a pro football team earlier in 1959. The National Football League would not say anything definite about expanding, so Winter, Boyer, and Skoglund acquired one of the eight franchises in a new league—the American Football League.

I still thought we would be better off waiting for the NFL to expand than to take a team in the AFL. My feeling was, if pro football was going to make it here—the Gophers were still big and about to go to the Rose Bowl for the first time—then it was going to have to be in the NFL, not a second-rate league.

I called NFL Commissioner Bert Bell a few times, and he indicated the NFL might do something. The guy I really drove crazy with phone calls was George Halas of the Chicago Bears. Papa Bear still was running the NFL at that time. He told me, "If Minneapolis waits, we're going to do something soon, but we're sure not going to expand if you already have an AFL team."

Later, the AFL filed a big antitrust suit against the NFL. Halas was on the stand, and he was asked, "How much involvement did you have in getting the NFL franchise for Minneapolis?"

And Halas said: "Have you ever heard of Sid Hartman in Minneapolis? Well, he's a newspaper guy up there, and he called me every day. Those were the conversations I had about Minneapolis." Halas's comments are in the court record.

Finally, there was a big meeting in Skoglund's office, to decide whether to go ahead with the AFL or wait for an NFL expansion team. The meeting started late in the afternoon and lasted until three in the morning. There were five people there: Skoglund, Boyer, Winter, attorney Sheldon Kaplan, and me.

Skoglund was pushing hard for the AFL. Joe Foss, the World War II hero and former South Dakota governor, was the first AFL commissioner. Skoglund and Foss were buddies. Skoglund knew it would hurt Foss and it would not look good for the AFL if Minnesota dropped out. Winter and Boyer outvoted him. They decided to wait for an NFL expansion team. In late January 1960, Oakland was given Minneapolis's franchise in the AFL.

There was an NFL meeting in Miami, and it went on forever. First, it took more than twenty ballots to elect a new commissioner—Pete Rozelle—to replace Bell. Then, the owners could not decide if they wanted to respond to the AFL by expanding.

After a few days, the Minnesota delegation that was at the meeting trying to get an expansion team gave up and went home. The only person who stayed was Max Winter. Paul Brown from Cleveland and George Preston Marshall from Washington kept saying to Max: "Stick around. The owners want to go to Dallas to keep the AFL from getting a hold there. If we vote in Dallas, we're not going to expand by one team but by two."

Max stayed and he came home with a franchise. The NFL decided to add Dallas as a thirteenth team for the 1960 season and to add Minnesota to get to an even number again in 1961.

The expansion franchises cost $600,000 apiece, but the owners only had to put up a small piece of that in cash. Winter, Boyer, and Skoglund brought in another partner, Bernie Ridder, the publisher of the St. Paul newspapers. Ole Haugsrud, the former owner of the Duluth Eskimos in pro football's early years, was allowed to buy a small piece of the team.

Rozelle was known to favor a national—rather than regional—TV package in which all teams shared revenue. It was an innovation in sports business that major league baseball still has not been able to figure out nearly four decades later. Rozelle's plan meant that it did not make any difference if a team was in Green Bay or New York—it would have an equal share of the TV money and thus would have a chance to compete.

For fifteen years, the Lakers were our only major league team. We lost them in 1960, but it still was the greatest year in the history of Minnesota sports.

First, the long battle for baseball came to an end when Calvin Griffith announced he was bringing his ballclub to Minnesota. Second, we were awarded an NFL expansion franchise. And, third, the Gophers beat Iowa in a game between the Nos. 1 and 2 football teams in the country, they tied for the Big Ten championship, and they earned a trip to Minnesota's first Rose Bowl.

Sluggers

Hank Aaron and Twins home-run king Harmon Killebrew share some secrets in the dugout. I was as amazed as anyone when the Twins became a good team after just a few seasons in Minnesota.

Chapter 7

Calvin and the Twins

The American Association days were fun, mostly because of the rivalry between the Minneapolis Millers and the St. Paul Saints. In the thirties and forties, the highlights of the holidays—Memorial Day, Independence Day, and Labor Day—were the doubleheaders between the Millers and Saints. There would be a morning game at Nicollet Park in Minneapolis and an afternoon game at Lexington Park in St. Paul, or vice versa.

The Millers were a Giants farm club after World War II. Mike Kelly owned the team, and Rosy Ryan was the general manager. The Saints were a Dodgers farm club. Walter Seegar owned the team, and Mel Jones was the general manager.

We had Ted Williams playing for the Millers in 1938. We had Willie Mays in 1951. Carl Yastrzemski played for the Millers after they moved to Met Stadium in Bloomington. Roy Campanella and Duke Snider played for the Saints. You could put together an all-time all-star team with the ballplayers who came through Minneapolis and St. Paul in the American Association days.

The biggest problem with being in Triple A baseball was that, if a player was doing well, he would get called to the big leagues. The fans were going crazy for Mays, but he was hitting over .400 and only stayed in Minneapolis for a month.

One of the best players the Millers ever had was third baseman Ray Dandridge who came to Minneapolis after a tremendous career in the Negro Leagues. Dandridge and pitcher Dave Barnhill were the first black players for the Millers.

Dandridge had the biggest glove I had ever seen and, goodness, could he use it. Halsey Hall always called Dandridge the best player he had seen. Dandridge was also a terrific person. He went in the Hall of Fame as a Negro Leagues star.

We had a lot of fun at Nicollet Park and Lexington Park. George Brophy was working in the front office for the Millers. Tom Briere was covering the team for the *Tribune*. We all had broken in together as sportswriters at the *Times-Tribune*.

In the 1950s, when we were a Giants farm club, the Millers had a ballplayer named Foster Castleman. Castleman and I were both vying for the affections of a woman named Joyce Waddington. Briere and Brophy decided to stir up the situation. They sent out wedding invitations to 150 people around the country announcing that Joyce and I were getting married.

I was mailed gifts from all over. I spent the rest of that summer returning gifts and calling people to say there was no wedding. Brophy and Briere thought it was the greatest practical joke of all time.

Minor league baseball started to lose its appeal in the mid-fifties. Milwaukee had landed the Braves in 1953. There were bus caravans going from Minnesota to Milwaukee to see big league games in the summer. The feeling was, if Milwaukee has a major league team, we should have a team.

When the Twin Cities started the effort to get major league baseball, the Washington Senators were the last team on our list. Far and away the first choice was the New York Giants and the National League. Dodgers owner Walter O'Malley jobbed us on that deal, convincing Stoneham to move to San Francisco so O'Malley could move into the gold mine in Los Angeles.

The next team we thought we had was the Cleveland Indians. Remember, in the fifties, Cleveland had some good ballclubs. The Indians won 111 games and played in the World Series in 1954.

The Senators were finishing last in the American League most every year. The Griffiths were known as the lowest-budget operators in baseball.

Washington Post columnist Shirley Povich was a friend. Povich liked Calvin's uncle, Clark Griffith. After Clark died, Calvin took over the club. Povich thought that Calvin was the biggest dummy in the world.

About the time Calvin announced he was moving to Minnesota, Bill Veeck came out with a book. Veeck wrote about the franchise moves that had taken place, and there was a sentence reading, "Sid Hartman, a Minneapolis sports columnist, did not want Calvin Griffith and the Senators to move to Minnesota." Charlie Johnson was the guy who did not want the Senators, not me. As far as I was concerned, we had to take anything we could get, even if it was the most horse-bleep team in baseball.

Calvin had seen Veeck's book, and his reaction was, "Who in the hell is this guy Hartman? He doesn't want me here?"

Veeck had gotten me off on the wrong foot. Mo Siegel, a sportswriter for the Washington *Star*, took care of me. He was close to Calvin and told him that I was the newspaper guy he wanted to get along with in the Twin Cities.

The Senators became the Minnesota Twins, moved into Met Stadium, took over the concessions business, and there were relatives all over the place: Joe Haynes, Thelma Haynes, Sherry Robertson, Billy Robertson, Jimmy Robertson. You didn't know who was in charge of what. Your reaction was, "What is this? We didn't get a ballclub. We got a family." It was like being around the Beverly Hillbillies.

And then there was this guy Howard Fox. He wasn't a relative, but he was the guy hanging out at Woodhill and Wayzata Country Clubs with Calvin. We wondered, "How does Fox fit in?"

The story went like this: There had been seven children in the Robertson family in Montreal, Quebec. Bruce died young. That left six siblings—Mildred, Calvin, Thelma, Sherrod ("Sherry"), and the twins, Billy and Jimmy. The family was poor. Two of the children, Calvin and Thelma, went to Washington, D.C. to live with their aunt Addie and her husband, Clark Griffith. Calvin and Thelma were raised as the Griffiths's children and took the name, although they were never formally adopted. The rest of the family, the Robertsons, moved to Washington not long after. They lived in a house down the street from the Griffiths.

Thelma married Joe Haynes, a pitcher. Mildred married Joe Cronin, a Hall of Fame shortstop and, later, the American League president. Calvin and Thelma inherited an equal share of Clark Griffith's 52 percent ownership of the Senators. Calvin had the authority to run the ballclub.

When the Twins arrived in November 1960, Calvin was the president and general manager. Joe Haynes and Sherry Robertson were the other family members in the baseball operation. Billy Robertson was in charge of stadium operations—basically, dealing with the Met Stadium commission on finances and the lease. Jimmy was supposed to be in charge of concessions, although his real title should have been "Executive Director of the Twins Room." That was the hospitality room for the scouts, press, and employees.

One of the demands the Griffiths made when they were looking over Met Stadium was to have a good-sized space for that Twins Room. You wondered why until you saw all the booze and food being wheeled into the ballpark with "Twins Room" marked on it. A lot of whiskey and steak from those deliveries wound up in the various family members' liquor cabinets and freezers. The Griffiths fed themselves out of that Twins Room for years.

Howard Fox was a Virginia gentleman—much smoother than the Griffiths. He had started working for the club as a young man in Washington. He moved up to the job of traveling secretary. That was an important position with the Twins. The traveling secretary was the only person from the front office who went on road trips on a regular basis. Calvin would get a lot of his information from Fox on how things had gone on a road trip. Fox could twist that information any way he wanted.

Calvin also had his spy in the clubhouse: Raymond Crump, the equipment manager and home clubhouse man. There were times with the Twins when you had the feeling the equipment manager had more to do with what players were on the roster than did the manager.

It was an odd organization, but who cared? It was terrific to have major league baseball. The Upper Midwest went crazy, sending buses throughout the summer from every little town in Minnesota, the Dakotas, Iowa, Nebraska, and even Montana.

The Twins had the goofiest promotions—Nuns Day, Campers Weekend, the Twins Fly-In—but they all worked because people were hungry to have major league baseball. In those early years, there was no comparison between the Twins and the Vikings when it came to importance. Baseball was much bigger.

You would walk in Calvin's office and wonder how he was going to get any more junk in there. Fans kept stopping by his office with gifts. Sid Freeman, a discount clothier downtown, was in there with free suits once a week. If you came from Frazee or Fulda and had a present for Calvin, you could get in to see him. He loved free stuff.

After all those years of scraping by in Washington, the Griffiths owned a ballclub that led the American League in attendance for the Twins' first decade—1961 through 1970. They were rolling in money.

Calvin knew a lot about baseball, although Haynes and Sherry Robertson were the two sharpest guys. The Twins also made a good decision when they brought in George Brophy to work for Sherry. George had worked for the Millers. Brophy could find ballplayers.

The first manager was Cookie Lavagetto. Calvin did not like him at all. He was too defiant. Calvin wanted the manager to come up to his office before batting practice and talk about the previous night's game. Calvin wanted to ask, "Why did you bunt there?" or "Why didn't you have a left-hander warming up to face Roger Maris in the seventh?" It was not as much second-guessing as the fact Calvin wanted to know what the manager was thinking. Lavagetto took it personally. He would come out of those meetings grumbling.

The first game was played in Yankee Stadium. Pedro Ramos vs. Whitey Ford. It was hard to believe—a ballclub from Minnesota playing the most-famous sports team in the world. And then Ramos pitched a shutout and the Twins won 6-0.

When the Twins came back to open the home season, there was snow on the edge of the warning track and in front of the stands. There had been heavy snow in the Twin Cities right before the Twins left spring training in Orlando, Florida, and now there was a picture of Met Stadium covered in snow on the front page of the Orlando *Sentinel*. Calvin was looking at the picture, feeling depressed and saying, "We won't be able to play a game for the whole month of April. Even when the snow melts, the field will be too wet."

Arno Goethel, the baseball writer for the St. Paul newspapers, said: "After the snow is cleared, Calvin, you could bring in a couple of jet engines to dry the field."

Calvin looked at Goethel and said, "How in the hell are we going to get a jet airplane inside that ballpark?"

That was vintage Calvin. He would say the goofiest things. And there were times when he was the most gullible person in the world.

Steve Cannon has been the afternoon drive host on WCCO-AM for a long time. Cannon has several fictional characters to keep him company while he is doing the show. One is a crusty fellow named Morgan Mundane. Cannon loved the free meals in the press room, and he did not want Calvin to get mad at him. When he thought Calvin and the Twins had screwed up, he would use his Mundane voice to rip them. When Calvin would see Cannon, he would complain about Mundane, and Cannon would say, "Those are Morg's opinions, Calvin. I try, but I can't do anything to straighten him out."

One day, I was having lunch in the Twins Room with Calvin, and this guy in work clothes was in there. He was a repairman, fixing something, and Jimmy Robertson must have invited the guy to have lunch.

Calvin said, "Hey, Sid, who is the guy over at that table? I've never seen him before."

I said, "Don't you know, Calvin? That's Morgan Mundane."

Calvin said, "That son of a bitch. He's ripping me all the time and now he is in here eating for free. I'm going to go over and throw him out."

I convinced Calvin not to do that. "He'll only rip you more if you do that," I said.

A couple of weeks later, Calvin said, "I haven't seen that Morgan Mundane around here again. He must have found out I didn't like him in the Twins Room."

It was a lot of fun being around Calvin because he was such a character. His biggest problem was he had only a modest appreciation for the truth. He would tell you whatever version of a story that came to mind as he was talking to you. There were times when Calvin would be saying he was going to make a trade in the Minneapolis *Tribune* and denying he was going to make a trade in the *St. Paul*

Pioneer Press—on the same morning.

I went to see Calvin every day. I would get some news from him before the game, then check again after the game to make sure his story had not changed. For me, the great thing about Calvin was that he couldn't keep a secret. If Calvin had the secret for the atomic bomb, I could have gotten it out of him within five minutes. Fox would be standing next to Calvin, saying, "Don't talk, don't talk. We don't want him to know about this." But Calvin would talk. You just had to make sure he was giving you the true version of the story, not the other version.

The Twins were short of pitching, and they had holes in the infield the first year. Zoilo Versalles was a twenty-year-old shortstop with wonderful ability, but he had the emotions of a twelve-year-old. He kept leaving the team and going to live with this family in St. Paul. He was homesick for Cuba and the young wife he had there.

Calvin could not wait to fire Lavagetto. First, they gave Lavagetto a leave from the team "to rest." Then, they fired him and put in Calvin's man Sam Mele, who had been a coach. Mele would go up to the office and answer Calvin's B.S. questions every afternoon, so Calvin loved him.

The biggest shock about getting major league baseball was this: We wound up with a good ballclub. We thought we were getting this lousy team, and by 1962, the second season, the Twins were in the pennant race.

The Senators moved to Minnesota just as some young players were ready to become stars: Harmon Killebrew, Bob Allison, Earl Battey, Jim Kaat, Versalles. Camilo Pascual still could pitch. Don Mincher was a slugger. In 1963, Jimmie Hall came along. In 1964, Tony Oliva—or Mr. America, as I've always called him—was the Rookie of the Year. If they had the same juiced baseball with that team as they had in the nineties, the Twins would have hit 300 home runs in a few of those early seasons.

The Twins could have been even better if not for a couple of bad breaks. Bernie Allen, a former Purdue quarterback and a left-handed hitter, was going to be an All-Star second baseman until he blew out his knee. Jimmie Hall set a record for home runs by a rookie before he was hit in the head by left-handed pitcher Steve Hamilton and never was the same.

Killebrew was the hero of the fans, with those majestic home runs he would hit. He was not the hero of the sportswriters. He was a decent fellow and polite, but he gave nothing to a reporter. Harmon was here fourteen years, and I don't think he ever gave anyone an interesting quote.

Allison and I never did get along. He was a jerk as far as I was concerned. We had been a minor league town, and Allison was really the first guy the Twin Cities sportswriters had "big league" us—meaning, he was condescending and arrogant for no reason other than he thought that was the way a major leaguer was supposed to act.

The best guy for the press with the early Twins was Kaat. He was a workhorse as a pitcher and a shoot-from-the-hip talker. He was as good with the information as a twenty-five-year-old pitcher as he has been over the past ten, fifteen years as the best baseball analyst on television.

Kaat never got along with Calvin. It drove him crazy that, no matter how good a season a player had, you had to fight Calvin to get a ten-dollar raise for the next season. In 1965, the Twins went to the World Series, and Kaat was 18-11 with a 2.83 ERA. Calvin said, "You only had seven complete games. Yes, we were in the Series, but you get paid by what you do individually. I can't give you more than a token raise." In 1966, Kaat won twenty-five games, had a 2.75 ERA, and a league-leading nineteen complete games. Calvin said, "The team had a lousy season. Yes, you had a good year, but you get paid by what the team does, not individual accomplishments. I can't give you more than a token raise." Every time Kaat was in a negotiating session with Calvin, he came out threatening to strangle him.

John Sain was the pitching coach in 1966. Kaat thought Sain had invented pitching. Sain's deal was to take over the pitching staff and separate it from the other players. Mele considered Sain an egomaniac and did not like him. The Twins fired Sain after the 1966 season. Kaat wrote his famous "open letter to Calvin" ripping him for firing Sain and sent it to the local media. Calvin was spitting mad at Kaat for that, but it made great copy for the newspapers.

Oliva was another of my favorites, although it was impossible to use him on my radio shows. Tony still had a thick Cuban accent. Before getting married, he was quite the ladies man. That's why I called him Mr. America.

The moment everyone remembers from 1965 came two days before the All-Star Game. The Twins were playing the Yankees on a Sunday afternoon at Met Stadium. The Twins were in first place. The All-Star Game was going to be played two days later at the Met. The combination of these two games had created more baseball excitement than ever in Minnesota—even more than in '61, when the Twins first came to town.

The Twins were down two runs in the ninth inning on that Sunday. There were two runners on and Killebrew was batting. A right-hander named Pete Mikkelsen was pitching for the Yankees. There was a full count when Killebrew touched off a long home run. Ray Scott was the play-by-play announcer. WCCO Radio must have replayed Scott's call of that home run 5,000 times in the years since then.

You knew when Killebrew hit it that something great was happening, that the Twins were going to the World Series. A team from Minnesota—the most horse-bleep team in the world we thought when we got it—was leaving the mighty Yankees for dead in the middle of July. You couldn't believe it.

And there was that same feeling in October: How can they be playing the World Series in Minnesota? The Dodgers, the greatest National League franchise, against the "Minnesota" Twins? The Twins beating Don Drysdale one day, Sandy Koufax the next, to start the World Series?

I kept looking down at the field from the press box and saying to myself, "You have to be kidding. All the times we got sent home from the major league meetings with nothing. All the times we were told, 'Minneapolis and St. Paul might never get a team.' And we're in the World Series? You have to be kidding."

After the Twins won the first two games in the World Series, we went to Los Angeles and lost three straight. The Dodgers had an infield as hard as concrete. Killebrew was playing third base, and Maury Wills and those guys were chopping the ball over his head.

Billy Martin was the third base coach. On the way back to Minnesota, he told Calvin Griffith, "When the Dodgers show up for the sixth game, we should have the slowest infield in the history of baseball."

Calvin asked Dick Erickson, the groundskeeper, if he could do anything to slow down the Dodgers. Erickson and his crew turned on the lights at Met Stadium late that night and folded a dozen wheelbarrows of sand into the dirt around first base.

The Dodgers started screaming during batting practice. The umpires made Erickson remove some of the loose dirt. But the grounds crew only took away a couple of wheelbarrows.

The Twins won that game. Jim ("Mudcat") Grant pitched and also hit a home run. The roar when he hit the home run rolled across the Bloomington prairie for five minutes. But Sandy Koufax was unhittable the next day and beat the Twins 2-0.

There were no hard feelings when it was over. The seventh game of a World Series had been played—in Minnesota! You had to be kidding.

The Twins would have been back in the World Series again in 1967, but two bad things happened. First, a couple of the relatives talked Calvin into firing Mele and replacing him with Cal Ermer. The Twins played well for Ermer that season, but in the long run, Mele was a much better manager.

Second, the Twins went to Boston needing to win one game out of two over the weekend to win the American League pennant. Kaat was leading and pitching great, then had something pop in his arm. He had to leave the game and the Twins lost.

Carl Yastrzemski was the best player in baseball that season, and he led Boston to the two victories that weekend. Yaz's biggest play came when he threw out Allison, trying to stretch a single to a double, by about twenty feet to take the steam out of a Twins rally.

There was an old baseball writer from the *Boston Globe* named Clif Keane. He was the smart-ass newspaperman of all time. Years later, Allison was at spring training in Orlando, Florida, hanging out with his buddy Jimmy Robertson. The Red Sox were at Tinker Field for an exhibition game. Keane was in the press box, which was twenty rows from the aisle where the fans walked in. Keane saw Allison walk in and he bellowed, so everyone in the ballpark could hear him, "Hey Allison, how far did Yaz have you out at second when you blew the bleepin' pennant?"

You could see the steam coming off Allison's neck. He was as strong as an ox. I thought Allison might come up and twist off Keane's head.

It was a strange feeling in Boston that weekend in '67. I've always rooted for the Minnesota teams to win, for two reasons: First, it makes my job easier; and second, I get to know the team officials, managers, coaches, and players, and wind up with a lot of friends.

I also always rooted for Yastrzemski. He was a nineteen-year-old kid when he played with the Millers. We would have dinner together. When the Red Sox came to town, Yaz and I would have lunch in the afternoon and then go to Market Bar-B-Que after the game. We were so close that, when I took my son Chad to All-Star Games, he would hang around with Yastrzemski's son Mike at the games.

Yeah, it might have cost the Twins the pennant when Allison was thrown out at second, but that was one of my best friends in baseball throwing out a guy I probably had more trouble with than any Minnesota athlete.

Chapter 8

Max Winter and the Vikings

I lived at 525 Humboldt Avenue North, and Max Winter lived across Sixth Avenue North on Elwood. I heard about Max when I was a young kid. He was a hot athlete at North High and Hamline University. Max won the conference medal as the outstanding athlete when he was at Hamline. Later, he coached an AAU basketball team on the North side called the Arrows. The players on that team—Mikey Alpert, Hashy Goodman, Len Siegel, Harold Sklar—were a few years older than me, and they were my heroes, the athletic stars of North High. The Arrows beat the best sixteen-year-old teams around town. I would go to those games.

After college, Max went to the Iron Range and ran a bowling alley for a time, then came back to Minneapolis. Max and his pal Ernie Fliegel were involved in managing fighters. Winter and Fliegel were great buddies of Jack Dempsey, Maxie Baer, and the rest of the New York boxing crowd.

When we were involved with the Lakers, Max and I would go to New York for NBA meetings. Winter would tell me to take care of the meetings, and he would head to Toots Shoor's restaurant to hang out with Dempsey and the rest of the New York sports figures. Of course, the underworld ran New York boxing, and Max knew those guys, too.

Max's strong point was promotion. He was the first guy to have a team band at a pro sports event. The Lakers were also the first pro team to have a highlight film. A guy named Dick Winick came to Max and said, "I've been trying to convince all these teams that a film would be great in promoting a team, but they all throw me out of the office." Max went for it, and we sold a lot of tickets by showing that highlight film to groups during the offseason.

Max also did a lot of work for Abe Saperstein and the Harlem Globetrotters. Max handled the promotion in the Midwest. He would also go to Europe and set up appearances for the Globetrotters.

Max drove me crazy promising tickets for a big game to his buddies—tickets that we already had sold. We were playing the Globetrotters, which was as tough a ticket to get as there was. I always had a supply of tickets in my desk drawer at the Lakers office. Max got in there and took out two hundred tickets and took care of all the big shots.

Unfortunately, they were tickets for a Philadelphia game. We had two hundred people—guys like Hubert Humphrey—showing up to sit in seats that already were sold. I had to round up every folding chair in the Auditorium and set up seats around the floor to take care of Max's guests.

Max and Fliegel opened a bar and restaurant on Hennepin Avenue called The 620 Club. The slogan there was "Where Turkey is King," but it could have been "Where Sports Talk is King." Max's joint was going strong when I started at the Minneapolis *Times* in 1944. There was a big, round table where a dozen people could sit. The table was occupied by the sports crowd at lunch time.

When Cullum was hard up for a column, he would write about the opinions that had been expressed at The Round Table. Thanks to Cullum, Max's joint, that table, and the people who had lunch there became a famous part of the Minneapolis sports scene. Dempsey would be there when he was in town. Mikan and Jim Pollard would come in. Old Gophers such as Louie Gross would be there. Mike Kelly and Rosie Ryan from the baseball Millers would be there.

Norm McGrew from the Minneapolis Chamber of Commerce was a regular. One time, I lost a twenty-five-dollar bet to McGrew, brought in the twenty-five bucks in bags of pennies, dumped the pennies on the table, then someone swept most of the pennies off the table. McGrew had to spend half the afternoon on his hands and knees picking up pennies.

If nothing else was on your schedule, you would go to The 620

Club for lunch, sit at The Round Table, and argue for a couple of hours.

Cullum was in there because of Tony Stecher, not Max Winter. Stecher was at The Round Table every day. He was the wrestling and boxing promoter in Minneapolis. Stecher was Cullum's man. Stecher would have preferred to promote only wrestling, but Cullum wanted to have big fights to write about. So, Stecher promoted fights.

Winter was an important guy on the sports scene—boxing, the Lakers, the Vikings—from the time I started as a sportswriter until Mike Lynn took charge of the day-to-day operation of the Vikings in the mid-eighties. I quoted him regularly in my column for over forty years. For many years, we would run a half-dozen small mug shots, called "half-column cuts" in newspaper jargon, with the column. Max's mug seemed to be in there a couple of days a week.

Max was also the leading proponent for building a dome in downtown Minneapolis. I lined up with him on that one, and we fought a bloody battle for a couple of years. When we won that one, the anti-dome people screamed about "Max and Sid." They spread the rumor that Max and I owned land around the dome site. Not true. They spread rumors that I owned part of the Vikings. Absolutely not true.

What all of this did was cement the idea that Max was my No. 1 connection—my godfather, my entry—into sports in the Twin Cities. That was never true.

There were many people I was closer to than Max. We worked well together with the Lakers. Because of my connection to the team, I wrote little about the Lakers. If I did, I would quote Max. He loved to get his name in the paper.

With the Vikings, he was a good source for me—most of the time. Max would get mad at me, just as he did other reporters. When Jim Finks left as the general manager of the Vikings, I criticized Max, and he did not talk to me for a long time.

Later, Max decided Mike Lynn was stabbing him in the back. Publicly, I stayed away from that issue. Privately, I told Max he was dead wrong about Lynn—that Lynn had done great things for him. Again, Max was upset with me.

Max was seventeen years older than me. Socially, we did little together. We respected each other. But the idea of an unbreakable, Max-and-Sid tie-in that was talked about for decades in Minnesota was always more legend than fact.

After the Twin Cities turned down the AFL and landed an NFL franchise, the owners had to put together an organization. Years later, Max Winter wound up getting most of the credit as our pro football pioneer. Mike Lynn insured Max's legacy by getting that facility built in Eden Prairie and then naming it Winter Park.

Bill Boyer had been the head of the Major League Baseball Task Force. He also was a leader of the Minneapolis Chamber of Commerce. The chamber was a big force in everything that came to town back then—not the ceremonial thing that it is now. Most people have forgotten that Boyer, not Winter, was the first president of the Vikings. H. P. Skoglund and Bernie Ridder were the real business people among the owners. Max was mostly in the background until 1964, when he took over for Boyer as team president.

Boyer was drinking too much. Skoglund and Ridder did not want him representing the Vikings with the league because of that. And, they were too busy running their companies to be the president of a football team. That's how Max wound up as president—basically, by default.

When the Vikings started, it was new NFL Commissioner Pete Rozelle who recommended that the Vikings hire Bert Rose as general manager. Rose was part of Rozelle's L.A. Rams connection. Tex Schramm had been the Rams' general manager, and Rozelle was his public relations director. Then, Rozelle became the general manager, and Rose was his P.R. director. Schramm wanted to get an NFL expansion franchise in Dallas. Rozelle was elected commissioner at the 1960 meeting in Miami, then the NFL awarded expansion franchises to Dallas for that season and to Minnesota for '61. The Rozelle connection is what allowed Schramm and his group to get a team in Dallas.

The least the Vikings could do after the help they received from Rozelle was to give his man Rose the job as general manager. Rose was given the power to make the football decisions. He felt it was important to hire a big name coach. Rose wanted Norm Van

Brocklin, another guy with a connection to the Rams as their one-time quarterback.

Hiring Van Brocklin, the Dutchman, turned out to be the dumbest thing ever done by Rose. Van Brocklin was power hungry. He wound up undermining Rose and getting him fired.

Van Brocklin took the Philadelphia Eagles to the 1960 NFL championship, beating Vince Lombardi and the Green Bay Packers. The Eagles had been an underdog team through that entire season. Van Brocklin came across as this hard-edged, shoot-from-the-hip, tough guy who had pulled together a team and refused to lose.

Van Brocklin was the right coach for an expansion team coming into a college football market. Remember, the football Gophers had gone to the Rose Bowl for the first time after the 1960 season and went back again after the 1961 season. Van Brocklin's personality was so strong that he gave the Vikings a lot of publicity. The image he brought with him gave the Vikings instant credibility.

It was that combination—the Dutchman's personality and image—that sold tickets for the Vikings in the early years. They averaged 36,000 at Met Stadium in 1961, which was better than a lot of people expected in a town that the Gophers still owned.

I never got along with Van Brocklin. That's not surprising. It was almost impossible for a newspaperman to get along with that ornery son of a bitch. He liked Dick Cullum, but that was about it.

I had a radio show with Van Brocklin. Half the time, he did not want to do the show. Then, when I did corral him, every question asked was a dumb question. He would say, "Why are you asking that stupid question?" He would say it on the air. He was getting paid and wouldn't do the show. We finally dropped it.

Van Brocklin also hung a nickname on me: "Cyanide Sid." We were on a Vikings road trip, and I called the room of Jim Finks, who had replaced Rose as general manager. Van Brocklin answered the phone. Finks asked, "Who is it?"

Van Brocklin said, "It's Cyanide Sid."

Finks thought that was great because he loved nicknames. Trainer Fred Zamberletti, the Vikings trainer for life, still calls me "Cyanide."

The Dutchman's biggest problem with me, other than the

radio show, was my relationship with Fran Tarkenton. Van Brocklin did not like the idea we were close friends.

The Vikings beat the Packers 20-17 in Green Bay in 1966. The great center, Mick Tingelhoff, had played the game with a fracture in his ankle. After the game, Vince Lombardi called Tingelhoff one of the toughest players he had seen.

Tarkenton also had an outstanding game, and I wrote the next morning how Tarkenton and Tingelhoff had studied films and come up with their own game plan.

Van Brocklin called and wanted to have lunch. Those lunches were always dangerous because, by the time you got there, Van Brocklin would have a few beers in him. He would holler and you would listen.

When I got there, he said, "You have to make up your mind whose side you are on. You're either on my side or Tarkenton's side. If you're on his side, stay out of here. You're either my friend or Tarkenton's friend."

I had taken enough of his garbage. I said, "I'll take Tarkenton."

Van Brocklin threatened to kick the hell out of me. He wanted to get into fights—physical as well as verbal—all the time.

Van Brocklin's biggest problem, along with being an egomaniac, was that he drank too much. Boyer drank too much. Rose drank too much. It was quite a thirsty operation in those early years.

When Van Brocklin would get drunk, he would become even more belligerent and more determined to get in a fight. He succeeded a few times, particularly with Jim Klobuchar, another volatile personality, who was covering the Vikings and Van Brocklin for the Minneapolis *Tribune*.

Klobuchar was working for the Associated Press when the Vikings were starting up. Charlie Johnson tried to hire him to write football for the Minneapolis *Star*. Klobuchar did not want to work for the *Star*, the afternoon paper.

Klobuchar had a reputation as a hard worker and an excellent writer. I took him to dinner and then went back to Charlie and said, "Can I hire Klobuchar for the *Tribune*?"

Charlie said, "You can try, but you're not going to get him."

I hired him. Charlie was mad as hell because I was able to hire

Klobuchar when he had failed to do so. I had problems with Van Brocklin. Klobuchar had problems with Van Brocklin. And Klobuchar and I had problems, the main one being this:

The *Tribune* had a small newshole—usually three pages with fourteen or fifteen columns—for sports during the week. Klobuchar wanted to fill up twelve of those columns by writing three, four stories a day on the Vikings.

We had a makeup editor for sports named Louie Green. Louie was a short little Jewish guy, over fifty years old, but he was as tough as nails. Louie would sit in the slot, surrounded by the sports copy desk, and he would go through the news wire. These were the stories that came off the Associated Press teletype. Louie would put the stories that he did not think he was going to use—but wanted to save, just in case—on the Spike. That's what it was, a spike with a sharp point that sat on a metal base, a couple of feet behind Louie and to his right. Louie would go through the roll of teletype, tear off the stories that he wasn't sure about and then, without looking, revolve his right arm back and put that piece of copy on the spike.

One evening, Louie did that and the palm of his hand came down on the sharp edge. The spike went into his palm about one-eighth of an inch. The blood was spurting out. Louie looked around and, with his palm still impaled, shouted:

"OK, who moved the bleepin' spike?"

That's how tough Louie Green was, and Klobuchar drove him crazy. He would cut the hell out of Klobuchar's copy, and they would get into these roaring arguments.

Klobuchar screamed at him once, "Let's go out in the alley, you old S.O.B." There was not an alley at the *Star* and *Tribune*, but if there had been, Klobuchar might have been in trouble.

Another time, Klobuchar had written a long story and Louie had cut its length substantially. Klobuchar went downstairs to the composing room, where the metal type was put on a form and turned into a page of the newspaper. Klobuchar saw what had happened to his story, and he had the printers restore his story and take out some other things. When the outstate edition came up and Louie saw what had happened with the Vikings story, I thought he was going to kill Klobuchar.

I had been told before hiring Klobuchar by several people, "You're going to regret the day you did this." They were right—I regretted the day, because he wanted to write the whole section.

Klobuchar and I had one last blowup. *Tribune* Managing Editor Darryl Feldmeier called me and said, "Well, Klobuchar has gone to work for the St. Paul newspaper."

I went upstairs to the office of John Cowles, Jr. and said, "I know you're in love with Klobuchar's writing. He might come back if I'm not involved with the *Tribune* sports department. If you want me to, I'll quit."

I have kept the note all these years that Cowles wrote: "Don't worry. You're the guy we want."

Klobuchar was in St. Paul for a short time, then *Star* and *Tribune* Executive Editor Bower Hawthorne brought back Klobuchar and teamed him with Barbara Flanagan as the *Star*'s co-columnists for the newside. They were a big hit. Klobuchar was a great writer. He had a terrific career. But when you were the guy running a sports department, it was impossible to work with him.

I'll admit it: In the early years, when Van Brocklin and Klobuchar would get in those fights, I was cheering for both of them to lose.

Van Brocklin's greatest moment as Vikings coach was probably the first game they ever played. The mighty Chicago Bears came to Met Stadium on September 17, 1961. Two weeks earlier, the Bears had overpowered the Vikings 30-7 in an exhibition game in Cedar Falls, Iowa. These were the Monsters of the Midway. They were coached by George Halas—Papa Bear, a founder of the league, a guy who had to say "yes" for Minnesota to get a franchise. And now here was this expansion team going to challenge the Bears!

You have to remember these were true expansion teams. There were no free agents to sign. These were the rejects—the over-the-hill and the never-were guys who were left over after the established teams protected their real players. Dallas had started a year earlier and had the first pick of the rejects. So, the Vikings were stuck with the previously rejected rejects.

Van Brocklin had a big asset as a coach: He could motivate through fear. He had the toughest practices you have ever seen. He

Fran Tarkenton's Hall of Fame induction

Max Winter and I were in Canton, Ohio, to celebrate Fran Tarkenton's induction into the Pro Football Hall of Fame.

took the players to Bemidji for six weeks of training camp and beat the crap out of them in practice.

Van Brocklin scared the hell out of the players before that opener versus the Bears. The players were worried that, if they stunk the joint out, Van Brocklin might practice for seven hours the next day. Van Brocklin had no heart when it came to players and practice.

George Shaw, a veteran, started at quarterback. He was a pocket passer, as Van Brocklin had been—as every quarterback in the NFL had been. Shaw was bounced around, and Tarkenton, the rookie quarterback from Georgia, came into the game. He started scrambling around, playing quarterback like it had never been played before in the NFL, and the offense caught fire. Tarkenton and the Vikings ran the Bears into the parking lot. The Bears had big, old linemen like Doug Atkins, who just collapsed into the Met Stadium grass after chasing around Tarkenton.

The Vikings won 37-13. You didn't have ESPN Sports Center or the network shows that you have now—you didn't have a thousand TV stations showing highlights—so there was no nineties-style hype of that upset. But the pro football world has never had a more surprising score.

Halas couldn't believe it. He thought it was a bad dream. He didn't say anything after the game, until the Bears got on the bus, and he told the players they were a bunch of "pussies." Years later, Halas told me it was the most embarrassing defeat of his life. All the next week, he was getting calls from other NFL coaches, asking how the Bears could lose to an expansion team.

In the long run, that amazing upset was probably the worst thing that ever happened to the relationship between Tarkenton and Van Brocklin. Tarkenton went crazy, making plays by running around. After one game, he was known as the Scrambler.

That is the one thing Van Brocklin did not want to happen. He could control Shaw and most of the team. He could not control Tarkenton. Van Brocklin was a dropback passer who couldn't run a lick. And there was Tarkenton, running all over the place—exactly the opposite of everything Van Brocklin had believed in as a pro quarterback.

They were two stubborn guys, two different guys. One was the son of a preacher. The other guy drank way too much and cussed out people all the time.

The people I felt sorry for were Van Brocklin's assistant coaches. The Dutchman was so moody. After a loss, he would threaten to fire all of them. They didn't know from one day to the next if they had a job.

Despite all of that, Van Brocklin knew football, and he could scare the players into playing hard in most games. There was a time, in 1964, when it looked as though Van Brocklin might get the Vikings over the hump. They were 8-5-1. They beat Green Bay and Lombardi for the first time that season—24-23 in Green Bay. They won three straight at the end of the schedule.

There was a lot of optimism going into the 1965 season. The Vikings went 5-0 in exhibition games. They were 5-3, then lost four

in a row. Van Brocklin quit in the middle of the streak, saying, "I've taken this team as far as I can take it."

Privately, all of the sportswriters were celebrating. We also knew that the son of a bitch was going to change his mind. He had told the owners he was quitting a few times earlier and always came back before it made the papers. We all wrote that Van Brocklin had done a good job and the Vikings should keep him. Sure enough, the next day the Vikings happily announced Van Brocklin was staying.

In reality, that was the end for him. After all the B.S. he had given the players about never quitting, the players looked at him as a guy who had quit. Players can see handwriting on the wall, and they react accordingly. They figured the Dutchman had become a short-timer with the Vikings, and that meant the fear factor was gone.

Jim Finks came in as the general manager after that season. He was not going to take on Van Brocklin right away. There was no need to. Van Brocklin blew himself up.

The Vikings went 4-9-1 in 1966. The final blow came with three games left, when Atlanta was playing at Met Stadium. The game was on television back to Atlanta—Tarkenton's home area. Out of spite, Van Brocklin benched Tarkenton and did not play him.

Not long after, Tarkenton called me and said, "I want you to know that I just told Jim Finks that I'm definitely not going to play any more football for the Vikings."

I said, "Let's have lunch."

We met at a joint in Bloomington. I tried to talk him out of demanding a trade.

He said, "No way. I wouldn't play for that man under any circumstances."

After Tarkenton's trade demand became public, Van Brocklin said he would quit. He was waiting for the owners to talk him out of it again. This time, Bernie Ridder went to Van Brocklin and told him he was finished.

The fans were not universally anti–Van Brocklin. Finks was as sharp as you could get. He knew it would be a bad situation to have Tarkenton looked at as the quarterback who had run off the coach. The Vikings did not really try to convince Tarkenton to stay, even with Van Brocklin gone.

Wellington Mara's team, the New York Giants, had hit the skids. Mara wanted to bring in Tarkenton and put some life in his franchise. Mara needed a personality to compete with Joe Namath and the Jets for headlines.

Tarkenton was intrigued by playing in the bright lights of New York. And Finks made a great trade—getting two No. 1s and a No. 2 draft choice from the Giants. Trading Tarkenton at that point was the second best move the Vikings ever made.

The best move was the one Max Winter and Finks made after Van Brocklin left: Hiring Harry Peter Grant to replace Van Brocklin.

Chapter 9

Bud Grant

Bud Grant was a tremendous three-sport athlete at Central High in Superior, Wisconsin. He went from there to the Navy and was assigned to the Great Lakes Naval Base. Paul Brown was coaching football, and Weeb Ewbank, another Hall of Fame football coach, was coaching basketball.

The Great Lakes basketball team came to Minnesota in 1945. I knew the Gophers would be recruiting Grant, so I made a point to meet him. We talked for a few minutes, and later I wrote a letter, thanking Grant for his time and suggesting that he come to Minnesota after the war.

When I started with the *Times*, Dick Cullum felt if you could sell a kid on the Gophers, there was nothing wrong with that. I was not the only sportswriter in the Twin Cities trying to help the Gophers. George Edmond was the sports editor in St. Paul, and he would call the kids over there and suggest they play for the Gophers. With all the Catholics in that town, Edmond would call the parish priest and ask if he could help convince a kid to play for the Gophers. The priests were willing to help as long as Notre Dame was not trying to recruit the same kid.

Paul Brown had said Grant was the best eighteen-year-old athlete he had seen, and as far as I was concerned, it was my duty to help the Gophers get him. Bud wound up making his college decision the same way he was to make decisions all his life: logically.

Grant had a girlfriend who wanted the relationship to be more exclusive than Bud wanted it to be. If the girlfriend had enrolled at

Minnesota, Bud would have gone to Wisconsin. Fortunately for the Gophers, she went to Wisconsin, so Bud came to Minnesota.

Bud played end along with Gordie Soltau on Bernie Bierman's postwar teams from 1946 through 1949. Bud's father, Harry, was a real character. Harry figured that, since I was a newspaperman, I would know what was going on with the Gophers. He contacted me as soon as Bud started at Minnesota.

It was impossible to get a hotel room in Minneapolis on a weekend when the Gophers were playing football. Harry Grant would have me use my connections to get the rooms he needed for himself and his buddies from Superior.

Harry was the fire chief in Superior. The New York Giants had their training camp in Superior for a number of years, and Harry would run a popcorn stand next to the practice field. He was the guy who introduced me to Wellington and John Mara, the owners of the Giants.

Bud did not make friends easily. He was aloof. We happened to hit it off. When he was at Minnesota, we would have a meal together most every day. My mother was still in the house on Irving Avenue, and she loved it when Bud came over for breakfast.

We used to drive my car to Superior to see his parents. I was driving one day and felt something inside my pant leg. It was a squirrel. I almost drove off the road and killed us. It was a squirrel that Bud had captured and domesticated.

When we got to the Grants' home in Superior, the squirrel was running around the house, and then it made the mistake of taking a nip at Bud's father. That was the end of the squirrel.

Bud also had a pet crow. He had the crow trained so it would land on a person's shoulder. If you didn't know the crow was around and it suddenly landed, it could give you a heart attack.

We were driving home from Superior late one night and had a flat tire. We were in the middle of nowhere and it was twenty below zero. I'm not the world's most knowledgeable outdoorsman. I saw this bright light in the distance. I figured it was a spotlight in the nearest town, so I started walking toward it. Bud did not say anything. I took a few steps and sunk up to my arms into a snow-filled ditch. Bud started laughing and said: "Hey, Sid, it's going to take you awhile to get to that spotlight. That's the moon."

Another time, I brought a brand-new car and was extremely proud of it. After a few days, the car started to develop this terrible stench. I thought it had something to do with breaking in a new engine—I'm not a mechanic, either—but the smell kept getting worse. I kept taking the car back to the dealer. Finally, they found a couple of decaying crows hidden in the car. It was no mystery where they came from. It had to be Grant.

Bud loved practical jokes. April Fool's Day was chaos at the Vikings offices. The secretaries knew that before the day was over they were going to open a drawer and a mammal or reptile of some kind was going to pop out.

Coaching football was an occupation for Grant. The outdoors, hunting and fishing, were his passion. Jim Finks, the general manager who put together those Vikings Super Bowl teams along with Grant, used to call him "Mark Trail."

Grant made a dumb move many years ago and went wolf hunting with a bush pilot and a couple of buddies in Canada. The newspapers found out about this and it was a big story. Grant has apologized a thousand times over and has become a tremendous conservationist. But after the incident with the wolves made headlines, a reporter called Finks, talked for a few minutes, then asked if Grant was around.

"Mark Trail? No, he's not here," Finks said. "He's probably out dynamiting walleye."

Take away that once incident and Bud always had the most common sense of any person I've met. I've never made an important decision in the past fifty years without talking it over with him. Bud Grant and Al Rubinger, my business partner and a fellow I grew up with in north Minneapolis, are my two best friends in the world.

Grant played four seasons of football, three seasons of basketball, and three seasons of baseball for the Gophers. The University of Minnesota never has had an all-around athlete to compare with Grant.

Getting a degree was never that important to Bud. He was more a student of the sports he played than of the classroom. He was fascinated by the way players would react to a coach's approach.

As I pointed out earlier, Bernie Bierman blew a chance to take the Gophers to the Rose Bowl in 1949. After they beat Ohio State, he beat up the players with tough, three-hour practices before the next week's game at Michigan. Then, he got the players to Michigan Stadium nearly three hours before the game. The Gophers lost their adrenaline—their energy—sitting around in that locker room, doing nothing.

Once he became a coach, Grant never took a team's physical edge away on the practice field, and he never took a team's emotional edge away by having the players sit and look at the locker-room walls for hours before a game.

After the '49 football season, Grant joined the Gophers basketball team for the month of December, and then we found out he was going to be ineligible. He was failing a class taught by a Jewish professor. I contacted the guy and asked for a favor, one Jewish guy to another, but it didn't work. Bud was ineligible. So, on Christmas Day, we announced that Bud had signed with the Lakers. He was in uniform that same night. We gave him a contract for $3,000.

Grant was an outstanding rebounder. He was the eighth or ninth man on that Lakers team and again the next season. The coach, Johnny Kundla, was not a big fan of Grant as a player. The other Lakers loved Grant because he was a such a competitor. George Mikan used to work with him all the time to improve Bud's basketball skills. Bud was proud of being a member of an NBA championship team in 1950. He always kept a team picture of the Lakers on his office wall.

The Philadelphia Eagles then drafted Grant on the first round. Bud stayed with the Lakers for another season. When the Eagles offered twice as much money as we were paying him, he went to the NFL. He would then supplement his income by pitching town-team baseball in the summer—just as he had done when he was with the Gophers and the Lakers.

Grant was an outstanding end for Philadelphia. When the Eagles would not give him the money he wanted, he refused to sign a contact. In addition to common sense, that was another Grant quality: stubbornness.

Bud became one of the first players to play out his option. After playing that season without a contract, he left Philadelphia and signed with the Winnipeg Blue Bombers in the Canadian Football

League. The general manager there was Bill Boivin, a fellow I got to know well after he signed Grant.

The Blue Bombers fired Allie Sherman as coach. Boivin called and asked if I thought Gomer Jones, the No. 1 assistant to Bud Wilkinson, would take the job. I called Jones, and he was not interested.

The surprise to everyone was that Grant, only twenty-nine, wanted the job. One thing that helped Bud to convince Boivin and team President Jim Russell to hire him as coach was when Wayne Robinson said he would come to Winnipeg to play for Grant.

Robinson was a great lineman for the Gophers in the early fifties. He was playing in Philadelphia and *Life* magazine came out with a story claiming that Robby was a dirty player based on quotes from Cleveland quarterback Otto Graham and other players. This was completely in contrast with Robinson's All-American boy image in Minnesota.

Charlie Johnson decided the *Star* should have a Robinson diary that would appear every week during the NFL season. Charlie assigned Halsey Hall to call Robinson after every game and then write the diary. When it came to getting quotes straight, Halsey was the classic example of the guy who could screw up a one-car funeral.

After one segment of the diary appeared, Robinson's teammates got their hands on the clippings. He called me and said: "Sid, I've been doing this diary only because you asked me to. Now, I'm the laughingstock of this locker room. They have the clippings all over with the quotes—things I would never say—circled. I'm not going to do it anymore."

Robinson complained for awhile, then I said: "I have an idea. Grant has a chance to be the coach at Winnipeg. How would you like to go up there and be an assistant coach for him?"

Robinson said he would go in a minute. He was an All-Pro player still in the prime of his career. The Winnipeg people had tried to sign Robinson when he came out of the University of Minnesota. Russell and Boivin were excited to have Robinson's name attached to the Blue Bombers.

Boivin wanted Bud to be a player-coach, but Grant figured coaching was a full-time job. Jim Finks was a rival with Calgary in the Canadian League. He was constantly amazed at the way Grant's teams could get outplayed for most of a game but still manage to stay close. Then, they would block a kick or hit on a long play at the end and win the ballgame.

"We could never beat that steely-eyed S.O.B. in a big game," Finks would say. "Never."

The big signing for Grant at Winnipeg was Iowa quarterback Kenny Ploen. Ploen won Grey Cups—the Canadian championship—for Bud. After he was finished at Iowa, Ploen was staying at his family's summer home in Brainerd, Minnesota. Winnipeg made a deal with him, and I took the contract to Brainerd for him to sign. On the drive back from the Twin Cities, I called Winnipeg from Royalton, Minnesota, to tell Bud, "I got your quarterback's name on a contract."

Ploen was part of a tremendous Iowa contact for Grant. Forrest Evashevski and Jerry Burns were my buddies, and they admired Grant. They helped him out a lot—getting Ploen, Frank Gilliam, Frank Rigney, Ray Jauch, Eddie Vincent, a bunch of Iowa players. Calvin Jones, Iowa's all-world tackle, was at Winnipeg until he was killed in a plane crash.

Bud already was an established winner in Canada when the Vikings started in 1961. Max Winter knew Grant from the Gophers and the Lakers, and wanted to hire him as the Vikings' first coach. Max did not have power among the owners then; Bernie Ridder had the power. Ridder and the other owners told Max that General Manager Bert Rose would make the decision on a coach. Rose wanted Norm Van Brocklin.

I don't think Bud would have taken the job in '61 even if it had been offered. As I've said, Bud has more common sense than any person I've met. He did not want to coach an expansion team. He felt an expansion team was a guarantee that a coach was going to fall on his ass.

Finks replaced Rose as general manager in 1965. As soon as Norm Van Brocklin was let go after the 1966 season, it was certain the Vikings would get Grant out of his contract in Winnipeg and get him down here.

When Grant came to the Twin Cities to negotiate the deal, Finks sent Publicity Director Bill McGrane to the airport to pick up Bud.

"I don't know Grant," McGrane said.

come out to Winter Park, the Vikings' offices in Eden Prairie. Then he said, "Grant and I are taking a flight and you are going with us."

We went to the airport. I kept asking, "What's going on?" They said, "We've made a huge trade with the Los Angeles Raiders. We want you to be there when we finalize the deal. It will be a big story for you."

We were flying out there and, the more I thought about it, the less sense it made. I kept asking Lynn and Grant what the real story was, and Bud finally said, "I'm retiring as coach, and we're flying to Hawaii to tell Max Winter before the announcement is made. We want you to be there."

The plane stopped in Los Angeles. I knew I had to write this story. Plus, I'm a coward when it comes to flying: I wasn't anxious to fly across all that water. I got off the plane, called the *Tribune* office, told them I would have a big story for the metro edition, and then flew back home.

There was never a lot of talk beforehand when one of Grant's main players would retire. Bud would give a veteran player an extra year after he was basically finished, then call him in and say, "It's time." There would be a small press conference, and that would be it. So, it was predictable that Grant was able to keep his intentions to retire completely quiet, until it was time to tell Max and then make it public.

I broke the story on the front page of the next morning's *Tribune*. The entire state was shocked.

On the day Grant had been hired to coach the Vikings, there had been a press conference at the Minneapolis Holiday Inn. Bill Boni was the sports editor and a columnist at the St. Paul newspapers then. Boni had come to Minnesota from the East—a nice man, but not someone who had been around when Grant played for the Gophers and the Lakers.

Grant walked into the room, put his arm around my shoulders, and said, "I guess I made the right decision."

And Boni said: "Oh, no. He knows this guy, too."

Boni had no idea how well we knew each other. He didn't know that, as far back as 1946, Bud Grant had been eating a couple of meals a week at my mother's house.

Bud never really said why he gave me the scoop on his first retirement. He probably figured I had earned it, not only because of our friendship, but for almost forty years he had watched me and knew that being a reporter was an everyday job for me.

Bud did not give me all the scoops. Ralph Reeve covered the Vikings for the St. Paul newspapers for a long time, and Bud loved Ralphie. I would go to Bud and scream, "You S.O.B.—you gave Reeve that story."

And Grant would say, "Yes, and I'll give Ralph stories in the future, too."

The toughest thing for Grant after he resigned was to call Jerry Burns and tell him that he was not going to get the job. Grant and Burns went back to the fifties, when those Iowa players were coming to Winnipeg to play for Grant. The Canadian League season started in July, so Burnsie would go to Winnipeg in the early summer to help Grant in training camp.

To replace Grant as head coach, Lynn had decided to hire Les Steckel, a young assistant the Vikings thought had a tremendous coaching future. Steckel brought in all of his young coaching buddies, and they pushed great coaches like Burns and Johnny Michels aside. It was a disaster. Grant went along with Lynn's decision—he thought Steckel had a future, too—but soon they both knew it had been a terrible mistake.

Steckel ordered the players to report to the Mankato training facility earlier and tried to turn it into a concentration camp. The players were pounding on one another every day in practice. This was exactly the opposite of Grant's approach. The Vikings were always the last team to report to training camp. One reason Bud came back was to prove that you couldn't coach like Steckel.

The Vikings went 3-13 with Steckel. Lou Holtz was coaching the Gophers and filling the Metrodome. Lynn had to do something dramatic.

I knew Lynn was trying to get Grant to come back, but Bud was vacillating. Bud was going to get every nickel, because he knew Lynn needed him in the worst way. He finally gave Grant the world, and Bud returned for the 1985 season.

Grant put the Vikings back on decent footing. They went 7-9. I think he enjoyed it, but he wondered how long it would be before

Super Bowl party, 1975

Although the Vikings lost to the Dallas Cowboys, just making it to the Super Bowl is always a thrill. Here we were out on the town before the 1975 game. From left: Vikings stockholder Don McNulty, then–Northwest Airlines President Don Nyrop, myself, Max Winter, and Hank Greenberg, former Detroit Tigers player and executive of the Cleveland Indians.

the Vikings would win again. After he quit the second time, the Detroit Lions offered Bud a contract worth $1 million a year. The money was tempting, but he decided it was not worth it because he wanted to win.

I'm a member of the NFL's Hall of Fame committee. We have the big meeting on the weekend of the Super Bowl. After Bud became eligible, I made a pitch for him at all of those meetings. He was 158-96-5 in the regular season, won eleven Central Division titles and four league titles.

Those AFC writers would always say, "Yeah, but the Vikings lost those four Super Bowls."

Finally, in 1994, common sense prevailed, and Bud was voted into the Pro Football Hall of Fame. He always presented that image of being a stoic, but Bud was emotional when he heard the news—and emotional again when he accepted the honor that summer in Canton, Ohio. Bud was the first person to be elected to both the NFL's Hall of Fame and the Canadian Football Hall of Fame.

I called him one day, looking for a note for my column, and asked, "Who is going to present you at the Hall of Fame ceremony?"

Without pausing, Bud said, "You are, Sid."

I thought he was joking. He made it clear he was serious. I was shocked. I started getting nervous right then. But it was the greatest honor I've had in my life.

Until that year, no sportswriter had ever been selected to make the presentation speech for an inductee at the Hall of Fame ceremony. In 1994, I presented Bud, and Chuck Heaton of the Cleveland *Plain-Dealer* introduced running back LeRoy Kelly.

Later, Pat Grant, Bud's wife, said, "I don't know why you were surprised, Sid. He always said, if he ever got in there, you were going to be the guy to introduce him."

Bud Grant once gave me another honor, in a much less formal situation. The Vikings' office used to be on France Avenue. Bud walked in and there were a couple of reporters talking, cutting me up about something.

One of them asked Bud, "What do you think of Sid Hartman?"

And Bud said: "I'll tell you what I think. I would trust him with my life. Is that good enough for you?"

Chapter 10

The Vikings' Town

There had been four teams involved until the last weekend in the 1967 American League pennant race. It now has a permanent place in baseball history as The Great Race. In Boston it is also remembered as The Impossible Dream, since the Red Sox had been in the tank for years before beating out the Twins, Tigers, and White Sox in the final hours of the schedule.

The Twins went backwards in 1968. Cal Ermer had replaced Sam Mele as the manager in 1967, did well initially, but it became apparent he was overmatched as a big-league manager. For the first time, attendance took a significant fall and there was serious grumbling among the fans.

After eight years, the honeymoon was over for Calvin. Instead of getting gifts from the fans, he was getting letters filled with criticism and advice. Most of the advice was this: Hire Billy Martin as manager.

Martin had been coaching third base for the Twins. He was the best third-base coach of all time. And, when it came to players, the tougher the case, the better Martin would handle him.

Rod Carew came to the Twins in 1967. Calvin saw Carew in spring training and told Mele that Carew was his second baseman. Mele called in the reporters before the start of the season and said, "I just want you to know that it's not my idea to play the kid. I don't think he's ready."

Carew was immature and moody at that point. Martin basically adopted him and turned Carew into the American League Rookie

Baseball at the Met
Second baseman Rod Carew was one of the great stars of the Minnesota Twins.

of the Year in 1967. When Griffith fired Mele, Martin should have been the guy to replace him.

That was obvious to everyone, but there was a big problem: Martin had a bitter enemy in Howard Fox. Billy had been full of booze one night, which was not unusual. He had been giving Fox some heat on a flight to Baltimore. When the Twins got to the hotel, Fox had this ritual of handing out room keys to the players and the rest of the traveling party. To agitate Martin, he waited until last to give the key to him.

Billy started bad-mouthing Fox. Howard's wife, Yvonne, was on the trip, so he must have felt he had to stand up to Martin. They shouted at one another, then Martin took a punch at Fox and gave him a cut on the face.

From that day on, Fox did everything in his power to prevent Martin from becoming the Twins manager—and to get him out of the organization.

Calvin used this excuse for not hiring Martin: Billy had not managed. He did not want to go to the minor leagues to manage. I told him after the '67 season, "The only way you're going to manage this club is to go to the Triple A club in Denver and do such a good job that Calvin has to hire you."

That's exactly what Martin did. He went to Denver and, with no players, tore up the league. Denver drew fans like never before. He won and he put people in the seats. After Ermer and the Twins flopped in '68, Calvin had no choice. He had to hire Martin.

Billy could be the dumbest S.O.B. in the world. He always drank too much. He was about as flawed as any person, but the people loved him. There was an amazing magnetism about him. He would go on the winter tour the Twins made throughout Minnesota, the Dakotas, and Iowa, and the people would go crazy for him.

As popular as Bud Grant became as a sports figure in the Twin Cities, Martin might have been more popular. The only sports figure who might have been bigger with the fans of Minnesota came later—Kirby Puckett.

The fans loved the aggressive baseball the Twins played for Martin. He had Cesar Tovar at the top of the order, followed by Carew, then Oliva, and Killebrew. Tovar would do anything to get on base for Martin. Carew was into every game, every inning, with Martin in the dugout. Carew stole home seven times that season.

The fans were never happier. Division play started that season, 1969, and the Twins won the A.L. West in a walk. If Martin had stayed, the Twins would have continued to lead the American League in attendance in the seventies, as they had done during their first decade in Minnesota.

Everything was going great, except Fox would come back from every trip and tell a horror story to Calvin about Martin. He made it sound as though the Twins would be unbeaten, not merely in first place, if it was not for Martin.

Twins Publicist Tom Mee told me this story: The part of the Twins delegation coming in for the 1969 All-Star Game already had arrived for the game in Washington, D.C. on a Sunday night. The team had been hot. Everyone was in Calvin's suite, drinking and celebrating. Most of the toasts were for Billy Martin, who had completely turned around the attitudes of the fans and the team from the seventh-place finish of 1968. Then, Fox came into the suite, loudly dropped his traveling bag on the floor and said, "Well, he did it again." He bad-mouthed Martin for a time and killed the party.

"Right then, I was fearful Martin would be fired at the end of the season, and I knew that would be a disaster for the Twins," Mee said.

Martin violated most of the cardinal rules, including the one about the manager not drinking in the same bar as the players. One night, Martin and a bunch of Twins were getting sloshed in the Lindell Athletic Club—the sports hangout in Detroit. Dave Boswell, a young, crazy pitcher, got in a fight with Allison. I would have been rooting for the young, crazy pitcher in that one. Boswell punched up Allison. Then Martin, who was a buddy of Allison's, took Boswell outside and shellacked him. The Twins begged the baseball writers to sit on the story. After a few days, the word got out, and the story made big headlines.

The Twins played Baltimore in the first American League playoff series. It was a best-of-five series and something brand new for the fans. They were saving their money for the World Series.

Then the Twins lost two terrific, one-run games in Baltimore—it was one of Earl Weaver's great Orioles teams—and came back to Met Stadium. The Twins only sold 33,000 tickets, 12,000 less than sellout,

World Series friends
Here I am down on the field before one of the series games with Joe DiMaggio and New Yankees manager Billy Martin.

and that made Calvin mad.

Calvin strongly suggested to Martin that Kaat start the third game. Martin said he would do it. Then the pitchers started getting ready before the game, and Calvin saw that Martin had Bob Miller warming up. Calvin went nuts in his private booth.

Martin had lost his confidence in Kaat. He was trying to be a genius by starting Miller, who had been a reliever most of the season. The Twins lost 11-2, and Calvin had to give back all the World Series ticket money—$2 million—that he already had in the bank.

Anyone who knows Calvin understands what giving back $2 million would do to his attitude. The rumors were out that Martin was going to be fired. I was writing in my column every day that this would be the stupidest thing that Calvin ever had done.

Martin also told me that he thought he was going to be fired. He went to Seattle to talk to General Manager Marvin Milkes about managing the Pilots.

Calvin was mad about Bob Miller starting, mad about giving back the $2 million, and mad that Martin was looking into job options when he had not been fired by the Twins. The one thing Calvin did not think about was the reaction he would get from the fans.

I was writing, "Don't do this to yourself, Calvin," and Dick Cullum was writing the same thing in the *Tribune*. The writers at the Minneapolis *Star* and the St. Paul newspapers were writing it: Don't be stupid, Calvin. Don't fire Martin.

Calvin was at the World Series in New York where the Orioles were playing the Miracle Mets. He called Tom Mee to his room and told him to prepare a release that Martin had been fired.

Natalie Griffith, Calvin's wife, was there. Natalie walked over to Calvin after he said that to Mee and said, "Calvin, this is going to be the biggest mistake you ever made in your life."

Natalie was right.

The worst screwing a team ever took from the officials came at Madison, Wisconsin, in November 1962. The Gophers were 5-1-1, and a victory was going to give them an outright Big Ten championship and a third straight trip to the Rose Bowl.

That was Warmath's best defensive team. He had the two best tackles in the country—not best combination, but *the* two best—in Bobby Lee Bell and Carl Eller.

The big worry going into the season was what the Gophers were going to do at quarterback without Sandy Stephens. As it turned out, the Gophers offense was better with Duane Blaska at quarterback than it had been with Stephens.

The Gophers had Wisconsin stopped and the game won, and the officials called the cheapest roughing-the-passer penalty on Bell against Badgers quarterback Ron Vanderkelen.

Then, after Wisconsin went ahead 14-9, the Gophers scored a touchdown that would have won it, and the officials called an "aiding the ball carrier." They said a Minnesota player had helped the runner into the end zone. That was the first and last time anyone heard of that penalty.

Jesse James never stole anything more blatantly than the Big Ten and its official stole the championship and the Rose Bowl that year. Wisconsin went out to Pasadena, and Vanderkelen put on a great second-half passing show in a loss to Southern Cal.

Warmath's teams stayed around .500, a little better, over the next six seasons. The Gophers tied with Purdue and Indiana for the Big Ten title in 1967. Indiana went to the Rose Bowl, even though the Gophers had beaten the Hoosiers 33-7 in the second-to-last game of the season.

There weren't two dozen bowl games back then. A Big Ten team was either the conference representative in the Rose Bowl or it stayed home. If current standards applied, Warmath not only would have had those Rose Bowls after the 1960 and 1961 seasons, but he would have been in New Year's Day bowl games in 1962 and 1967, and in some kind of a bowl game in 1964, 1965, and 1968.

There's no doubt Murray Warmath was a good coach for the Gophers—outside of Bierman, the best we have had. But he had three straight losing seasons, 1969 through 1971, and all the attention had turned to the major league sports. Memorial Stadium was half full, and the athletic department needed to sell more tickets to pay its bills.

At Wisconsin, the Badgers had faced a similar problem and brought back an old hero, ElRoy ("Crazy Legs") Hirsch, as the athletic director. Hirsch drank about as much as anybody, but he was an outstanding salesman, and the Badgers started drawing a big crowd again at Madison.

Marsh Ryman was the athletic director at the University of Minnesota. He could not have sold an ice-cold beer to a man crawling across Death Valley on his belly. The boosters and the administration decided that the Gophers had to do the same thing as Wisconsin and bring back a hero as athletic director.

Paul Giel was working as the sports director at WCCO Radio and doing the radio analysis on Gophers games. And he was the all-time Golden Gopher with the public. Giel had come out of Winona, Minnesota, as a tailback in 1950. But freshmen were not eligible for varsity competition. Still, the Gophers were drawing a few thousand people to watch Giel play freshmen games. I was giving regular updates in my column on how great Giel was in practice.

The fans could not wait. The combination of Giel and Wes Fesler, a coach with a wide-open offense, was going to take the Gophers to the Rose Bowl for the first time. Fesler failed. Giel was a tremendous player. In 1953, when Giel was a senior, the Gophers were a .500 team, but still he was the runner-up to Notre Dame's Johnny Lattner for the Heisman Trophy.

Giel was also an outstanding pitcher. This was in the days when baseball had bonus babies: If you gave a player so much money to sign, you had to keep him in the major leagues for two seasons before sending him to the minors. The Millers had been the New York Giants' farm club. That meant the Giants' scouts were in town often. They fell in love with Giel as a pitcher. The Giants offered a huge bonus—$54,000.

Giel did not know what to do. I remember calling Frank Lane, the sharpest general manager in baseball at the time, and asking him what Giel should do. "Take the money," Lane said.

Giel took the money. The signing took place in Milwaukee, where the Giants were playing a series against the Braves. I went to Milwaukee for the signing.

I remember that well, because I fell asleep coming back on the train. They made a stop in Wisconsin and disconnected the car, putting it on another line. I woke up at a stop in some small town in Wisconsin and had to pay someone to give me a ride to Minneapolis.

The money was great, but Giel was a much better football player than a pitcher. He never made an impact in baseball. The Twins gave him a brief shot when they came here in 1961, then traded him to Kansas City for center fielder Bill Tuttle.

Giel's baseball mediocrity did not affect his status with Minnesota's sporting public. He still was a Minnesota hero—good looking, personable, articulate. He had stayed in front of the public by doing a terrific job on WCCO. In 1971, the University of Minnesota needed to do something to reinvigorate its athletic program. Football attendance had gone in the tank, and the athletic fundraising was almost nonexistent. The university needed Giel much worse than he needed the university.

One day, *Star* and *Tribune* Editor Bower Hawthorne asked me to come up to his office. This was unusual, because I had more trouble with Hawthorne than any editor we had at the newspaper. Les Malkerson, a member of the university's Board of Regents, was sitting there. Hawthorne said, "Les wanted to know if you thought Paul Giel would be interested in the Gophers athletic director job. He would like you to sound out Paul."

I went to Giel, and he was willing to talk about it with the university people. He came back to the university out of loyalty, nothing else.

The idea was to replace Ryman and Warmath. One thing Giel insisted on: He was not going to take the job and then have to fire Warmath. Don Knutson and a few of Murray's buddies went to Warmath and persuaded him to quit. It was announced before the 1971 finale against Wisconsin. The Gophers went out and beat the Badgers for Warmath.

It took some time to work out the Giel deal. Finally, the meeting was set when Giel would meet with the Board of Regents and get approved as athletic director. My mother died. The funeral was the same morning as the regents meeting.

Giel called University President Malcolm Moos and said, "I can't be at the meeting. I'll be at the funeral for Celia Hartman."

Moos became all upset. The regents felt they were the most important people in the world. Moos did not know how they would react to being stood up. He called me and asked if we could change the time for the funeral.

I said, "Dr. Moos, I don't want to talk to you right now. I'm a little upset myself, with my mother dying."

Paul Giel reminded me again what friendship means. He came to my mother's funeral. The regents had to wait.

Cal Stoll was a backup end on Bernie Bierman's teams in the late forties. Later, he was an assistant coach at Michigan State for Duffy Daugherty when the Spartans were getting the best players in the country—by hook or crook. Stoll had gone to Wake Forest, a perennial loser, as a head coach. He won an Atlantic Coast Conference title there. He was the guy I wanted to replace Warmath. Stoll was a good recruiter and a head coach on the rise.

Harvey Mackay, a friend of Giel's and a big Gophers booster, was also involved in trying to get Stoll. Cal kept saying he did not want to leave his "kids" at Wake Forest. He was sincere in his feeling about the players he recruited to a school.

Stoll turned down Giel. He turned down all of us. He had a meeting with his Wake Forest players at noon one day and said, "I'm staying." When a coach tells his players that, it's a powerful thing to overcome.

Stoll also felt that if the Michigan State job opened up in a couple of years, he was in line for it. Giel was ready to give up on Stoll. Mackay and I kept working on him. I called up Stoll and said, "Listen, you S.O.B. I've done you a million favors. Come to Chicago and meet with us. You don't have to take the job. Just talk to us."

Giel, Mackay, and I met Stoll at the Marriott Hotel at O'Hare Airport and talked him into taking the job.

Stoll recruited some outstanding offensive players. He had a running back named Larry Powell who had a disease called French polio that ended his career. If Powell had not gotten sick, the Gophers would have won nine or ten games a couple of seasons, and Stoll would have coached at Minnesota for another ten years.

Giel fired Stoll after a 4-7 season in 1978. Giel said he could not sell Stoll to the public anymore. Stoll was 39-39 in seven seasons. Considering the trouble the Gophers have had in football since he was fired, that record makes Stoll look like the second coming of Bernie Bierman.

Bud Grant came in, took the Vikings to the NFC title game in his second season, then took them to the Super Bowl after the 1969 season, his third year on the job.

Calvin had fired Billy Martin. Gophers football was struggling. Suddenly, the Twin Cities and the state belonged to the Vikings. It stayed that way for a long time.

The football Gophers always had been No. 1 for me. I sort of switched my allegiance to the Vikings and so did most of the writers in town. The Vikings were as big in the seventies as the Gophers had been after the war and through the Rose Bowl years—as big as the Twins had been in the sixties.

Jim Finks was able to get the Vikings NFC dynasty started with some unbelievable trades. Finks turned the three draft choices he received from the New York Giants for Tarkenton into offensive tackle Ron Yary, receiver Bob Grim, and running back Clinton Jones. Even better, Finks put a package together for the Los Angeles Rams for a No. 1 pick that he turned into Alan Page, the amazing defensive tackle from Notre Dame.

Finks and Grant were an outstanding combination. Another

catalyst for getting the Vikings to the Super Bowl was Joe Kapp. After the Tarkenton trade, Finks and Grant knew they needed a quarterback. They both had backgrounds in the Canadian Football League and had respect for the talents of players—and quarterbacks—in that league.

Kapp was the all-time team guy. He refused the team's most valuable player award after the 1969 season. He said, "There is no MVP. This is 40 guys for 60 minutes."

People ate that up. Forty for sixty. And with Kapp, it was no B.S. That's the way he felt. If Kapp thought someone had let up for one play, he would grab him by the jersey and threaten to kick the hell out of him.

Kapp and his teammates would go out, drink tequila and, sometimes, wind up fighting each other. Kapp and Lonnie Warwick, the middle linebacker who was just as fierce about competition as Kapp, got drunk one night in Duff's—the big hangout on Hennepin Avenue in downtown Minneapolis—and beat the hell out of each other.

If that happened today, it would be a big scandal—a sign of dissension. With those Vikings, it was looked as part of their deadend-kid image. Old-time Vikings fans still love to tell that story, about Kapp and Warwick brawling.

That team was full of beauties. They loved to give me a hard time. One day, after a game the Vikings had won in Dallas, I was standing with the reporters, waiting to get in the locker room. All of a sudden, these two cops came out of the room and started whisking me away. One of the coaches saved me from being arrested.

When I got back in the locker room, the players were all laughing. I found out what happened. Linebacker Wally Hilgenberg had called the cops over, pointed at me, and said: "See that guy over there? He tried to grab my privates."

Another time, we were playing the Lions at the Pontiac Silverdome. Tarkenton was back with the Vikings by then. While en route to the Silverdome, I went to the restroom on the bus. Tarkenton and a couple of his buddies jammed the door and locked me in. I was in there screaming for an hour, before the driver finally came back to the bus and heard me. It was the middle of the first quarter before I got into the stadium.

Then there was the time at a Vikings banquet at the Radisson

Sid —

You are a genius —

a literary Giant —

a man for all seasons —

And you always told

me I am full of Shit —

seriously you are

a great great friend

I love you

Fran Tarkenton

Tarkenton's note

Here is Fran Tarkenton's autographed note to me in a copy of his autobiography, Tarkenton, *by Jim Klobuchar and Fran Tarkenton.*

South in Edina. I sat down and found a bowl of cold soup at my table. I thought, "Cold soup. This is really a fancy dinner." I gobbled it up, and everyone at the table started laughing. Tarkenton had put the bowl in front of me. It was Green Goddess salad dressing for the entire table. Later, Tarkenton gave me a plaque with a bottle of Green Goddess attached to it.

Kapp could have been the Vikings quarterback for another five years. He really screwed up. After the '69 Super Bowl season, he got hooked up with John Elliott Cook, an eighty-year-old lawyer who convinced Kapp he could beat the NFL in court and bring true free agency to football.

Oakland owner Al Davis got involved. He said, "We can't lose this case." Davis told Commissioner Pete Rozelle to hire Joe Alioto, once the mayor of San Francisco. Rozelle and Davis had a horrible relationship, but Rozelle took Davis's advice this time.

Alioto won the case. When he came back, Kapp was never the same quarterback. He wound up in New England, where he did not have the same defense as he had to lean on in Minnesota. No one had a defense like the Vikings had for seven, eight years with the Purple People Eaters: Alan Page, Carl Eller, Jim Marshall, and Gary Larsen.

I don't know of any defensive tackle, Mean Joe Greene included, who has had the talent of Page. He was a private guy. He didn't have much to do with Marshall, Eller, anyone on the team, really. Page was aloof. He thought he was brighter than most football players. I guess he was right. He's now a Supreme Court judge for the state of Minnesota.

The real character was Jim Marshall. He was like Zoilo Versalles with the Twins. Marshall spent considerably more money than he was making, and he once had a car repossessed from the parking lot while the Vikings were practicing. Max Winter paid off the loan so Marshall could get back the car. I put that in my column, thinking it would shed a positive light on Max, who did not have a reputation as a big spender.

Max called and raised holy hell. He said, "Sid, you dumb S.O.B. Now, they are going to repossess the other car that he's behind on, because they will think that I'm going to pay it off, too."

After Kapp left, the Vikings tried a bunch of different quarterbacks—Gary Cuozzo, Bobby Lee, Norm Snead. It did not work. So, they brought back Tarkenton for the 1972 season. He was the king when he came back.

Francis was full of confidence. He was the best quarterback in the world because he believed he was the best quarterback in the world. He was quite a promoter. If there was a Viking getting paid for a television or radio ad, it was Tarkenton.

There was a considerable amount of jealousy. Ron Yary, for one, could not stand Tarkenton. Francis did have his pals—Mick

Vikings training camp
I have been to many a Vikings' training camp, during the reigns of both coaches Bud Grant and Jerry Burns.

Tingelhoff, Grady Alderman, Paul Krause.

The Vikings were 7-7 in Tarkenton's first year back. He had been a .500 quarterback in New York, too. Beano Cook, the character you hear talking about college football on ESPN now, had a crack after that season: "The engraving on Tarkenton's gravestone is going to read 7-7."

That became a popular one-liner, but Tarkenton proved Beano and everyone else wrong. He took the Vikings to three Super Bowls.

Newspaper editors tell you that reporters are supposed to be objective. I was never objective. I was at my worst with Grant's teams in the seventies. I made an ass out of myself, cheering for the Vikings and bitching about the officials, almost every Sunday in the press box. I never knew how bad it looked. I didn't care. It was more important to me to see Bud and the Vikings do well than how the other sportswriters felt about me.

The playoff loss to Dallas in '75 was the worst. Grant felt that was his best team. The front four still was overpowering. Tarkenton was playing great, and Chuck Foreman, the Pro Bowl runner they always needed, was in his third season—a wonderful offensive weapon.

Then Dallas receiver Drew Pearson pushed Nate Wright to the ground and caught that game-winning pass. An official, Armen Terzian, was hit in the head by a whiskey bottle thrown by an irate fan. Terzian was led off the field, with a bloody towel wrapped around his head. They took him to the officials' locker room. Terzian was being attended to after the game, when I came storming in there. I blasted the officials for not calling the pushoff by Pearson. The officials were incensed. Their guy was bleeding, and I was telling them how horse-bleep they were.

The NFL started a new rule after that. Only pool reporters designated before the game were allowed to talk to the officials, and they weren't allowed to interview them—only to ask for an explanation of a call. Many of my sportswriting colleagues refer to this as the Sid Hartman Rule.

Going after the referees after that game was not my greatest moment, but I react emotionally to games involving Minnesota teams. To me, it was a heart-breaking event—a terrible, terrible loss. That was also the day that Fran Tarkenton's father had a heart attack and died.

Has there ever been a tougher day for a Minnesota team? I went to Bud's house later that night. He always felt the officials were after him. He felt Commissioner Pete Rozelle was after him because of his campaign for full-time officials. Most times, Bud could handle defeat, but that day he felt he had been screwed royally.

The other infamous losses—in the Super Bowl—bugged me only because of the abuse Grant had to take. It took awhile to get Grant into the NFL Hall of Fame for one reason: the 0-4 record in the Super Bowl. When you look at it, the three losses with Tarkenton as quarterback were to the three best teams the AFC has ever produced: Shula's great Miami club, Pittsburgh's four-time Super Bowl champs, and Al Davis's best Oakland teams. If the NFL had teams like that in the eighties and nineties, I can guarantee that San Francisco, Dallas, and Washington would not have the multiple Super Bowl championships they have won.

The Steelers were a young team, and the Vikings did have a shot to beat them after the 1974 season. The trouble was Tarkenton had injured his arm during that season, and he could not throw the ball from one end of a room to the other. The Vikings kept it quiet going into the Super Bowl, but there was real concern Tarkenton's career might be over. For some reason, the strength just left his arm.

Jerry Burns was tight with some guys on the Michigan State staff. They told him that baseball pitcher Mike Marshall, a Michigan State alumnus, had developed a series of exercises that had brought a number of dead arms back to life for several pitchers. Tarkenton and Marshall got together after that season, Marshall gave him an exercise regimen, and Tarkenton's arm came back.

Covering the Super Bowl always has been tough because the access most reporters get is in group interviews. I had a big advantage. Grant let me into the Vikings' practices.

Before the Vikings played Oakland in Pasadena in January 1977, Al Davis came up to me and said, "I hear you have been at the practices all week. What are the Vikings going to do?"

I didn't know anything about strategy, so I said, "Al, I think they are going to block a Ray Guy punt." Guy never would get a punt blocked. Davis laughed and walked away.

Then, the Vikings blocked a punt. Davis came back and said, "You S.O.B. You knew that was going to happen."

Unfortunately, Brent McClanahan fumbled on the two-yard line, and then Ken Stabler and the Raiders caught fire. That was the last Super Bowl for Grant, Tarkenton, and all those friends of mine.

The night before the Oakland game in Pasadena, I had stayed with Grant in his suite at the Huntington Sheraton. Bud said, "We're bunking in my room tonight."

The people at the hotel had been told that Bud loved ice cream. They sent about three quarts of it to his room. We sat up, eating ice cream and talking about old times.

I don't know if he realized this was going to be the last Super Bowl and was feeling nostalgic. Maybe Bud thought having me around would change his Super Bowl luck.

It didn't.

Chapter 11

Building the Metrodome

Vikings General Manager Jim Finks held private conversations on a new stadium with the Minneapolis City Council. There was a press conference, and Finks announced plans for a football-only stadium in downtown Minneapolis, near Hennepin Avenue. Finks's announcement was a bombshell. The community activists started raising hell immediately, demanding pollution studies and traffic-pattern studies and all of that nonsense.

Finks was popular and smart. He would have had an easier time selling a new stadium to the public and the politicians than anyone. Unfortunately, Finks had a disagreement with Max Winter, John Skoglund, and Bill Boyer, and he wound up leaving the Vikings in 1974.

Finks wanted to buy a 5 percent share of the team and was turned down. He knew that, with new television contracts and with a better stadium, the value of the Vikings was going to skyrocket. It only made sense for Finks to get some of the financial reward for building the team and leading the push for a stadium.

Winter, Skoglund, and Boyer did not want to sell the stock to Finks. Among the owners, only Bernie Ridder, publisher of the St. Paul papers, was willing to do it. He felt the Vikings should do whatever it would take to keep Finks.

Ridder's newspaper chain was in the process of merging with the Knight newspapers. As part of that merger, he sold his Vikings stock to the other owners.

There was more to Finks's departure than the refusal to sell him 5 percent. Max was driving him crazy. NFL Commissioner Pete

Rozelle had told the NFL owners at a meeting that they should be more involved in the day-to-day operation of their club. Finks called Rozelle and said, "Thanks a lot. Max was giving me enough problems before. Now, you're telling him to get more involved."

Finks was getting all the credit for turning the Vikings into a powerhouse. Max wanted some of the publicity, even though he had nothing to do with personnel decisions.

On the day he resigned, Finks called me at Met Stadium, where the Twins were playing a game. He said, "Bernie Ridder knows I've resigned. I'm sure he is going to tell Ralphie Reeve. I didn't want you to get beat on the story."

Ridder gave the story to his football writer, Reeve, who had the Finks story in the *St. Paul Pioneer Press* the next morning. Thanks to Finks calling me, so did the Minneapolis *Tribune*.

I had breakfast with Finks that morning and tried to talk him out of it. He was not going to change his mind. Finks was a temperamental guy. He left the Chicago Bears years later, when George Halas—after agreeing to give Finks all of the managerial power—started to interfere.

I ripped Max Winter in my column for not doing what was necessary to keep Finks. He called me and said, "Whose side are you on?"

I said, "Not your side. You blew this one."

Max didn't talk to me for six weeks after that. The Vikings had been a smooth operation from the time Norm Van Brocklin left after 1966 until Finks's departure in 1974. Finks was tough as nails in negotiations, but the players respected him. They also enjoyed playing for Grant, because he didn't beat the hell out of them in practice, and they knew they were going to get a playoff check.

Finks had his trouble with Winter, and Grant started to have trouble with his No. 1 player, Alan Page. Grant let Page skip training camp to attend law school one year. Page wanted to do the same thing the next year. Grant did not think he could sell that to the rest of the players a second time.

Grant and Page never did get along that well because they both were stubborn guys. The final blow came when Page decided to become a recreational runner. He showed up in training camp down forty pounds—from 270 to 230. Grant was fuming. There was no way Page could continue to be an All-Pro defensive tackle at that size.

Early in the 1978 season, at Chicago, Page was getting handled by the Bears, and he was taken out of the game. Then, someone was hurt, and Page was told go back in. He refused.

Grant said, "You go back in." Page went in, but the next day he was cut, claimed on waivers by the Bears. The only defensive lineman ever to be the NFL's most valuable player was gone for the $100 waiver price.

The honeymoon was over for the Vikings. From the 1969 season through 1977, nine seasons, the Vikings won nine playoff games and went to four Super Bowls. From 1978 through 1996, nineteen seasons, the Vikings won four playoff games and made it to one NFC title game.

Winter was in big trouble after Finks left. He had a dozen or more players with no contracts, and Max had no idea how to go about signing them. Max could not negotiate because he hated to pay anybody. He wanted to pay NFL players in 1974 the same $4,000 salary we were paying ex-Gophers to play for the Lakers twenty-five years earlier.

Max met Mike Lynn at NFL meetings. Lynn was at the meetings as part of a Memphis delegation trying to get an expansion team. Max brought Lynn to practice, and the reporters were asking, "Who's this guy?" He was always with Max. Lynn was standing there next to Max, shivering, at the Super Bowl in Tulane Stadium in New Orleans after the 1974 season. That's the one the Vikings lost to Pittsburgh.

Lynn did not have a title when he started with the Vikings. He studied the NFL salary structure and did some paperwork, and told Max what to say when the agents came to negotiate contracts. Lynn started to learn the football business, and within a year, Max was trusting him with everything.

Lynn was given Finks's title as general manager. Minneapolis *Tribune* sports columnist Joe Soucheray gave him another title in print: the Remarkably Slick Mike Lynn. That was a backhanded tribute to Lynn's amazing rise to power in the Vikings organization.

Finks had raised the issue of the Vikings needing a new stadium, and then we started to worry about what was going to happen with the Twins.

Firing Billy Martin had proved to be the P.R. disaster that many people told Calvin Griffith it was going to be. The Twins won the West Division title again with Bill Rigney in 1970, but the fans were still mad.

Harmon Killebrew started to tail off. Tony Oliva blew out his knee. The team started to go in the tank. The Twins went from the top of the American League in attendance to the bottom.

Calvin started to get the roving eye again, looking for greener pastures. He once said, "The Braves went from Boston to Milwaukee and then to Atlanta. Maybe a team has to move twice to keep going financially."

Seattle had lost its expansion team after one season in 1969, when the Pilots were sold to Bud Selig's group in Milwaukee and became the Brewers. Seattle was suing Major League Baseball and the American League. The other owners were looking for a team to move to Seattle and take them off the hook.

Calvin liked Minnesota. He did not really want to move. But with attendance falling into the 600,000s in 1974, Calvin was taking money out of the bank, rather than putting it in the bank. "I don't like to pay interest," Calvin said. "I like to collect interest."

There were family members telling him to move. Seattle had agreed to build a domed stadium, the Kingdome, and the feeling was it could be another financial bonanza—that the family could be rolling in money again for a few years.

Joe Haynes and Sherrod Robertson, Calvin's top advisers during the sixties, had both died. Howard Fox had become Calvin's No. 1 guy. Fox was working behind the scenes with other American League people to kill the move to Seattle.

There was a meeting of the five-person American League executive committee in Milwaukee. They were going to make the recommendation on the Twins' move to Seattle. John Fetzer from Detroit was on the committee. I had a good relationship with him from when we were trying to get baseball in Minnesota. I made a lot of calls to Fetzer. We had him on our side. We also had the Milwaukee and Cleveland votes. We were able to block the move.

CHAMBERS OF
JUSTICE HARRY A. BLACKMUN

August 29, 1983

Mr. Sid Hartman
Sports Department
The Minneapolis Tribune
425 Portland Avenue South
Minneapolis, Minnesota 55488

Dear Sid:

It was good of you to join Doctor Merritt and me at the Metrodome last Tuesday evening and to take us up to see Mr. Griffith and Mr. Fox. I very much enjoyed visiting with you. As I told you, I have always enjoyed your columns when I am in the Minneapolis area or whenever friends clip them and send them on to me. Keep up your good work.

I presume to send you a copy of Flood v. Kuhn. It is hard to believe that it is over ten years old. I think I enjoyed writing this one more than any other. The local sports writers were not very happy with my sentimental journey in part I. I suspect they felt I was impinging on their turf.

Sincerely,

Harry A. Blackmun

Letter from a baseball fan, 1983

U.S. Supreme Court Justice Harry Blackmun was a big baseball fan, and whenever he came to Minneapolis–St. Paul, he would catch a Twins game. In 1983, Bud Merritt, Blackmun, and myself watched a game together at the new Metrodome.

Minnesota people never did understand how close we came to losing the Twins to Seattle. The American League wound up settling the suit by putting expansion teams in Seattle and Toronto, in 1977.

Fox had convinced Calvin to hire Gene Mauch as manager in 1976. Frank Quilici had been managing the Twins. Frank is a wonderful person, but he had no clout with the front office. Calvin took advantage of him—didn't give Quilici a chance to win. For instance: The Twins had an outfielder named Steve Brye. He broke his hand. The doctor put a cast on Brye's hand, but Calvin would not put him on the disabled list.

Quilici said, "What am I going to do with Brye? He has a cast covering his whole hand. I can't play him."

Calvin said, "Use him as a pinch-runner."

Mauch would not put up with that nonsense. He brought professionalism and a sense of direction back to the Twins. Free agency and Mauch came at the same time. Mauch would have won the West Division in 1977—with Rod Carew, Larry Hisle, and Lyman Bostock—if Calvin had only signed Bill Campbell, his No. 1 relief pitcher. Calvin wouldn't give Campbell a contract for $28,000 in the spring of 1976, so Campbell was a free agent after the season, went to Boston for a million bucks, and Mauch ran out of pitching.

Next to Martin, Mauch was the best manager I've seen. He also was the worst loser. The Twins had a postgame food spread in the clubhouse every night. About twice a season, Mauch would go in there after a loss, tip over the table, and all that food would go flying.

Mauch could dress faster than any guy I've seen. It took about five minutes to get from the press box to the home clubhouse at Met Stadium. Sometimes, you would get there, Mauch's uniform would be sitting in a pile in the middle of his office, and he would be gone.

Eventually, Calvin's cheapness became more than Mauch could take. He quit late in August 1980 and went back to California, where he had his heart broken in two playoff series as manager of the Angels. He never did get to his World Series.

The Twins were dying. The Vikings had started to demand a new stadium. It was obvious the Twin Cities needed to do something to keep the major league sports we had worked so hard to get fewer than twenty years earlier.

It was the influence and the financial power of Minneapolis that got Met Stadium built in Bloomington. It was the influence and financial power of Minneapolis that got major league sports here in 1961. It was the influence and financial power of Minneapolis that was going to get a modern stadium built.

Minneapolis people always have carried the ball for Minnesota when it came to sports. So, people in Minneapolis started saying, "If we're going to build a new stadium, why should football and baseball continue to be in Bloomington? Why shouldn't we get the benefits downtown?"

Mike Lynn wanted an open-air stadium next to the ballpark in Bloomington. Max Winter was the guy pushing for a dome in downtown Minneapolis.

Max had been prominent in Minnesota sports for forty years, but he never had been an insider with the rich folks—with the Wayzata crowd. To people old enough to remember, Max still was known as the promoter of fights that occasionally had some strange results. Max was the guy who had promoted the Globetrotters, who had run a turkey joint on Hennepin Avenue.

Now, the Wayzata folks started courting Max. John Cowles, Jr. was the publisher of the *Star Tribune*. He thought a dome was a great idea. Cowles was the head of the downtown group of businessmen that agreed to buy and donate the land. Most of it was *Star Tribune* land, and John, Jr. basically gave it away. The Dome would not have built if the Minneapolis people did not come up with the free land.

Max loved the attention he was finally getting from the downtown business people. Getting the Dome became his dream. Lynn fought the battle for him, even though he did not believe in the Dome. Lynn was the guy who went to Memphis, Phoenix, and Los Angeles to check the stadium situations there, and he gave Minnesota politicians the message that the Vikings were willing to leave if a stadium bill was not passed.

Lynn might have preferred a football-only stadium in Bloomington, but he was smart enough to cut himself a deal in the Dome. The Vikings set up a company to build and operate the suites at the

Metrodome. Lynn still collects $250,000 a year as the head of the company.

The political fight over the stadium was the toughest I have ever been through—tougher than the battle to get major league baseball. The St. Paul legislators were working to kill the stadium. The St. Paul people always had a better relationship with the outstate legislators than the Minneapolis politicians. Publicly, the St. Paul politicians were not lobbying against it, but privately they did not want a stadium in Minneapolis, and that is what made it such a bloody battle.

I was deeply involved and did some things I would never do today, or my rear end would be fired by the newspaper. Harvey Mackay was lobbying harder at the Legislature than anyone. Harvey talked me into meeting with some of the legislators who were swing votes, to do some arm twisting.

When the stadium bill was in the Legislature, I was getting death threats. My phone number was listed in the book, and people were calling in the middle of the night, screaming things like, "You're going to die, you Jew bastard."

It became a bitter situation. My son, Chad, was getting abuse in school. My daughter, Chris, was getting insulted. A lot of people were getting heat. The reporters at the *Star Tribune* decided to take out an ad protesting John Cowles, Jr.'s involvement in getting the stadium built. I was going to take out an ad myself, praising John, Jr. for his concern for Minneapolis, but I was talked out of it. That would have led to the *Star Tribune* getting even more abuse.

The stadium debate still was going on at the end of the legislative session. The stadium bill went down in a vote, and it looked as though it was dead. Harvey Mackay and other pro-dome people worked the floor as hard it has ever been worked, brought the bill back to life at midnight, and it passed.

If it had not passed, the Twins and the Vikings would have been gone. The Twin Cities would have been a "cold Omaha." Hubert Humphrey was the first guy to say that about the impact of major league sports, and it's the greatest description ever of what the Twins and the Vikings (and now the Timberwolves and the Wild) mean to this area. I've stolen that phrase—"We would be a cold Omaha" —a thousand times from the late, great Senator Humphrey.

To make the Metrodome happen, we still needed to get Calvin Griffith to agree to go downtown. John Cowles, Jr. and the rest of the downtown business people had spent all their time schmoozing Max and the Vikings. They had not done a good job of selling the Dome to Calvin.

I don't think Calvin ever wanted the Metrodome to be built. By then, he wanted to move to a warm-weather location and get his bank account back to where it had been before he fired Billy Martin.

Dan Brutger, a construction guy from St. Cloud, was the head of the stadium commission. He went out to Met Stadium and begged Calvin to sign a Metrodome lease. The business people told Calvin they were going to buy more season tickets if he came downtown and cancel season tickets if he stayed in Bloomington. Calvin was told he would have a tough time getting a new radio and television deal if he did not go along with the Metrodome. Wheelock Whitney, an old friend of Calvin's, finally met with Calvin and convinced him to sign a lease. Even then, Calvin wound up outsmarting Brutger and the stadium commission. They had to give him an escape clause that would allow the Twins to get out of the lease if attendance averaged less than 1.2 million in the first three years.

Brutger did not have much choice. Calvin was not going to sign without it. The modified version of Calvin's original escape clause is part of the reason Minnesota was in danger of losing the Twins again in the late nineties.

The real problem with the Metrodome is that Brutger and his executive director, a bureaucrat named Don Poss, cut every corner in building the stadium. They were not satisfied to come in on budget. They wanted to come in under budget and come off as big heroes.

If they had built a three-deck stadium, with suites and a mezzanine on the middle level, there would be enough seats between first and third base, and Carl Pohlad, the owner after Calvin, would have signed a lease to stay in the Metrodome. We made a trip to the Pontiac Silverdome. We showed Brutger and Poss the press box and said, "Here, build this." They squeezed in two cheap press boxes. They squeezed in everything. If Brutger and Poss had built it first class and had come in over budget, nobody would have given a damn. But to save money, they built a football stadium with the minimum requirements for baseball.

When the astronauts first started going into space, they told their colleagues who made a mistake in flight that they had "screwed the pooch." When it came to building the Dome, Brutger and Poss did exactly that. They screwed the pooch.

Chapter 12

Lou Holtz

After Cal Stoll was fired as the University of Minnesota's football coach in 1978, there was a big movement among the players from the Rose Bowl teams of the early sixties to bring in Joe Salem. Everyone called him "Smokey Joe." He had been a backup quarterback, and whenever he came in the game, the Gophers would start to move. The fans loved him and so did his teammates.

Salem had been a successful coach at the University of South Dakota and then Northern Arizona. He was a sought-after coach. He had a chance to go Kansas or to West Point to coach Army.

Athletic Director Paul Giel was not sure he wanted Salem. There were some high school coaches in Minnesota pushing Monte Kiffin, an assistant at Nebraska. Kiffin had recruited Minnesota for Nebraska, and he was popular with the high school coaches.

For a time, Giel was going to hire Kiffin, but then Smokey Joe's old teammates were able to convince him to hire Salem. The first thing the university did was have Bob Naegele donate some of the best billboard spots in the Twin Cities. Then, they put up a likeness of Salem with a rose in his teeth on those billboards. Salem's critics in the media used that to ridicule him for the next five years.

It might come off as ridiculous when you consider Salem lost eighteen of his last nineteen games, but I think he was a fine coach. His first three teams were close to going to bowl games. Then, in 1982, they were decimated by injuries. Every football team suffers injuries, but no team has ever been destroyed like the '82 Gophers.

They won the first three games. They were rated in the top

Minnesota football coaches

The Vikings' Bud Grant and the Gophers' Lou Holtz were two of the best football coaches Minnesota has ever had.

twenty. Illinois came to town, and the Metrodome was sold out. Everything looked great. Then, after trailing the Gophers going into halftime, Illinois came back in the second half and won the game. The Gophers' injuries kept mounting, and everything came apart for Salem's program.

Salem's biggest problem was this: He had an outstanding coaching staff when he came to Minnesota. He had Mike Shanahan, now coaching the Denver Broncos and considered by many football people to be the sharpest offensive coach in the game. Shanahan left for Florida after one season with the Gophers. One after another, other schools came after Salem's coaches. He had started off with a low-budget staff, and when the offers came in, Giel and his assistant, Bob Geary, would not give Salem the money to keep the coaches.

Salem could coach, but he never had a chance. While he was here, Minnesota was not willing to pay the price—for coaches, for facilities—to be competitive.

I was so close to Iowa coach Forrest Evashevski and his assistants—especially Jerry Burns—that I would cover a couple of Iowa games every fall. Evashevski liked to pull pranks. One of his favorites was to put five or six people in the car and drive to some country joint for lunch, then figure out a way to strand one guy out there, ten or fifteen miles from town.

One time, Burns tipped me off that I was going to be the victim, so I made an excuse and didn't go to lunch. I went back in the office and there was this little blond guy with glasses—a young assistant I had seen around but didn't really know. I said, "What are you doing for lunch?" And this young coach said, "Nothing," so we went to a nearby restaurant. That was the first time I had a conversation with Lou Holtz.

Burnsie already had told me: "This Holtz kid is going to be a great coach. He understands the game and he understands people."

Burnsie played a big part in Holtz getting his first college head-coaching job at William and Mary. I had him on my *Sports Hero* show a few times when Holtz was coaching at North Carolina State and Arkansas. I would run into Holtz at NCAA coaches meetings. I knew him well.

I still didn't believe it when Burns kept telling me: "Holtz likes the Big Ten. Holtz would take the Minnesota job if the Gophers went after him."

I told Burnsie he was nuts. I should have listened to him. Burnsie had been right about Holtz in 1976, when he told Lou it would be a mistake to take the job as the coach of the New York Jets. Joe Namath was on his last legs. The Jets' management made Holtz keep some assistant coaches who already were in place. They second-guessed Holtz and drove him crazy. It was a mess there, and Lou quit with one game left in a 3-10 season and went to Arkansas.

The Gophers fired Salem after the 1983 season, and Harvey Mackay came up with the wild idea of trying to hire Holtz. Lou had an outstanding seven seasons at Arkansas. He had a couple of disagreements with Arkansas Athletic Director Frank Broyles over assistant coaches.

As it turned out, Harvey's idea was not so crazy. Holtz was ready to move, although I still didn't believe he could be convinced to come to Minnesota.

I blew the potential scoop on the story. I was in Florida, taking a few days off. Gil Brandt, the scouting director for the Dallas Cowboys, called and left a message on my answering machine back in Minnesota. He was calling to tell me that Holtz had decided to take the Minnesota job. I didn't return the call for a couple of days. By then, the word was out. I had myself to blame for not having that story first.

Mackay and businessman Jaye Dyer had been able to get Holtz to come to Minnesota and talk to University President C. Peter McGrath. First, Holtz told McGrath that Minnesota was going to have to do what it was unwilling to do for Salem, and pay what it took to put together a top coaching staff. Second, McGrath agreed to build a football facility. Salem had asked for the same thing and didn't get it.

Before Holtz was in the picture, the Gophers had offered the job to Les Steckel, an assistant with the Vikings. Steckel also said that he needed a football facility and could not get that promise from the university.

Steckel and I had a long conversation. He asked my opinion on the football situation. I told him that, with the lousy facilities and with what traditionally had been a lukewarm commitment to football by the university administration, I didn't think a coach could win with the Gophers. A month later, Bud Grant quit, and Steckel wound up getting the Vikings job, which he could not handle.

As soon as Holtz took the job, he went to work hiring a first-class coaching staff. He had been trying to hire some new assistants at Arkansas. He brought those guys to Minnesota. He hired John Gutekunst, who had done an outstanding job at Virginia Tech, as his defensive coordinator.

Holtz talked to me about who would be a great Minnesota guy to hire. I recommended Butch Nash, who had been around forever and was liked by everybody. So he hired Nash.

Holtz did not arrive in town until January 1984. He swept into town like a tornado. It was three months before spring practice would start, but Holtz was quoted in the newspapers and was on radio and television every day. He brought optimism to Gophers football, something that had been in short supply since Minnesota last tied for a Big Ten title in 1967. After the 84-13 loss to Nebraska in September 1983, people were feeling that Gophers football was hopeless. Holtz came to town and changed the whole attitude, immediately.

The fellow who was moved into the background was Paul Giel. Giel had been the dominant figure in the athletic department since he gave up his job at WCCO Radio to become the A.D. in 1971. Paul was in the hospital, undergoing bypass surgery, when Holtz was hired. Some boosters—Mackay, Dyer, a couple of other business-men—handled the Holtz deal. Giel had little to do with getting him in here. Giel was used to dealing with coaches—Cal Stoll and Joe Salem answered to him. Holtz ran the entire football operation and was demanding.

After seeing the scores from the 1983 season, Holtz figured he was inheriting the worst players in America. He was amazed when he started looking at the tapes and saw the talent Salem had left behind. When he saw the tapes and the offseason workouts, Holtz said the talent at Minnesota was as good as what he had at Arkansas.

Holtz felt the big problem was getting the linemen who were already in the program to become stronger—to make sure the whole squad was in better shape. That first winter, Holtz demanded that the players work harder in the weight room and on conditioning than Minnesota football players had ever worked.

It was miraculous, what Holtz did for Minnesota football. One year earlier, they had canceled the annual spring game because of injuries and a lack of interest. For Holtz's first spring game, local businesses went out and hustled. They sold 42,000 tickets for $2 apiece. A crowd of 28,000 people showed up at the Metrodome to see a spring game for a team that had been 1-10 the previous season.

Holtz made the Gophers competitive again in 1984. They had a four-game losing streak late in the season to drop to 3-7, then the Gophers beat Iowa 23-17 in the last game at the Metrodome. Sixty thousand people were in there screaming, and the fans were left with a great feeling at the end of Holtz's first season.

In 1985, Oklahoma came to the Dome rated No. 1 and beat the Gophers 13-7. Rickey Foggie, the quarterback Holtz had recruited from South Carolina, threw four passes into the end zone at the end of the game. If one of those passes had been complete, all Holtz and the Gophers would have had to do was kick an extra point to beat the No. 1 team in the country.

Ohio State came to Minnesota with an outstanding team. The Gophers were 3-0 in the Big Ten. The Gophers were marching down the field to beat the Buckeyes. Foggie pulled up lame on about the twenty-yard line. Ohio State survived 23-19, but that was another game when the Metrodome was jammed with people screaming for the Gophers.

Some people have questioned it, but there is no doubt about this: Holtz had a Notre Dame clause in his Minnesota contract—an agreement that he could get out of the deal if he was offered the job at Notre Dame. Holtz put that in there because coaching at Notre Dame was something that had been in the back of his mind for years, and everyone knew that the guy at Notre Dame, Gerry Faust, was not going to last much longer.

I'm convinced Holtz wanted to stay here. During the week before the Ohio State game, Holtz had a meeting scheduled with University President Dr. Kenneth Keller, to talk about a few things involving the football program. Holtz was protective of his time when preparing for a game—especially a big game—and Keller kept him sitting outside

Football friends
We took time out from a banquet at the Wayzata Country Club for a photograph with, from left, Lou Holtz, myself, legendary Ohio State coach Woody Hayes, and Murray Warmath.

the office for almost an hour. Holtz was fuming. Keller was the most anti-sports president we've ever had at the university. I don't think he cared if Holtz stayed or left.

There was a possibility Giel would have to have another bypass surgery. Because of his health, Paul wanted less pressure, so he said to Holtz: "I would like to have you take over as athletic director as well as football coach. I would be the assistant in charge of fundraising. I could represent Minnesota at Big Ten meetings and the Rose Bowl, things like that, but you would run the show."

Holtz was excited about that. He went home and talked to his wife, Beth, and they agreed he would sign a long-term contract—with no escape clauses—to be the athletic director and football coach at Minnesota. Then, Giel had some doubts if he really wanted to step down, and that conversation ended.

Holtz raised more money than any football coach in Minnesota history. The men's athletic department was getting money from people that it had never heard of previously. Holtz would visit a

Minnesota business executive and come out of the meeting with a check for $25,000 or $50,000 for the Williams Scholarship Fund. Holtz was so good at this that the university's fundraising foundation became upset. Holtz was getting big donations from people and companies that had turned down the foundation. Out of the clear blue, Holtz received a memo from Keller telling him what companies he could go to and what companies he had to stay away from. I've never seen such a bunch of goofballs in my life as Keller and his buddies in the university administration.

By early October, it was obvious Notre Dame was going to change coaches. The first coach Notre Dame tried to hire was George Welsh at Virginia. It also talked to UCLA coach Terry Donahue.

Once Notre Dame zeroed in on Holtz, it was not 100 percent certain that he was going to leave. He knew about the pressure a Notre Dame coach faced. I don't think the decision was as easy for Holtz as people thought.

Holtz is more than a top-notch salesman and motivator. He is also as good a coach as I've ever seen. If the offensive line played lousy, Holtz would be with the offensive line in practice the next week. He can coach any phase of the game.

No coach puts more pressure on assistants than does Holtz. One of his assistants said, "On the Sunday after we lost a game, we would have the meeting with Lou and leave there feeling as though you had let down everyone—that you were worthless. But by Thursday, Lou would have you convinced that there wasn't a team in the world that could beat this coaching staff and this group of players."

Minnesota had seven or eight players locked up that backed out after Holtz left, going to Notre Dame or other big-time schools. Tony Rice was set for Minnesota. He would have taken over at quarterback after Foggie was finished. Rice wound up going to Notre Dame, sitting out a season because of academic restrictions, and then he led Holtz and the Irish to the national championship.

Minnesota missed its chance to keep Holtz when the proposal to make him athletic director fell through. He loved Minnesota, but when Notre Dame made the offer, it was too hard for Holtz to say no.

Holtz stayed at Notre Dame for eleven years. He coached more games there than anyone in history. The reason Holtz quit late in the

1996 season was exactly what he suggested at his press conference in South Bend: He felt Knute Rockne's record for victories was sacred and that he should not pass it. When I wrote that in a column, some people scoffed, but it is absolutely true. Three, four years before he quit, Holtz was telling me about Rockne's record. He was paranoid about that record. Holtz grew up loving Notre Dame, and with people like that, Rockne is almost a saint.

No one forced out Holtz at Notre Dame. He could have stayed there forever. Father Joyce wrote a letter to Holtz, saying exactly that, and telling Lou what a sad day it was for all Notre Dame people when he resigned.

It was one of my saddest days as a sportswriter when Lou Holtz left Minnesota. If he had stayed, Holtz would have taken the Gophers to the Rose Bowl a few times. There's no doubt about that.

I went to Notre Dame for one of Holtz's first games in fall 1986. He invited me to attend the Mass that the football team went to on the morning of a game. When the players stood during Mass, I would stand. When they knelt, I would kneel. I was kneeling and somebody poked me in the back. It was Moose Krause, the former Notre Dame athletic director and a longtime friend of mine. Krause said: "Sid, I knew us Catholics would get you, sooner or later."

Chapter 13

From Buyout
to the World Series

Gene Mauch quit as the Twins manager with a month left in the 1980 season. Free agency was in full swing, and Twins owner Calvin Griffith refused to spend the money. The ballclub's public image and talent pool was at an all-time low.

The collapse had started at the end of the 1978 season. First, Calvin made his famous speech to the Waseca Lions Club. Then, he traded Rod Carew to the California Angels for one talented player who was weird, Kenny Landreaux, and a bunch of stiffs.

Calvin was doing a favor for a friend in going to Waseca to make that speech in the last week of the 1978 season. He had a few drinks and started talking. A reporter, Nick Coleman, Jr. of the Minneapolis *Tribune*, was visiting his in-laws at the time and went to the Lions Club function with his father-in-law. Calvin said the main reason the Twins had moved to Minnesota was there were so few black people. "Blacks don't go to ballgames, but they go to the rasslin' matches and put up the damnedest chant you ever heard," he said.

He said ballplayers should take advantage of the "free love" that was available on the road. He was asked about Jerry Terrell, a former Twins infielder who was from the Waseca area, and Calvin said it was a "disgrace to baseball that Terrell had been able to play in the big leagues."

It was outrageous stuff, even for Calvin. Coleman wrote a story for the Sunday *Tribune,* and people went crazy. The newspapers published editorials saying Calvin had to step aside as president of the Twins.

Calvin said he had an agreement before he appeared at the Lions Club that everything was off the record. Later, he insisted he was misquoted. Clark Griffith, Calvin's son, said: "Calvin has convinced himself he wasn't even in Waseca on the night in question."

The Twins had an executive board consisting of Clark Griffith, Bruce Haynes, and Howard Fox. The board went to Calvin and told him it was time to resign. Calvin responded by disbanding the executive board.

How bad were the Twins? John Castino led the team in baseball's power categories in 1980 with 13 home runs and 64 runs batted in. By comparison, Philadelphia's third baseman Mike Schmidt let the major leagues with 48 home runs and 121 RBIs. In 1981, attendance was going to be at an all-time low—less than 600,000—until there was a long strike at midseason. The league wound up playing a split season, and that helped cover up how bad things were for the Twins.

Moving to the Metrodome should have been a boost for the Twins, but the first thing Calvin Griffith did was trade away the most-recognizable players: shortstop Roy Smalley, catcher Butch Wynegar, and relief pitcher Doug Corbett.

Billy Gardner was managing, and he had fifteen rookies on a twenty-five–player roster. In the long run, this was going to pay off for the Twins, but it was a disaster as far as selling tickets in 1982 was concerned.

To get him to move to the Metrodome, the Metropolitan Sports Facilities Commission had given Calvin an escape clause in his lease. If the Twins did not average 1.2 million in attendance for three years, the lease was broken, and Calvin could leave.

The Twins did not reach 1 million in attendance in their first season inside the Dome. We were in trouble right off the bat as far as keeping the Twins was concerned. It was obvious Calvin was not going to do anything to improve the product and sell tickets.

Calvin and some other members of the family now had their eyes on Tampa–St. Petersburg. Calvin and his sister, Thelma Haynes, owned 52 percent of the ballclub. A Washington businessman named Gabe Murphy owned 42 percent. Tampa Bay had completed a deal to purchase Murphy's stock. Calvin and Thelma were going to sell next. The Tampa people were willing to pay a big price for the stock, and they were willing to give the Griffith family a contract to run the ballclub for a certain number of years. The escape clause would kick in after the 1984 season, and Calvin had a deal with Tampa–St. Petersburg waiting.

When I started in the newspaper business, Jack Mackay was the political writer for the Associated Press. The stories Mackay wrote on politics and the State Legislature would appear in every outstate daily newspaper. Mackay had a lot of power at the State Capitol and he used it. If you wanted something to happen at the State Legislature, you had to get Jack Mackay on your side. I knew Jack, but we did not travel in the same circles. He was much more powerful than I was when it came to making things happen.

Jack's son, Harvey Mackay, was a golfer at the University of Minnesota. Harvey learned a lot about how to influence people from his father. A few years back, Harvey wrote his bible for the business world, *Swim With the Sharks Without Being Eaten Alive*, and he hustled enough copies to make sure it appeared on the *New York Times* best-seller list. It was No. 1 on the *Times* list for fifty-four weeks. Harvey is now one of the most successful authors in the world.

I first got to know Harvey at the university. Then he started Mackay Envelope Company and turned it into a big success. He was the national president of the University of Minnesota Alumni Association and also president of the M Club—for athletic letter winners—at Minnesota.

Harvey first was visible as a booster when Bill Fitch replaced Johnny Kundla as the Gophers basketball coach in 1968. Harvey was involved with the recruiting of Jim Brewer, a high school All-American from the Chicago area who the Gophers took away from all the big schools in the country. Even though Harvey helped get Brewer for him, Fitch left after the 1969–1970 season to coach the Cleveland Cavaliers, an expansion team in the NBA.

Harvey Mackay was the main man in hiring Lou Holtz in December 1983. He is also the reason the Minnesota Twins are not the Tampa Bay Twins. He saved the day in 1984, when Calvin had one foot out of the Metrodome's revolving doors and his ballclub on the way to Florida.

The Twins needed to sell 1.8 million-plus tickets to keep Calvin from breaking the lease and selling to the Tampa group. There were a lot of meetings among the downtown business people to try to decide what could be done to stop the move. The consensus was that this time we were out of luck. We had stopped the Twins from moving to Seattle several years earlier, but there did not seem to be any way to head off the move to Tampa–St. Pete.

Finally, Harvey said: "There is only one thing we can do. We have to buy the tickets. That will lock in Calvin for awhile and give us the time to get a local buyer."

Harvey went to all the businesses in town and raised $6 million in cash within thirty days for the buyout. The idea was to buy the cheap seats in the outfield second deck in bulk. The Twins also had scheduled some half-price ticket promotions. That's when Harvey was really in his glory.

On May 16, 1984, the Twins had a weekday afternoon game against Toronto with half-price tickets. All the television cameras—local and national networks—were in front of the Metrodome. Harvey marched up to the ticket window with his briefcase full of money at the start of the game. He bought all the tickets that were left.

There were 6,000 fans in the Metrodome that afternoon, but the official attendance (tickets sold) was 51,863. It is still a Twins record for a weekday afternoon game.

Harvey continued to buy out the cheap tickets every day for a week, spending a total of $1.1 million. Finally, both sides announced the buyout was being suspended while Calvin undertook serious negotiations to sell the team to a local buyer.

Harvey's buyout plan sounded ridiculous. It looked even more ridiculous with all those empty seats. But it worked.

Carl Pohlad was the guy they had found to buy the team. He was primarily a banker—not well known in the media, but one of the richest people in Minnesota. A few years earlier, he had tried to buy the Philadelphia Eagles with a partner. There were a lot of people—including me—telling him what a hero he would be in the community by buying the Twins and saving baseball.

Even though he had a home in Orlando, Twins Vice-President Howard Fox did not want to see the Twins move to Tampa–St. Pete.

Fox had been inseparable from Calvin around the ballpark for years. When Pohlad surfaced as the leading candidate to buy the team, Fox became attached to him. Fox saw this as his chance to become the team president. He had dreamed about that for years, but was unlikely to accomplish it with the Griffith family owning or running the team. Fox's strategy worked. When Pohlad completed the sale, he named Fox as president.

Clark Griffith, Calvin's son, was the holdout against selling—to the Tampa group or to Pohlad. His feeling was the family could make it in the Metrodome, if they operated aggressively and wisely to put a good product on the field.

Thelma Haynes, Calvin's sister and partner, wanted no part of that. She wanted to get her money and move to Florida. So did her son, Bruce. Thelma and Bruce were pushing Calvin to sell to Pohlad, and so was Fox. They had much more influence with Calvin than did Clark, who had feuded with Fox for years and had been turned into the organization's outcast.

Pohlad knew Yankees owner George Steinbrenner and called to ask for advice. Steinbrenner said if he could get the team for $38 million—$24 million to Calvin and Thelma, $11 million to the Tampa Bay people who now owned Gabe Murphy's 42 percent, another $3 million for the Griffith family—then it was a hell of a deal.

Pohlad and Fox told Calvin that he would be a consultant. Calvin took that to mean the family would be running the team, as would have been the case if he had sold to Tampa–St. Pete. There was never a chance that was going to happen with Pohlad.

A tentative agreement to sell was announced in June, and the formal sale took place on September 7, 1984. By then, an amazing thing had happened. All those rookies from '82—Kent Hrbek, Gary Gaetti, Tom Brunansky, Frank Viola—were starting to become outstanding players. A little rookie also had showed up to take over in center field a month into that season. His name was Kirby Puckett.

There were only mediocre teams in the American League West. The Twins had a five-game lead in the division in late August. The Twins no longer needed Harvey Mackay at the window with a briefcase full of money to sell tickets. The fans were starting to rally around Billy Gardner's ballclub.

Pohlad's business associates had said when he bought the team,

World Series stars
This photo was taken during Kent Hrbek's last year with the Twins. From left: Kirby Puckett, myself, and Hrbek.

"The guy has a magic touch." That luck carried over to baseball. In June, Pohlad made an agreement to buy what looked like a terrible ballclub. By early September, when he officially owned the team, the young players had started to jell, and Pohlad had a pennant contender.

The football Gophers of the late forties contained a collection of memorable characters: Leo Nomellini, Bud Grant, Verne Gagne, Billy Bye, Clayton Tonnemaker, to name a few. The championship Lakers teams were another interesting group: George Mikan, Jim Pollard, Vern Mikkelsen, Dugie Martin. And the Vikings Super Bowl teams were that way, with the outgoing Fran Tarkenton, the aloof Alan Page, the flamboyant Chuck Foreman. That's the great intrigue of sports. You mix all these personalities and talents together. Sometimes, the chemistry is right, and you wind up with a group of people you will never forget. And sometimes you get rotten eggs—a team you can't wait to forget.

The Twins of the eighties wound up with the greatest chemistry of any team we've had in Minnesota. It is no coincidence they became the first group to bring a professional world championship to the Twin Cities since the Lakers in 1954.

Kent Hrbek was the ringleader of that effort. Hrbek grew up a few blocks from Met Stadium in Bloomington. When he was a kid and there was a night game at the Met, the lights would shine into his bedroom window. Hrbek was a left-handed hitter, and his hero was another left-handed hitter, Tony Oliva.

How could anything be more perfect than a hometown kid taking the Twins to the World Series? That seemed a long way off when Hrbek was a seventeenth-round draft choice out of Bloomington Kennedy High in 1978.

Normally, players picked that late do not get a lot of money. Hrbek was going to the University of Minnesota. Dick Siebert was coaching the Gophers. He told me: "The Twins really should sign this kid. He's more of a ballplayer than he is a student. He has a chance to be a great power hitter."

One of the smart things Calvin did was to come up with $30,000 to sign Hrbek. Calvin's brother, Jimmy Robertson, and one of Jimmy's guys in the concessions department, Tom ("The Greek") Bourdakalis, convinced Calvin to scout Hrbek in a game. Hrbek hit a couple of home runs with that beautiful swing of his, and Calvin was convinced.

Hrbek came out of Visalia in the Class A California League to the Twins in August 1981. He hit a game-winning home run in Yankee Stadium on his first night in the big leagues.

Gaetti, Viola, catcher Tim Laudner, and outfielder Randy Bush all came from the Class AA Orlando team that Tom Kelly had managed in the Southern League in 1981. Shortstop Greg Gagne came in a trade with the Yankees.

The best hitter in that whole group of rookies might have been Jim Eisenreich, a left-handed hitter out of St. Cloud. Eisenreich had a wonderful swing, and he could play center field. Unfortunately, Eisenreich's career in Minnesota was ruined. He would go into uncontrolled twitching and was unable to stay on the field. One night in Milwaukee, he started to hyperventilate, and his condition became so bad the players and trainers pinned him on a table in the clubhouse. The same thing happened in Boston. Billy Gardner said: "It was the damnedest thing I've ever seen. I thought Eisey's heart was going to explode."

The Twins doctors kept saying he had a nervous disorder. It turned out to be Tourette's syndrome, which can be treated by medication. The Twins screwed it up, and Eisenreich wound up going back to St. Cloud. Later, he was put on the proper medication, the Twins gave up their claim to him, and Eisenreich made a comeback in Kansas City. Now he's in his late thirties, makes $2 million a year with the Florida Marlins, and remains an outstanding hitter.

It's not often a farm system can produce two great center fielders in such a short time, but George Brophy, the Twins minor league and scouting director, did it. With Eisenreich back in St. Cloud, the Twins brought Kirby Puckett to the big leagues in May 1984.

The Twins were still a young club when they blew the lead in the American League West in 1984. They had a relief pitcher that season named Ron Davis. He was a big, goofy-looking son of a gun who would sing "Jimmy Crack Corn" on the way to the mound. He also could give up more home runs in the most crucial moments of any pitcher in history. Davis blew the division title on the last weekend in Cleveland in 1984. Then, in 1985, the Twins were leading a game in the ninth inning in Yankee Stadium, and he gave up a home run to Don Mattingly. It was the third time he had done that in a couple of weeks.

The fans were ready to kill Davis. *Star Tribune* sports columnist Doug Grow might have saved his life. He wrote a column about how Davis had taken some underprivileged kids fishing on his day off, after the Mattingly home run. When the Twins played at the Metrodome after that column appeared, the fans applauded for Davis.

Soon, he was giving up home runs again, and the fans were booing him again. The Twins had poor seasons in 1985 and 1986, and went through Ray Miller as a manager.

After the 1986 season, Pohlad phased out Fox and put Andy MacPhail in charge of the team. Tom Kelly had managed the last twelve games in '86, and MacPhail was pushing for him to be the permanent replacement for Miller. It took MacPhail a long time to convince Pohlad.

There was a perception that I was working against Kelly. The fact

In the Twins dugout
Here I am interviewing Twins star shortstop Roy Smalley.

was I didn't think he was going to get the job, so I was mentioning other candidates in my newspaper column. I knew Pohlad was looking for a more experienced manager.

Jim Frey, who had been the Chicago Cubs' manager, could have had the job, but he wanted to be a general manager more than a manager. Chuck Cottier, who had been the Seattle Mariners' manager, was given an interview. Finally, Pohlad gave the go-ahead on hiring Kelly. It turned out to be the smartest thing Pohlad has done as a baseball owner.

Kelly has a lot of Bud Grant in him when it comes to personality and the way he runs a team. They both knew enough about handling players to have staying power. Kelly did not have Grant's personality in public, however.

Bud also had a greater fondness for money. Bud would go out and make a speech for $2,000. Kelly would rather hang out at the greyhound track in Hudson, Wisconsin, where he owns a kennel.

They are both private people—Kelly more so than Bud.

Grant and Kelly could find a way to get inside a player's head. They both wanted a few stars and a bunch of other players who can fill roles. Grant kept some marginal players around, and I would ask: "Why are you keeping that stiff?"

The answer was: "He will make the routine plays. He will do what he is told. He won't bitch about playing time. He won't lose a ballgame for me."

Kelly has been the same way with the Twins. Jeff Reboulet. Al Newman. Chip Hale. Randy Bush. He loved having players like that around.

Kelly had a terrific relationship with his first group of Twins. He had managed most of them somewhere along the line in the Twins farm system. When they were rookies in 1982, he was the third-base coach, and he was their buddy.

Hrbek, Gary Gaetti, and Tom Brunansky were the real characters. They had a sign above the door to the clubhouse weight room that read, "Nobody but Sid goes past here." They wanted me to come in there so they could pull pranks on me.

Hrbek would wrestle you to the floor. He hurt himself wrestling with Bobby Dorey, the clubhouse cook. He wrestled me to the floor, and I had a bad back for several weeks. Hrbek was a beauty.

In '87, the Twins played Kansas City on the second-to-last weekend of the season. The Dome was jammed. Kansas City started Charlie Leibrandt in the Sunday afternoon game, and the Twins slaughtered him in the first inning. I never heard a stadium as loud in Minnesota as the Metrodome was that afternoon. It would get louder.

The Twins reduced their magic number to one that day, and then wrapped up the division title the next night in Texas. They then surprised everyone by beating Detroit in five games in the American League Championship Series.

People remember Hrbek's grand slam home run in the World Series against St. Louis's Ken Dayley. They remember the parade, when it seemed like everyone in the metropolitan area lined the streets in Minneapolis and then St. Paul to see the Twins. They remember Kirby Puckett riding in the parade in that Snoopy Air Force hat.

To me, the most fantastic moment was the homecoming at the

Dugout interview
Here I am in the dugout interviewing Twins manager Tom Kelly.

Metrodome, after the Twins came back from winning the pennant in Detroit. I flew back with the team. Originally, the plan was the players were going to wave to a couple thousand people greeting them at the charter terminal, get in their cars, and drive home.

Then we heard on the plane that the police were nervous that too many people would show up, so the welcome was moved to the Metrodome. We heard that there might be 10,000, even 15,000, people at the Dome to welcome back the Twins.

The players went downtown on a couple of busses. I had my car parked at the airport. I drove downtown, saw the traffic and could not believe it. I had to beg ten cops to let me drive through to the Metrodome.

I got there at the same time as the Twins and walked in the tunnel with the players. Fifty thousand people inside the dome greeted the Twins. There was more noise than I heard at the World Series. The ballplayers were overwhelmed. They did not want to leave. They walked around the floor of the stadium, talking to people, signing autographs.

The Homer Hankies—the idea of Terri Robbins from promotions at the *Star Tribune*—became a national symbol for the baseball madness we had in Minnesota in October '87. The paper still gets letters asking to buy Homer Hankies.

The Twins played St. Louis in the World Series. Cardinals Manager Whitey Herzog told me, "I never believed there was much of a home-field advantage in baseball, but there is in this dome. This is one time in my life I'm worried about noise beating my team. Some of my players will be able to handle it, but some won't."

When it came to Game Seven, Whitey started a pitcher who could not handle it. He sent Joe Magrane to the mound, and the guy apart like a cheap suit. The Twins were world champions.

Most of the players were leftover from the Griffith era, but the glory went to Pohlad. Those business associates of his were correct. Pohlad did have a magic touch.

Chapter 14

Sports Capital of the World

My friend Bob Knight, the Indiana basketball coach, was in town. I left the Metrodome early and was driving Knight back to his hotel in Bloomington. It came on the radio that the Twins had traded right fielder Tom Brunansky to St. Louis for second baseman Tommy Herr.

This was early in the 1988 season. The Twins were coming off the World Series victory. They were the biggest heroes we've ever had around here. I couldn't believe General Manager Andy MacPhail would mess with the chemistry of his team like that. I called MacPhail at home at midnight and said, "What the hell is going on?"

Brunansky was having a bad spring. Brunansky always had been a streaky player. You knew he could win a couple of games a week for the Twins when he came out of his slump and went on a hot streak.

The Twins convinced themselves Brunansky could not throw the ball from right field anymore. Manager Tom Kelly pushed for the trade. He thought Herr, a switch-hitter, would give more balance to the lineup.

It turned out to be a disaster. Herr spent the whole season in the trainer's room. Even worse, he was pushing religion in the clubhouse. He gave Gary Gaetti a pamphlet about the world coming to an end. Gaetti jumped into religion with both feet, so much so that he went downhill as a player for a few years.

Hrbek and Gaetti had been the best of friends. They would go into a room in the clubhouse after the game, have a couple of beers,

Spring training break, 1992
Taking a break from Twins spring training for dinner with, from left, my son Chad Hartman and his wife Kathleen, my daughter Chris Schmitt, Twins owner Carl Pohlad and his wife Eloise, and myself.

smoke cigarettes, and talk baseball. Herr ruined that when he turned Gaetti into a God Squadder.

It looked as though the born-again Christians were taking over the clubhouse for a while. One night in Seattle, about a half-dozen players got together and stayed up praying because of another world-is-ending prediction. The world did not end, and the Twins had an afternoon game in the Kingdome. Kelly was not too happy when all his Christians showed up blurry-eyed from praying all night and then played a lousy game.

It did not take long for MacPhail to realize he had made a horrible move with the Herr trade. He told me, "From now on, I'm going to check out players more closely from a personal standpoint before I make a trade."

That was a bad deal, but MacPhail was the best sports executive we had around here since Jim Finks. He came from a great baseball family. His father, Lee, a longtime executive with various American League clubs and then the American League president, was first class in every way, and he passed that along to Andy.

MacPhail could handle employees and the media. He was extremely well organized. He surrounded himself with sharp baseball people—Bob Gebhard as a vice-president, Terry Ryan as the scouting director, Kevin Malone as a regional scouting director. There is no comparison between the front office MacPhail had and the one the Twins have been working with since Andy went to the Cubs as team president in September 1994.

The Brunansky trade hurt the Twins for the time, but they still had Hrbek and Kirby Puckett. In 1991, they added designated hitter Chili Davis, Jack Morris (as a No. 1 starter to replace the traded Frank Viola), and Mike Pagliarulo (as a third baseman to replace Gaetti—gone as a free agent), and won another World Series.

We had been through it only four years earlier. Things were not as crazy with the public in October 1991 as they had been in '87, not until the Twins came back from Atlanta trailing three victories to two. Then, Puckett hit the winning home run in Game Six, and Morris pitched ten shutout innings in Game Seven, and the Twins-Braves series went down as one of the greatest World Series ever played.

For Minnesota, the World Series came in the middle of a stretch of eleven months that has never been duplicated by another city. We had the Stanley Cup finals with the North Stars in May 1991. We had the U.S. Open at Hazeltine National in June. We had the World Series in October, then the Super Bowl in January 1992, and the NCAA Final Four in early April 1992.

It was amazing. People were so excited about sports around here that I'm surprised Harvey Mackay did not put together a committee to try to get the Kentucky Derby to move to Canterbury Downs, Minnesota's new racetrack.

The shock to me was getting the Super Bowl. I did not think we had a chance. The idea first came from Governor Rudy Perpich. He pushed sports more than any politician we've had in Minnesota.

Perpich put together a Super Bowl task force that was led by Marilyn Carlson Nelson, the daughter of Curt Carlson, head of the Radisson Hotel chain and one of the richest people in Minnesota. Nelson's task force did a superb job.

As usual, Harvey Mackay also had a big role. He went to see several of the key owners, including Lamar Hunt in Kansas City and Norman

Braman in Philadelphia. Braman was the head of the NFL's Super Bowl site-selection committee, and Harvey was able to convince him that Minneapolis was capable of pulling this off.

Still, there is no way the Super Bowl would have come to Minnesota without three people: Max Winter, Mike Lynn, and Jim Finks.

Max had been less influential than the other partners when the Vikings started in 1961. Bill Boyer was the president and Bernie Ridder and H. P. Skoglund were the smart business people. Eventually, Boyer drank himself out of the president's job. Ridder and Skoglund did not have the time, so Max became the president.

There was a certain group of owners that ran the NFL: Art Modell of the Cleveland Browns, Carroll Rosenbloom in Baltimore and then L.A., Wellington Mara in New York, Art and Dan Rooney in Pittsburgh. Max was smart enough to align himself with those people.

After Finks left as general manager in 1974, Max decided not to hire a new general manager; he was going to run the show. Then, he found out he did not know how to negotiate a contract. That's when he brought in Mike Lynn from Memphis. When Lynn started, Max gave him a few little jobs. Soon, Lynn became indispensable. Max would go to Hawaii in November and stay for weeks at a time, and Lynn would run the whole operation.

Lynn was loyal to Max. He convinced the owners to build the office and practice complex in Eden Prairie and to name it Winter Park, in Max's honor. That certainly has added a lot to the legend that Max was the pioneer of the NFL in Minnesota.

In the eighties, the next generation of the Boyer and Skoglund families did not want Max in there. Jack Steele, Bill Boyer's son-in-law, or John Skoglund, H. P.'s son, wanted the job. It was Lynn who kept Max in the president's job and kept turning a big profit for the owners.

Only one Super Bowl had been played in the north—in Detroit at the Pontiac Silverdome in 1982—and it was a disaster. The weather and the organization were both terrible. The only reason Detroit had been given a game was that the automotive companies were big NFL sponsors, and they put on the pressure to get a Super Bowl. The feeling was there would never be another Super Bowl played in a northern climate.

On his way to the Twins

Here I am with Paul Molitor in the days when he wore a Milwaukee Brewers cap.

The big contribution Lynn made to the Minnesota effort was pushing through a motion at an NFL meeting that one of the next five Super Bowls had to be played at a northern city. Once that happened, it was obvious the game would have to be played in a dome—the Silverdome, the Kingdome in Seattle, or the Metrodome. The disadvantage for Minneapolis was the size of the Metrodome. The NFL wanted at least 70,000 seats. The capacity of our Dome was 63,000.

One smart thing the Minnesota delegation did was produce a film with Max Winter, sitting alone in the Metrodome, asking his friends to come join him for the Super Bowl. Max was well liked by the older owners, so that gave Minnesota a sentimental advantage.

I still thought it was a pipedream. I was talking to my friend Art Modell, and he was telling me Minnesota had no chance—that the northern Super Bowl was going to Seattle. I was writing in my column that Minnesota wasn't going to get a Super Bowl. Then, on

Close personal friends
Here I am with Twins star Chuck Knoblauch.

a Saturday morning, Finks called and said: "Cyanide, stop writing that Minneapolis is not going to get the Super Bowl. You're going to look like a jackass. We're going to get it for you."

And Finks was the guy who made it happen. He was running the New Orleans Saints at the time. He had left Minnesota under unfriendly circumstances with Max, but over the years, they had patched up their relationship. Finks was a first-class guy and a straight shooter. He loved Minnesota and felt, if a northern site was going to get the Super Bowl, we deserved it. He knew the Max angle was going to play well with many of the owners. Finks went into the meeting and made a speech. He said, "Do it for Max, who has done a lot for this league. Do it for Minnesota, which has gone to four Super Bowls and now deserves to have one in its backyard."

Some of the owners were afraid they would come up here and run into the Blizzard of the Century. But Finks sold them, and when the Super Bowl came here, it could not have worked out better. The weather was mild and the organization of Marilyn Carlson Nelson's task force was remarkable.

The officials of the NFL still tell me they have never been more pleased with the community involvement and the operation of the Super Bowl than they were with that one. One example: The NFL had a history of using a lot of local kids to dance and sing as part of the pregame and halftime shows. In every other town, they would have 30 percent no-shows. In Minnesota, every kid showed up for practices and the game.

Mike Lynn's goal was to have the Vikings in the Super Bowl after the 1991 season. That's why he made the Herschel Walker trade. He felt that, with a big-time running back, the Vikings could be the dominant team in the NFC Central over the next few years. Lynn's theory was if the Vikings could win enough to get a first-round bye and at least one home playoff game, they could go back to the Super Bowl. The Dallas Cowboys wound up double-crossing him on the Walker trade.

Dallas had an option in the trade to keep the five players they had obtained from Minnesota or turn them into draft choices. Dallas's Jerry Jones and Jimmy Johnson had told Lynn they were going to keep the players. In Lynn's mind, he did not feel he was giving up all those draft choices.

I remember going into Lynn's office the day after the trade was announced and saying, "In Dallas, Jones and Johnson are saying you gave them all these draft choices."

And Lynn said: "Forget the draft choices. We gave them five players and a No. 1 draft choice. They are going to take the players, not the draft picks."

Lynn soon realized he had been misled. I've always felt that, if Herschel Walker had not had such a great debut in his first game for the Vikings vs. Green Bay in the Metrodome, Lynn would have sent Herschel back to Dallas and canceled the deal. But Herschel ran for a total of 150 yards; he kicked off his shoe and kept rambling on one play; and everyone—the team, the fans, and the media—thought he was going to be the guy to put the Vikings over the top.

The first people to realize that would not be the case were the

Dawn of the Herschel Walker era, 1990
We all had high hopes that Dallas Cowboy running back Herschel Walker would be the man to put the Vikings on top. Here, we celebrated the arrival of Walker with the team. From left, Walker, myself, former Viking player and current scout Scott Studwell, and WCCO sports announcer Mark Rosen.

coaches. Jerry Burns was the head coach of the Vikings, and he could not believe the limited number of things a team could do with Walker in the offense. The Vikings were not made to be a power-running team, but that was the only way to use Walker.

It turned into a terrible situation. Several of the local sportswriters started ripping Walker. He was not happy here. The fans turned on Lynn. He resigned during the 1990 season. He was out of the picture by the time the Super Bowl came in 1992, which was sad, since he had pushed through the northern-site proposal that gave Minneapolis a chance to host the game.

The Walker trade was only one of Lynn's problems. He also

wound up in a feud with Max and a court fight for control of the team. Max was old and not nearly as sharp as he had been. His relatives convinced him to try to run off Lynn, so they could take control of the club.

Richard Cohen, Winter's son-in-law, poisoned Max on Lynn. Cohen had a buddy he was going to put in as the CEO. Cohen thought he could convince Jack Steele and John Skoglund to vote with Max and get Lynn out of there.

Lynn was close to Steele and Skoglund. Lynn had taken care of himself financially, yes, but he also had taken care of the owners. There were only three votes with the owners, and Lynn had two of them.

Lynn had a contract that gave him authority to run the club, and he had the votes. When it was obvious that Winter's family could not get him out, Max sold his stock to Irwin Jacobs and Carl Pohlad for $25 million.

Jacobs and Pohlad sued to try to get control of the team. They tried to bring out a lot of embarrassing stuff about Lynn, such as flying to Beverly Hills on a private jet to buy suits. Steele and Skoglund stuck with Lynn, and eventually, they outlasted Jacobs and Pohlad in court.

Jacobs and Pohlad did not come out poorly on the deal. They never do. They wound up getting $50 million, double their money, for the stock from an ownership group of ten people that Lynn put together.

Lynn did an outstanding job in running the Vikings. He sold tickets. When things had the potential to turn sour, he cut his losses quick in 1984 and fired Les Steckel after one disastrous season. Then he gave Bud Grant a tremendous deal to come back and put the franchise on a solid footing again.

The one thing I have against Lynn is that he was responsible for Jim Finks not becoming the NFL commissioner. When Pete Rozelle resigned in 1989, it was all set that Finks was going to be his successor.

Art Modell of the Cleveland Browns, Dan Rooney of the Pittsburgh Steelers, Wellington Mara of the New York Giants—they were all behind Finks. It was such a cinch Finks would get the job that he had made a deal for a home in Chicago. He was going to move the

NFL office from New York to Chicago.

Lynn did not want Finks to get the job. Maybe it was jealousy. After Finks left the Vikings, they went to two more Super Bowls in the seventies. The sportswriters—including myself—were still giving the credit to Finks, since the nucleus of the team had been put together by him.

Lynn rallied the newer owners and the malcontents and convinced them that Finks represented the "old guard," and the old guard had been running the league long enough. Finks was not able to get the necessary votes, and the owners wound up electing NFL attorney Paul Tagliabue as the commissioner.

It broke Jim Finks's heart, not getting the commissioner's job. I'll never be able to forgive Lynn for that.

Minneapolis was just another Midwestern town before the Twins and the Vikings came here in 1961. When we would go to the New York with the Lakers in the fifties, you would hear everyone saying, "Mindianapolis is playing tonight." They had heard more about Indianapolis than Minneapolis, so they gave our town the Indianapolis pronunciation.

Sports made this a big-league area. From May 1991 into April 1992, we were the Sports Capital of the World.

The Timberwolves had brought the NBA back in 1989 and set an all-time attendance record at the Metrodome. Target Center opened for the 1990-1991 season, and they sold every ticket—19,006 per night—that season.

Then, in the spring of '91, the North Stars made the miracle run to the Stanley Cup finals. The crowds at Met Center were crazy, and the new owner, Norm Green, was the biggest hero in town.

The U.S. Open came to Hazeltine, and the whole world found out that Minnesota was nuts for golf. We drew the largest crowds ever for an Open. There was a Monday playoff, and the U.S. Golf Association was expecting 5,000 people to show up as had been the case with playoffs at other courses. At Hazeltine, more than 30,000 ticketholders came to watch Payne Stewart and Scott Simpson play as a twosome. Hazeltine sold $6 million worth of merchandise—sweatshirts, golf shirts, umbrellas, etc. One year later, the Open was held at Baltusrol outside of New York City, and that course was bragging

Golf friends, 1997
Minnesota golfer Tom Lehman and myself.

about having sold $1 million worth of merchandise.

The Twins won another World Series in 1991. They sold an average of 2.4 million tickets per season for six years, from 1987 through 1992.

Then came the two biggest events in the country—the Super Bowl and the NCAA Final Four early in 1992. Even the critics had to admit the Metrodome turned out to be a fantastic facility.

It's amazing that so many politicians and so much of the public has forgotten what sports means to Minnesota. Because they built it cheap, without a mezzanine level and without enough seats near home plate, the Metrodome always has been more of a football stadium than a ballpark.

There is no doubt the Metrodome has outlived its time as a two-team stadium. There's no doubt the Twins need a ballpark, and it's ridiculous they have been made to fight so hard to get one.

We don't have community leaders like we used to have. Worse than that, we now have professional politicians in the State

Legislature. Serving in the State Legislature was never intended to be a full-time job. But that's what it has turned into, and the losers become the people of Minnesota. You have a bunch of lightweights in the Legislature who are only interested in appealing to groups of activists so they can get re-elected.

If we were to lose major league sports, what do you think the convention business would be in the Twin Cities? I'll tell you: zero. People get game schedules before they come here for conventions. They want to know when the Twins are in town, when the Timberwolves are in town.

There's my pro sports speech. Maybe you have heard it or read it before. You'll hear and read it again. We lost the North Stars in 1993 because the Metropolitan Sports Facilities Commission would not let Norm Green develop a shopping mall around the Met Center.

Norm Coleman, the one politician in this state with some vision, was able to beat the odds and get the NHL back to Minnesota. As the mayor of St. Paul, he landed an expansion team to start in the year 2000. It will wind up costing more than $200 million to get the NHL back—$80 million for an expansion franchise and $130 million for a new arena in St. Paul.

The Twins and the Vikings are the big, big prizes. If we lose either of those teams, it is anyone's guess as to how much we will have to spend a few years down the road to replace them. If we lose either major league baseball or the National Football League, we will become "Mindianapolis" all over again.

Chapter 15

The Hockey State

Eveleth was a small mining town on Minnesota's Iron Range that became the hockey capital of the United States. A major reason was John Mariucci, a big, tough Italian who was one of the great athletes and greatest characters this state has ever produced.

Mariucci and Butch Nash were the ends for a Big Ten championship football team at Minnesota in 1938. Mariucci never paid any attention to what defense the Gophers were supposed to be playing. He knocked down the guy in front of him and looked for the ball carrier.

There is a myth that the first national championships won by the Gophers in hockey came with Herb Brooks coaching in 1974, 1976, and 1979. Actually, Mariucci was the star defenseman on a Gophers team that went 18-0 in 1940 and won the national AAU title—the only championship available for a college hockey team at that time.

Mariucci played five seasons for the Chicago Blackhawks. There were only a handful of U.S. players in the National Hockey League and most of them were from Eveleth. Mariucci earned a reputation as the toughest man in the NHL. He had a fight with Detroit's goon, Jack Stewart, that went on for a half-hour.

In 1952, Minnesota Athletic Director Ike Armstrong was looking for a hockey coach to replace Doc Romnes. I said to him, "The only guy for the job is Mariucci."

Armstrong could not stand me, so there must have been other people giving him the same advice. Mariucci coached the Gophers for thirteen seasons. Everyone called him "Maroosh." Even the newspaper headlines would read, "Maroosh sees tough series vs. North Dakota."

The Canadian players were completely dominant in college hockey. Mariucci became the first crusader for the U.S. player. He started using almost all Minnesota kids against teams that were filled with older, more talented Canadian players. Doug Woog, who has been the Gophers' hockey coach for the last ten years, has a policy of offering scholarships only to Minnesota kids. That does not put him at much of a disadvantage. It was a huge disadvantage for Mariucci when he was trying to play with a roster of Minnesotans in the 1950s.

I would take a few trips with Mariucci's team back then—not because I was a big hockey guy, but because it was so much fun to spend time around Mariucci.

His big rivals were Fido Purpur at North Dakota and Al Renfrew at Michigan. Purpur and Mariucci had played against one another in the NHL. They did not like each other. Maroosh was a holy terror on those trips to Grand Forks, North Dakota. One night, I was sleeping, and he came into my room and said, "Let's go." It was 1 A.M.

I said, "I'm not going anywhere."

Maroosh dumped a bucket of water on my bed.

So, we hit the streets of Grand Forks. We went to this ballroom with a bar in the front. The bartender was cleaning up. "We're closed," he said.

Maroosh said: "You were closed."

We stayed there for four hours, with Maroosh drinking and telling stories.

Mariucci was a true Iron Ranger. As a kid, he was outdoors playing hockey every day of the winter, so the cold did not bother him at all. He never wore an overcoat. It could be thirty below and Maroosh would not wear a coat.

Mariucci and football coach Murray Warmath got along great. They were both physically tough men. One day, Mariucci was in Warmath's office, and they decided to thumb wrestle. Maroosh broke Warmath's thumb.

When you got a few drinks in Maroosh, look out. He would start wrestling with anybody. Mariucci was a forty-years-earlier version of Kent Hrbek with the Twins. A big teddy bear, he loved to agitate people with humor and loved to wrestle.

Mariucci was so upset about the fact U.S. kids were not getting a chance to play hockey at many colleges that he helped convince the Gophers to stop playing Denver in 1960. Denver was using all over-age Canadians. Minnesota and Denver did not play for a dozen years. More than winning, Mariucci's goal was to give the U.S. kid—especially the Minnesota kid—a much larger opportunity in college hockey. He succeeded in doing that.

Marsh Ryman had been the interim coach for Mariucci in 1955–1956, when Maroosh was coaching the United States to a silver medal in the Olympics in Cortina d'Ampezzo, Italy. I've always regretted not pushing the *Tribune* to cover the Winter Olympics in '56. It would have been the best time ever—being in the Italian homeland with Mariucci for a couple of weeks. And his team beat the Canadians. I can guarantee you that Maroosh kept a couple of Italian bartenders up later than they wanted to be that night.

Ryman became the athletic director after Ike Armstrong left. In 1966, Ryman decided to get rid of Mariucci. He thought Maroosh was drinking too much. That was funny, since Ryman drank more than Mariucci.

If he had to get fired, the timing could not have been better for Mariucci. The National Hockey League was starting a whole new conference of six expansion teams for the 1967–1968 season, and the Minnesota North Stars were one of those teams. One of the first things the new organization did was put Mariucci on the payroll as a scout and the guy to represent the team in the community.

The NHL always had been a controlled operation. Arthur Wirtz and Jim Norris owned Chicago Stadium, the Olympia in Detroit, and Madison Square Garden in New York. They controlled three of the six teams in the NHL—the New York Rangers, Detroit Red Wings, and Chicago Blackhawks. The government told them they had to unload one of the teams for antitrust reasons. I don't know how they got around that, but they kept right on operating three teams.

Finally, the NHL expanded, and it was a surprise to a lot of people that Minnesota wound up with a team. There was a feeling the NHL might go to a couple of the bigger cities in the East—Washington or Cleveland—rather than Minnesota.

The big problem here always had been the absence of a big-league arena. That was the main reason Ben Berger and Morris Chalfen sold the Lakers to Bob Short's group. That's the main reason the Lakers wound up moving to Los Angeles: no arena.

The Gophers would not let the Lakers play in Williams Arena. Ike Armstrong looked at pro sports as competition. When I was with the Lakers, we were stuck in small buildings—the Minneapolis Auditorium, the Minneapolis Armory, and the St. Paul Auditorium. There were even times in the spring when the boat and car shows were booked, that we had to use Hamline's tiny fieldhouse for play-off games.

The Minnesota group promised the NHL a new building. Bob McNulty was the hero when it came to getting hockey here. He was one of the owners, and his company put a new building, Met Center, on the ground for $6 million. It was an amazing construction feat.

The North Stars hired Wren ("The Bird") Blair as general manager and coach. Blair had been here previously, running the Minneapolis Bruins in the Central Hockey League for the Boston Bruins organization. Blair was the second coming of Norm Van Brocklin—a crazy, hard-drinking, hard-nosed son of a bitch. I didn't get along with Van Brocklin, and I didn't get along with The Bird.

Blair was always screaming about how I didn't know anything about hockey. He was right about that, but you hate to hear it every day. He was like Van Brocklin. He would get drunk and want to fight.

Blair also was like Van Brocklin in that he could get his name and the name of his team in the newspapers. The Vikings needed a guy like that out front when they started in 1961, because Gophers football still was the big thing in town. The North Stars needed a guy like that out front when they started in 1967, because the Twins still were riding high and the Vikings were just starting their upswing with Bud Grant.

Lou Nanne had been a star for the Gophers. He got out of the university in 1963 and played semi-pro hockey for the Rochester Mustangs in the United States Hockey League. And, he was selling envelopes for Harvey Mackay.

The North Stars were putting their team together, and I started writing how they should sign Lou Nanne. I wrote it a dozen times. I was driving Blair crazy. He was willing to sign Nanne, but Lou was asking for a $6,000 contract, and Blair thought that was way too much to pay for an envelope salesman. Finally, Blair called me one day and said: "I signed your boy Nanne, so now will you shut up?"

Blair was an old-time hockey coach. He never got close to the players. I had my favorite players with the North Stars. He would trade one of my favorites and I would rip him. Then, he would be even madder at me.

You knew Blair was going to flame out in a few years, just as Van Brocklin had done. You can't make that many enemies and survive.

Minnesotans were amazed by Blair that first winter. They thought going to an NHL game was like going to the theater. The rich people from Lake Minnetonka would show up in their suits and mink coats and sit in the high-priced seats. Then, Blair would start screaming on the bench and turn their ears blue with cuss words. It was R-rated dialogue, before there was such a thing as an R rating.

Blair always could stir the pot. He could not believe how quiet the fans would be at times. One night, he ripped the Met Center crowd by saying Minnesotans were a bunch of "phlegmatic Swedes." We all ran to the dictionary to find out what phlegmatic meant—"not easily moved or excited"—and then we said, "I guess he's right."

Blair was fired in 1974. By then, the hockey honeymoon was over. Jack Gordon was moved up from coach to general manager. He was not exactly a ball of fire. Neither was Ted Harris, the guy who took over as coach.

Glen Sonmor, Mariucci's replacement with the Gophers, had left the university and was running a World Hockey Association team, the Fighting Saints, at the St. Paul Civic Center. Between an unexciting team and the competition in St. Paul, the North Stars were dying. The arena was half full and the original owners—Walter Bush, McNulty, Gordie Ritz, Bob Ridder, and the other partners—were losing a ton of money.

Even after the Fighting Saints went out of business, the crowds at Met Center were terrible, because the North Stars were terrible.

McNulty called me and said: "We have a crazy idea. We're thinking about taking Lou Nanne off the ice and making him the general manager. What do you think?"

I said, "That's the smartest thing you could do. Louie will shake up things, if nothing else."

It was February 1978. The first thing Louie did as general manager was to name himself as interim coach. "I had one goal in mind," Louie said a few months later. "I was going to make sure we finished last, so I could draft Bobby Smith, the No. 1 player in junior hockey."

The North Stars owners were fortunate to have Nanne. After that season, they pulled off an unprecedented deal by selling the Stars to the Gund brothers, the owners of the Cleveland Barons. Then, the two teams were merged into the North Stars. It took a hustler to grease the skids for a deal like that with the other NHL teams. Nanne was a hustler.

After Louie finished maneuvering, Walter Bush's group was out from under; he had owners with deep pockets in Gordon and George Gund; he had Bobby Smith; he had the best players from two teams (Minnesota and Cleveland); and he had a team that was off the bottom of the league and on the way up.

In spring 1981, the North Stars reached the Stanley Cup finals against the New York Islanders. Nanne had hired Sonmor as assistant general manager in 1978 and then named him coach a few games into the 1978–1979 season.

Sonmor might not have been the greatest coach in the world, but he was a wonderful talker. The newspapers were full of Sonmor's one-liners. He was popular with the players and the media. Sonmor's only problem was the same one so many people in hockey seemed to have: booze. Eventually, he was fired after getting drunk on a road trip and punching a customer in a Pittsburgh bar.

That was later, well after Sonmor had taken the North Stars on that journey to the Stanley Cup finals. Bobby Smith had become a star, as Nanne had anticipated. Neal Broten, a Gophers and Olympic hero, and Dino Ciccarelli were two new stars.

The state went crazy. The fans lived and died with the North Stars for almost two months, before the team finally lost in six games to the Islanders.

Last year of the North Stars

Before the North Stars moved on, I covered many a hockey game. Here I am in the locker room with Bobby Smith.

I enjoyed it immensely. Wren Blair might have been right when he said I didn't know anything about hockey. But I was right when I told McNulty in 1978 that the smartest thing the North Stars could do was to hire Louie Nanne to run the team.

Billy Martin was the greatest baseball manager we've had in Minnesota. Bill Musselman was the greatest basketball coach we've had in Minnesota. Herb Brooks was the greatest hockey coach we've had in Minnesota. And they all have had this in common: They are stubborn S.O.B.'s. They would rather get fired than take advice—even if the advice offered makes perfect sense.

University of Minnesota hockey had been a pleasant, weekend diversion in the winter when Mariucci and Sonmor were the coaches. The rivalries with North Dakota, Michigan, and Michigan Tech—and later Minnesota-Duluth and Wisconsin—were fun, but Gophers hockey never was life and death. Not until Herbie became the coach.

Brooks had been hanging around as a volunteer coach. Sonmor left for the WHA team in St. Paul after the 1972 season. Herbie begged Athletic Director Paul Giel for the job. Since he was willing to work cheap, Giel gave it to him.

Brooks had a lot of theories about how the game should be played. He could ramble on for hours about hockey "systems." Most of all, he could motivate players. He did that by putting the fear of the Lord in them. He would get the players in the locker room before a game or between periods, grit his teeth, get the fire in his eyes, and players would be gritting their teeth and getting a fire in their eyes at the same time.

The Gophers won national championships in 1974, 1976, and 1979. They also made it to the final game in 1975. One perfect example of a Herb Brooks team that I'll never forget:

They were playing a WCHA playoff at Notre Dame in 1977. This was Herbie's only losing team in seven seasons at Minnesota, and Notre Dame was making a big hockey push back then. It was a two-game, total-goal series. The Gophers lost 5-1 on the first night.

They were on the road and went into the second game four goals down. The season was over, right? Nope. Brooks put the fire in those kids, and they went out and beat Notre Dame by seven goals. That was a preview of what was to come in the 1980 Winter Olympics in Lake Placid, New York.

Brooks had the Olympic team together for months, and he played with the players' minds every night. They would get in Herbie's doghouse, and they had to work so hard to get out, they would not screw up again. Just like with Bob Knight and Indiana basketball.

A few days before the Olympics started, the United States played the Soviet Union in Madison Square Garden. The Russians won 10-1. Everyone connected with U.S. hockey was depressed. Everyone connected with Minnesota hockey was depressed, since so many of the players on that team were Minnesotans. Everyone was depressed except Brooks. Getting bombed in the Garden was great. Now, the Russians were overconfident, and Herbie had his players' complete attention. They beat the Russians in the game that mattered—the Olympic semifinals—at Lake Placid, then beat Finland to win the gold medal.

Miracle on Ice. It did more than make Herbie Brooks a national hero. It made the announcer, Al Michaels, a hero. He has been living off that "Do you believe in miracles?" for almost twenty years.

Brooks had a million job offers after Lake Placid and could not decide on one. A sportswriter in St. Paul wrote: "It's obvious there is only one job offer that will satisfy Herb Brooks—Emperor of the World." First, Brooks appeared on TV shows for a few months, then went to Davos, Switzerland, and coached for a winter. The New York Rangers wanted to hire him in the worst way.

Art Kaminsky was his agent. Usually, the reporters are calling the agents, asking for information. But Kaminsky was calling me. He would say, "What the hell am I going to do? The Rangers want an answer, and I can't get the S.O.B. to make a decision."

I finally said, "Art, there's only one thing to do. Call his wife, Patti. When push comes to shove, she runs the show. She'll give you an answer."

The next day, Herbie finally took the job. He was a great coach with the Rangers, but of course, he ended up feuding with everybody. In 1987, he finally landed his dream job—coach of the North Stars. His best friends, Nanne and Sonmor, were there. The North Stars had gone downhill again, but these three guys made a commitment to a new beginning.

University of Minnesota friends
Here I am with, from left, Gophers football coach Joe Salem, myself, and hockey coach Herb Brooks, in about 1982.

Then, Louie took the job as club president, and Herbie felt as though he had been double-crossed: Jack Ferreira was brought in as general manager. I still believe Brooks could have stayed as coach but he was mad at the Gunds—for the team they had given him and for not giving him a shot to be general manager as well as coach.

I said, "Don't bad-mouth the Gunds to the media, and it will be OK." Of course, he bad-mouthed the Gunds. What should have been a great job turned into one unhappy season for Herbie.

Herbie has feuds, but also a great sense of loyalty. He feuded with Craig Patrick when he left the Rangers, and now they are buddies. He was mad at Nanne after the North Stars fiasco, but now they are buddies again.

The Timberwolves brought the NBA back to Minnesota in 1989, and they became the hot attraction. A new building—Target Center—opened in downtown Minneapolis in fall 1990. The Gund brothers had a poor team, the North Stars, and a building that was outdated.

The Metropolitan Sports Facilities Commission owned the Met Center. The North Stars' original owners had given the building to the public.

If you're looking for a reason that Minnesota lost its NHL franchise, the people to blame are the members of the sports facilities commission. They had two chances to save hockey and blew it both times.

First, Gordon and George Gund went to the commission and asked for $10 million to $15 million in improvements at Met Center. The corridors would have been remodeled, and more suites would have been added. It would have allowed the Gunds to stay somewhat competitive against Target Center in the ice show and concert market.

Gordon Gund talked to a meeting of the commission, and he was basically laughed at. This man and his brother had pumped millions into the North Stars and the building out there, and they were treated like dirt.

Gordon Gund wanted to stay in Minnesota. His brother George wanted to move the team to the San Francisco Bay area, where he lived. They had an agreement: If the commission would give them some improvements at Met Center, they would commit to staying in Bloomington. If not, they would move the team to California.

The North Stars were headed to San Jose until Nanne saved the NHL for Minnesota—temporarily. He convinced the league to split the team—half the players staying here as the North Stars, half going to San Jose as an expansion team. Then, when local groups would not come up with the money, Louie found Howard Baldwin and a couple of partners to buy the North Stars.

One of the partners was Norm Green, a minority owner of the Calgary Flames. Baldwin did not have the money to make the deal work, so Green became the sole owner in the summer of 1990. The Montreal Canadiens came to Met Center in December of that year, and there were less than 5,000 people in the building. Green was ready to kill himself.

Green was an off-the-wall character, always changing his mind on how to go about selling the team to the public. He was extremely impulsive. He went to a Timberwolves game, saw the dance line, and tried to have a dance line at hockey games. Nothing worked.

Then, the North Stars started to win some games late in the season. The coach, Bob Gainey, was as low key as you could get, but he knew how to prepare a team for the playoffs. The North Stars upset Chicago, St. Louis, and then Edmonton. Unbelievably, they were in the Stanley Cup finals vs. Pittsburgh, at the end of Norm Green's first season.

Norm had a private box in a corner of Met Center. It was open and the fans could see him up there, in his $2,500 suits and silver hair, with his young, beautiful wife, Kelly, and their important friends. Frank and Kathie Lee Gifford came to sit next to them for a hockey game. During the playoffs, the people in the sellout crowds would shout "Norm, Norm, Norm," and he would wave from the box, like Julius Caesar.

The North Stars lost in six games to the Penguins. The winning coach was Bob Johnson, a Minneapolis guy. He had been the coach at Minneapolis Roosevelt High, then started the hockey program at the University of Wisconsin. He became known as Badger Bob and was Herbie Brooks's bitter rival.

Badger Bob was an optimistic, outgoing person who had a million friends. The final game of the series was played at the Met Center in Bloomington, so he won the Stanley Cup a mile from a pond where he had often taken his Roosevelt teams to practice in the winter.

If ever there seemed to be two guys on top of the world, it was Norm Green and Badger Bob Johnson—proving again that you never know what will happen next.

Johnson was diagnosed with a brain tumor a couple of months later and was dead within a year. With Green, it was his reputation in Minnesota—not his health—that was ruined. In two years, the chants at Met Center went from "Norm, Norm, Norm" to "Norm Sucks."

Again, you can blame the Metropolitan Sports Facilities Commission. The Mall of America was opening across the way from Met Center. Green had been a shopping-center developer in Calgary. He unveiled a plan to remodel Met Center and put a small shopping center around it. He was going to pay for it and wanted a ninety-nine-year lease on the land. The commission told Green he would have to buy the developmental rights. He was not going to pump millions into the building and also pay for the land. The commission blew its second chance to lock up the hockey team.

Timberwolves owners Marv Wolfenson and Harvey Ratner had gone way over budget on Target Center. The basketball crowds were great, but the building needed another tenant. They made a deal with Green to give him all of the suite rental revenue if he moved the North Stars to Target Center. Then, Wolfenson and Ratner went to the city of Minneapolis and said, "Buy this $104 million building for the $75 million we owe on it, and you have a modern arena, a basketball team, and a hockey team in downtown Minneapolis."

The politicians blew that one, of course. A sexual harassment allegation against Green surfaced, and that was it. His wife, Kelly, went to their home in Palm Springs and said, "I'm never coming back to this state."

In February 1993, Green made a deal to move the team to Dallas. He sold the franchise a couple of years later for a big profit. The hockey fans still look at Green as the villain in losing the NHL.

They got the wrong guy. The geniuses on the stadium commission first ran the Gund brothers out of town, then they created the situation that allowed Green to leave town. With friends like the members of the stadium commission, the pro sports teams in Minnesota need no enemies.

The first NHL star for Minnesota was Bill Goldsworthy. He was to the North Stars what Harmon Killebrew was to the Twins. After scoring a goal, he would skate on his left skate, kick his right leg, and pump his right fist. The Goldy Shuffle became so famous that youth hockey players in Minnesota still can be seen doing it, twenty years after Goldsworthy played his last game for the North Stars.

Goldsworthy also became more than the first NHL hero for Minnesota. He became the first prominent sports figure in this state to die from AIDS.

Goldy had a serious drinking problem. Glen Sonmor had sobered up, and they became the best of friends. Sonmor was Goldsworthy's mentor in the fight against alcoholism. Goldsworthy had long stretches of sobriety. In 1991, the North Stars had a young player named Neil Wilkinson with a drinking problem. Goldsworthy took Wilkinson under his wing and helped him gain sobriety.

But Goldy could never stay sober himself. He would get drunk and spend the night with women he did not know. He wound up with

AIDS. Gary Olson of the *St. Paul Pioneer Press* broke the story. There was an outpouring of affection for Goldy, and for a few months, he was a public person in the fight against AIDS.

Then, Goldsworthy started drinking again—heavily. He did not give the new AIDS drugs a chance to prolong his life. Goldsworthy died in 1996.

It was much different for John Mariucci when he died. Maroosh had cancer. All of his friends were able to see him and have long talks with him before he died. I went to Mariucci's home with Herb Brooks, his brother Dave Brooks, and WCCO radio personality Steve Cannon, who was an Eveleth guy like Maroosh. We were there for four, five hours, telling stories about Maroosh, listening to his stories. He laughed at everything. I should have taped that session. A week later, the Godfather of Minnesota hockey died.

Chapter 16

Hoops: Almost a Career

I got out of the Minneapolis Lakers operation in 1957, when the team was sold to Bob Short's group. Max Winter and I still had many friends in the NBA, and all those championships with the Lakers showed that we knew how to run a basketball team.

We put together a group that paid $150,000 to the NBA for an expansion franchise that was supposed to start play in Chicago for the 1960–1961 season. This was truly the first expansion team in major league professional sports. The NBA awarded us the team in 1959, a year before the NFL and major league baseball expanded, and way before the NHL expanded.

The sum of money we were paying was enormous. We were going to get a bunch of No. 1 draft choices. The only team that was protected was the Cincinnati Royals: They were going to get Oscar Robertson as a territorial choice. We were going to get Jerry West, Darryl Imhoff, and several other terrific college players.

Our major investors were Munya Goldman from the Twin Cities and Dave Traeger from Chicago. They were partners in the insurance business. We also had the guy who owned Sara Lee, we had the old Chicago Bears quarterback Sid Luckman, and several other people.

The holdup was that we could not get into Chicago Stadium. Arthur Morse was working for Arthur Wirtz, the owner of the Chicago Blackhawks and the stadium. Morse was promoting college basketball doubleheaders. Morse felt if we came in with pro basketball, it would kill his doubleheaders, so he convinced Wirtz to keep us out.

NBA owners and directors, 1960s

The NBA board of directors and team owners gathered in the early 1960s in New York at a birthday party for NBA Commissioner Maurice Podoloff. Seated from left: Madison Square Gardens owner Ned Irish, Detroit Pistons founder Fred Zollner, Podoloff, Walter Brown of the Boston Celtics and Bruins, and Ed Gottlieb of the Philadelphia Warriors. Standing second from left is Munya Goldman, who was associated with our Chicago Zephyrs and Baltimore Bullets. Next to him on the left is Morris Chalfen of the Minneapolis Lakers and Chicago Zephyrs. I am at Chalfen's right.

We started up for the 1961–1962 season playing in the Chicago Amphitheater, which was a real dump. The NBA was not as impressed with $150,000 as it had been—not after baseball and the NFL had expanded—and it gave us only one first-round draft choice: Walter Bellamy, the seven-footer from Indiana.

The first coach I hired was Jim Pollard. As it turned out, Pollard had been a better player than he was a coach, and we replaced him with Bobby Leonard.

We were the Chicago Packers the first season, then came up with a livelier nickname—the Zephyrs—for the next year. The nickname change did not help, because we still were stuck in the Amphitheater. The owners decided to move the franchise to Baltimore and become the Bullets for the 1963–1964 season.

We had a general manager by the name of Paul Hoffman. He had the title, but I made the personnel decisions. There was a redeye flight from Minneapolis–St. Paul that would land in Baltimore at four in the morning. I was on that flight all the time, spending the day in the Bullets office, going to a game, then flying home.

Considering we had started as an expansion team two years earlier, I was able to put together a hellacious lineup in Baltimore: Bellamy at center, Gus Johnson and Bailey Howell at the forwards, and Rod Thorn and Kevin Loughery in the backcourt. I made a trade with Detroit—sending Terry Dischinger to the Pistons for Howell, Loughery, and Les Hunter. Ned Irish, who ran the Knicks, got up at a league meeting and said: "This trade is highway robbery. It's going to kill the Detroit franchise. The league should cancel the trade."

We were drawing OK in Baltimore, but the owners were Chicago guys. They wanted to either move the team back to Chicago or to sell it to someone in Baltimore.

I was called to a meeting in Chicago, and the owners told me: "We want you to quit your job at the Minneapolis newspaper, move to Chicago, and run the club. We have a good club, and we finally have a deal with Wirtz to play in Chicago Stadium. Once we get our money out, we'll give you 20-percent ownership in the team."

I couldn't have asked for more than that. Chicago always had been a tough nut for pro basketball to crack, but everyone figured that, with a good club, it would be a gold mine.

I thought a long time about taking the offer. Finally, I decided my roots in Minnesota were too strong. I turned it down. The team was sold to Abe Pollin and eventually became the Washington Bullets.

There would be no Chicago Bulls today if I had given up the newspaper business and decided to become an "official" general manager in basketball. We would have moved back to Chicago.

There is another twist to this: When we were starting as an expansion team in Chicago, Bill Veeck called me. He was running the White Sox. Veeck said he had a young guy named Jerry Krause who was working part time for him and needed to make a few bucks in the winter. I put Krause to work as a basketball scout.

Jerry Krause, of course, wound up as the general manager of

the Bulls, producing a dynasty in the nineties. Krause takes nothing but heat from the media in Chicago, but everything he does—drafting Scottie Pippen, signing Toni Kukoc, trading for Dennis Rodman—proves that he is smarter than the sportswriters and the other geniuses.

John Wooden should have been the University of Minnesota's basketball coach—not UCLA's—starting with the 1948–1949 season. Wooden had tentatively accepted the job, with the provision he could bring an assistant coach. A snowstorm messed up communications, and by the time Minnesota Athletic Director Frank McCormick was able to get back to Wooden, he had taken the UCLA job.

Minnesota hired Ozzie Cowles away from Michigan. The rumor was that Michigan Athletic Director Fritz Crisler was about to fire Cowles anyway. When McCormick called to ask for permission to talk to Cowles, Crisler almost jumped through the phone, he was so happy.

Cowles did a decent job at Minnesota. He had the ability to teach spot-up shooting. Bud Grant could not shoot a lick when he played for Dave MacMillan. Cowles came in and made a black mark on the floor. He had Grant shoot from that spot all the time in practice. Next thing you knew, Grant was making baskets.

Cowles had some good clubs. He was 18-3 his first season with Jim McIntyre, Grant, Whitey Skoog, and Harold Olson. He was 17-5 with Ed Kalafat, Chuck Mencel, and Dick Garmaker in 1953–1954. The next season, with Mencel, Garmaker, and Boots Simonovich, a seven-footer from the Iron Range, the Gophers were beaten by one and two points in two games against Iowa and finished second in the Big Ten to the Hawkeyes.

The problem for Cowles—as it was for every Minnesota coach until Clem Haskins—is that there were not five or six Big Ten teams going to the NCAA tournament. Until the mid-seventies, only the Big Ten champion qualified for the tournament.

Cowles had six teams that finished third or better in the Big Ten in eleven seasons, but the Gophers never won the league, so they never made the NCAA tournament. In his first ten seasons, Haskins never had a team finish as high as third in the Big Ten, yet his Gophers were in the tournament four times.

Obviously, with a sixty-four–team NCAA tournament, the standards for what qualifies has changed a lot in thirty-six years—from 1949, when Cowles had an 18-3 team that stayed home, to 1995, when Haskins had a 19-11 team that went to the tournament.

Cowles was fired after the 1959 season. John Kundla left the Lakers to replace him. Kundla did nothing in his first few years at Minnesota. More and more, the black athletes were starting to take over basketball. Minnesota still was trying to compete with white kids from the Upper Midwest. Recruiting black football players from the South and from Pennsylvania had allowed the Gophers to go to two Rose Bowls, but basketball had not gotten the message.

Finally, Glen Reed, Kundla's assistant, went out and got some big-time talent. He recruited Lou Hudson from North Carolina, Archie Clark from Detroit, and Don Yates from Pennsylvania—three outstanding black kids.

The Gophers were 10-4 and third in the Big Ten with Hudson, Clark, and Yates as sophomores in 1963–1964. The Gophers beat Michigan 89-75 on a night when Williams Arena—the big, old barn—had 20,000 people in it.

The Gophers had a chance to be national contenders in 1964–1965, with Hudson, Clark, and Yates, plus two outstanding Minnesota kids—Terry Kunze from Duluth and Mel Northway from Minneapolis. Then, Kunze was caught having someone take a final examination for him and was thrown out of school.

Without Kunze, the Gophers went 11-3 in the Big Ten. But they lost twice to Michigan and finished second in the Big Ten. No tournament. Then, in 1965–1966, Yates flunked out, and Hudson had to play left-handed for most of the season. Sweet Lou had a cast on a broken right hand, his shooting hand.

Once Hudson and Clark were gone, Kundla was short of talent again, and that meant disaster. The Gophers sank to the bottom of the league, and Kundla was axed after the 1967–1968 season. They brought in Bill Fitch.

Harvey Mackay started getting involved in the recruiting. Mackay landed Jim Brewer—a top national recruit—from Chicago. Fitch would have won if he had stayed at Minnesota. But he bailed out after the 1969–1970 season and went to the NBA to coach the expansion team in Cleveland.

More than quarter-century later, Fitch was still coaching in the NBA. And, more than thirty years later, Gophers basketball still is a premier wintertime attraction in Minnesota thanks to one person. Not Bill Fitch. The other Bill—Musselman.

One of the hottest young coaching prospects in the country in 1970 was Bob Knight. That's because he was winning at Army, which was considered impossible. Knight agreed to take the Wisconsin job, but asked the people there to keep it quiet until he could tell his superiors at Army. The story leaked in the Madison media, and Knight called and told Wisconsin to forget it.

Knight came from Ohio State, and he wanted a Big Ten job in the worst way. After Fitch quit and Knight got mad at Wisconsin, he came to Minneapolis to interview for the Gophers job. The search committee consisted of Fitch, Athletic Director Marsh Ryman, and faculty representative Stan Wenberg.

Knight was interviewed at the old Sheraton-Ritz in downtown Minneapolis. When a coach was brought in to interview for a big-time job, most hosts took him out for dinner. That was common sense. Only the University of Minnesota could handle something so simple with so little class. When Knight's interview was over, Wenberg and Knight walked out of the hotel together. Wenberg pointed down the street and said: "You'll be able to find a place to have dinner down there a couple of blocks."

Knight could not believe the way Minnesota had handled the whole deal. He went back to Army, and the Gophers wound up hiring George Hanson, Fitch's assistant. Hanson was the most overmatched coach in the history of the Big Ten. Williams Arena was empty, they had a junior college player named Ollie Shannon who played completely out of control, and Hanson was fired after one season.

I called Knight and said: "Are you interested? After a year of Hanson, I'm sure the Gophers will realize you would be doing them a favor to take the job, not the other way around."

Knight said: "I have something to tell you in confidence. I'm going to be named the coach at Indiana tomorrow."

Ryman wound up hiring Cal Luther, the coach at Murray State in Kentucky. Luther took the job, spent a day looking at the ancient facilities at Williams Arena, and went back home to Kentucky.

The Gophers had decided to go with Luther because he had more experience than Bill Musselman, a thirty-three-year-old coach at Ashland College in Ohio. When Luther backed out, Minnesota hired Musselman.

There was not much interest in Gophers basketball at the time. They were averaging 6,000 people a game and the top-priced ticket was $3.50.

Musselman had learned the art of promotion from Ray Mears, his college basketball coach at Wittenberg University. Mears had a pregame show in which the players did ballhandling routines. Musselman took that with him to Ashland and then he brought it to Minnesota.

I didn't think the pregame show would work at a Big Ten school. I thought it was a high school stunt. After Paul Giel became the athletic director, I didn't think he would go for it. I was wrong. The public loved the pregame show. It was a big reason Musselman was able to fill up Williams Arena almost immediately.

Musselman was the Lou Holtz of basketball. He came to town and started selling. He took his players around the state for intra-squad games.

For talent, he went to the junior colleges and brought in play-ers—Ron Behagen, Clyde Turner, and Bobby Nix. He put them with Jim Brewer and had an outstanding team immediately.

The rest of the Big Ten coaches were fuming when Musselman recruited Behagen from Southern Idaho Junior College. Behagen came from New York City, where he had a fantastic reputation as a player and a terrible reputation as a citizen. The Big Ten coaches had a gentlemen's agreement not to recruit Behagen. Musselman was not going to pay attention to something like that.

The interest Musselman created in a period of five weeks was amazing. The Gophers played their first game on December 1, 1971, before the usual small crowd. By January 4, 1972, when they opened the Big Ten schedule against Indiana, there were 20,000 people in Williams Arena.

Minnesota beat Indiana 52-51 that night. Brewer blocked a shot at the buzzer. Knight was certain his player had been fouled, and he chased the referees off the floor. It might have been the loudest night ever in Williams Arena. That was the night that made Gophers basketball into a big event—and it has stayed that way for twenty-five years.

The fire marshal imposed new rules after the Indiana game and would only let the Gophers put 17,000 people in the building. The fans would all be in their seats a half-hour before tip-off, so they would not miss a second of the pregame show.

Ohio State had been the dominant team in the Big Ten, with Fred Taylor as coach. They came to Williams Arena on January 25. Again, the Barn was rocking, because the Gophers had a chance to move into a first-place tie with a victory.

How big had Gophers basketball become in less than two months with Musselman? The NHL All-Star Game was played at Met Center on the same night. And most of the media attention in the Twin Cities was focused on the Gophers–Ohio State game.

It was a fierce, low-scoring game—as most of them were with Musselman coaching. Luke Witte was the Ohio State center and the star, along with guard Allen Hornyak. When the first-half buzzer sounded, Witte swung an elbow in the face of Nix, the Minnesota point guard. A referee was standing right there and did not call a thing.

At halftime, the Gophers were all talking about getting revenge on Witte. Then, late in the second half, Ohio State started to pull away. Behagen fouled out. Witte was knocked to the floor by Turner on a lay-up. The Gophers' Corky Taylor held out a hand to pull up Witte from the floor. As Taylor raised up Witte, he kneed him in the groin. The players on the floor started to tangle, then Behagen came off the bench and stomped on Witte's head. It turned into a riot, with fans jumping onto the elevated floor to chase Buckeyes.

Dave Winfield was on that Minnesota team; Musselman had recruited him off an intramural team. Winfield put two Ohio State players in the hospital. He did not sneak up on them, though. Winfield fought with them face to face.

It became known as The Brawl and was a national scandal. *Sports Illustrated* wrote a cover story that did everything but proclaim Musselman to be the second coming of Mussolini.

The Big Ten suspended Taylor and Behagen for the rest of the season. Ohio State also wanted to have Winfield suspended. Someone from the conference called and asked me about Winfield. I lied. I said,

Minnesota boys

Dave Winfield and I, fellow Minnesota boys. Winfield has been on several Minnesota teams, playing basketball with the Gophers and baseball with the Twins.

"I didn't see Winfield hit anyone." They did not have videotape and replay to check. So, Winfield escaped. After the Gophers lost Taylor and Behagen, they basically had five players—Brewer, Turner, Nix, Winfield, and Keith Young. They became known as The Iron Five.

The Gophers were two games behind Ohio State after they lost that game in Williams Arena. The Buckeyes faded, and the Gophers wound up winning the Big Ten title. It was the first conference title since 1937—in Musselman's first season.

But the fight was going to cost him, eventually. Fred Taylor was an influential person in college basketball. He was angry when Musselman recruited Behagen. After the fight, he hated Musselman, and Ohio State hated Musselman. With Ohio State's clout, it was only a matter of time before the NCAA would investigate the Minnesota program.

There were accusations of big cash payments, but it was never proved. The NCAA settled for doing what it does best when it wants to get someone: It piled up dozens of Mickey Mouse allegations.

The Gophers had choked away another Big Ten title in the 1972–1973 season. They were mediocre in 1973–1974. Then, in the 1974–1975 season, Musselman put together what would have been one of the most powerful college teams the Big Ten had seen. He had a front line of Mychal Thompson, Mark Olberding, and Mark Landsberger—later all NBA players—with Ray Williams (another NBA player), Flip Saunders, and Osborne Lockhart as guards. The next year, Kevin McHale would be coming in from Hibbing. That would have been Musselman's nucleus in 1975–1976: Olberding, Thompson, Landsberger, McHale, Williams, Saunders, and Lockhart. Forget the UCLA dynasty. Musselman would have won a national championship with that team.

Minneapolis *Star* sportswriter Chan Keith had as much to do with the NCAA investigation as Ohio State. He did an investigative series on Musselman for the *Star* but nothing came of it. Keith was upset no one was paying attention to his investigation locally, so he started calling the NCAA office to get it interested.

Musselman quit in the spring of 1975, before the NCAA came in with its report. He became the coach of the San Diego Conquistadors of the American Basketball Association. He signed Olberding to play in San Diego. Landsberger saw the investigation coming and transferred to Arizona State.

Michigan assistant coach Jim Dutcher was hired to replace Musselman. Dutcher had a team that went 24-3 in 1976–1977—without Olberding and Landsberger. It's hard to imagine how good that team could have been.

The Gophers tried to disassociate themselves from Musselman after he left. The truth is Minnesota football attendance had gone in the tank. If Musselman had not come in and started to fill up Williams Arena, the men's athletic department would have been swimming in red ink. From the time he came until the time he left, Gophers basketball attendance improved by 10,000 people per game and ticket prices tripled.

Dutcher took over the Gophers for the 1975–1976 season, and he kept filling Williams Arena. The Gophers won a Big Ten championship in 1982 with Trent Tucker, Darryl Mitchell, and Randy Breuer. Dutcher had a club that was probably going to the NCAA tournament in 1986, when three players—Mitch Lee, Kevin Smith, and George Williams—were taken off a plane that was bringing the Gophers back from Madison. They were jailed and charged with rape.

University President Kenneth Keller threw the athletes out of school and decided to forfeit the next game at Northwestern. Basically, Keller dismantled the basketball program, without waiting to find out if the three players were guilty or not. Dutcher quit in protest of the decision to forfeit.

Lee was a bad actor, but the other two kids were decent guys. All three players wound up being found not guilty. I'm still amazed that none of them chose to sue the university.

Jimmy Williams, Dutcher's assistant, coached for the rest of the 1986 Big Ten schedule, then the Gophers had another search. Giel had made the decision to hire Tennessee coach Don DeVoe. University Vice-President Frank Wilderson overruled him. Wilderson, a black man, decided the Gophers needed a black man as coach.

Wilderson was also the guy who had allowed Luther Darville to have access to the football team when Joe Salem was the coach. Darville was working in the minority affairs department at the university. He was giving cash to some of the black players, while Wilderson looked the other way.

The fact Darville was hanging around then led to problems for Lou Holtz. After Holtz left for Notre Dame, the *Star Tribune*, the university, and the NCAA all did investigations into Darville's involvement with the men's athletic program. After all that effort, they did not come up with much against Holtz. There was also an investigation after Dutcher left. The stuff the *Star Tribune*, the university, and the NCAA found in their investigations of Dutcher's program were the most pissant collection of violations of all time.

Dutcher was an underrated basketball coach at Minnesota—just as Cal Stoll was an underrated football coach. Dutcher and Stoll were two of the best recruiters we had at Minnesota. They did well enough to keep their jobs for much longer than they were allowed to by that screwed-up university.

After Wilderson rejected DeVoe as Dutcher's replacement, he called John Chaney at Temple. Wilderson could not even get an interview with Chaney. Then, Wilderson called Clem Haskins at Western Kentucky, which was Clem's alma mater.

Haskins told me that, if he could have gotten a long-term contract at Western Kentucky, he would have stayed. The university was desperate. The Gophers offered Clem a five-year deal for big money, so he took the job.

After Keller had run off half the team, it took Haskins a couple of years to reinforce the roster. Clem became a big hero when the Gophers made it to the final sixteen in 1989, his third season, and then to the final eight in 1990. Three players Dutcher had already recruited as incoming freshmen for the 1986–1987 season—Willie Burton, Melvin Newbern, and Jim Shikenjanski—were a big reason Clem was able to make those tournament runs.

As I said, Dutcher might have been the best basketball recruiter we had at Minnesota.

Musselman had a wild ride after leaving the university. He went to San Diego to coach an expansion team in the American Basketball Association. The team lasted for seven games, and the owners folded it. Musselman then coached the Virginia Squires, also in the ABA. Eventually, he hooked up with a crazy fellow named Ted Stepien, the owner of the Cleveland Cavaliers.

Musselman went from coach to general manager, back to coach. Stepien also owned a slow-pitch softball league. One time, Stepien brought in the coach of a softball team to be the G.M. and Musselman's boss.

The Cavaliers were out of control, making trades. They traded so many No. 1s that the NBA passed a rule that a team could not trade its top draft choice in consecutive years. The Cleveland disaster seemed to guarantee that Musselman would never get another chance to coach in the NBA.

Musselman went to the Continental Basketball Association and dominated that minor league. He also had coached the Reno Bighorns in a short-lived minor league—the Western Basketball Association.

I had introduced Musselman and Billy Martin, and they had

become buddies. Musselman had Martin in Reno to make a promotional appearance at a game. They went out that night, and Billy wound up in an altercation in a bar. Musselman called up George Steinbrenner, Billy's boss with the Yankees, to convince him that Billy was not at fault.

The NBA was getting ready to expand again in the mid-eighties, and Marv Wolfenson convinced his business partner, Harvey Ratner, that they should get a team for Minneapolis. Wolfenson had been a big pro basketball guy when the Lakers were here.

A lot of people felt pro basketball would not make it in the Twin Cities—that the North Stars and hockey were too dominant in the winter. I never felt that way. Despite the mythology, there is much more interest in basketball in Minnesota than there is in hockey. If you draw a line from Moorhead on the North Dakota border to Mankato in the southern part of the state and continue to the Iowa border, there isn't much hockey south of the line. That's 40 percent of the state. I've always said this: Hockey is a cult sport and basketball is a general interest sport, along with football and baseball.

Part of the reason there was pessimism about pro basketball for the Twin Cities was that two American Basketball Association teams had folded at Met Center. The Muskies started the same season as the NHL and the North Stars—1967–1968. They folded after one season and were replaced by the Pipers, the team that had won the first ABA title a few months earlier in Pittsburgh.

The Twin Cities had big-league baseball, the NFL, and the NHL. They weren't too interested in what was perceived to be a second-rate league. Jim Klobuchar wrote a satirical column in the Minneapolis *Star* about going to an ABA game at Met Center. Klobuchar called to order tickets and then asked, "What time does the game start?" The answer was, "What time can you get here?"

It was a whole different story when Marv Wolfenson and Harvey Ratner went after pro basketball twenty years later. This was the NBA. With Michael Jordan, Magic Johnson, and Larry Bird, the league was bigger than it had ever been.

Still, I thought Wolfenson and Ratner were crazy when they agreed to pay the expansion fee of $32.5 million. When the NBA saw that kind of money hit the table, it gave franchises to all four bidding cities—Charlotte and Miami for 1988 and Minneapolis and

Orlando for 1989.

Once Wolfenson and Ratner had a team, I started working on them to hire Musselman. The other reporters in town kept quoting a Timberwolves source as saying Musselman had no chance. The source was Bob Stein, the team president and Wolfenson's son-in-law. Stein did not want Musselman, but Wolfenson knew Musselman was a good coach. He overruled Stein and told him to hire Musselman. Stein also hired Bill McKinney as the director of player personnel.

It did not take long for McKinney and Musselman to be fighting for power.

I'm also of the opinion that you can't work for your father-in-law. Stein was married to Marv's daughter, Ellen, and they started having trouble in their marriage, and that only made things more chaotic with the Timberwolves operation.

Musselman won twenty-one games with a first-year expansion team and twenty-nine games the second season. He was coaching his rear end off, as always, and filling the arena. The Timberwolves set an all-time NBA attendance record in the first season in the Metrodome, and they sold out every game in the Target Center in the second season.

Musselman won the power struggle with McKinney, but he still had Stein against him. The Timberwolves had a rookie named Gerald Glass in the second season. Musselman thought Glass was fat and lazy and would never be a player. Wolfenson kept telling Musselman to play Glass, to see if he could be a scorer. Musselman would say OK, then sit Glass for the whole ballgame.

That was Musselman. If you told him he had to do things one way, he was going to do it the opposite way. Wolfenson let Stein fire Musselman after the second season. It took another half-dozen seasons—until 1997—for the Timberwolves to win as many games as the twenty-nine won by Musselman with a second-year team and to make the playoffs.

Musselman reminds me of Billy Martin in baseball and Herb Brooks in hockey. None of them could get along with the boss. They were stubborn as hell and drove everyone they worked for crazy. But if you let them alone, you could be sure of this: They were going to win.

There were four years when University Athletic Director Paul Giel had both Musselman and Brooks working for him. That alone should have earned Mr. Giel a reservation in Heaven.

The best line of all on the Timberwolves operation came from Harvey Ratner. He said, "Marv got me into basketball and made me a millionaire."

The background note to that was, before they started the Timberwolves and built Target Center, Harvey had been a multi-millionaire.

The biggest mistake was that Marv and Harv should have stayed in the Metrodome for another season, continued to draw those huge crowds, and allowed the contractors to build Target Center at a reasonable pace.

Instead, they fast-tracked Target Center, kept making improvements on the fly, and a building that was supposed to cost $80 million came in at $104 million. Marv and Harv also lost their financing—and a bundle of money—when Hal Greenwood's savings and loan, Midwest Federal, collapsed.

Attendance was excellent, but Wolfenson and Ratner were in trouble financially. The city of Minneapolis had a chance to take over Target Center and have both the Timberwolves and the North Stars as tenants. The politicians screwed it up, of course, and finally Wolfenson and Ratner made a deal to sell the team to a New Orleans group.

They did not want to see the team move, but Marv and Harv had to do something to wake up the politicians. The team would have been gone, just like the hockey club, if was not for NBA Commissioner David Stern.

I had plenty of conversations with Stern—a commissioner who has done as much for the NBA as Pete Rozelle did for the NFL—during that whole episode in 1994. There was no way Stern was going to let the Timberwolves leave here. He saved us until an excellent owner, Mankato businessman Glen Taylor, could be found.

The Wolves were an embarrassment for a long time, but Taylor finally found the right guys to run the basketball operation—Kevin McHale and Flip Saunders. I was as close to those two guys when they were at Minnesota as I have ever been to any Gophers athletes. I feel like they are my sons. Count on it: Kevin and Flip will win an NBA championship with the Timberwolves.

But will they win six titles in seven seasons, like we did with the Lakers from 1948 through 1954? I wouldn't bet on that.

Chapter 17

The Final Four

The Minneapolis Lakers were the dominant team in pro basketball from 1947 through 1954, winning one National Basketball League championship and five NBA titles in seven seasons. At the same time, Adolph Rupp and the Kentucky Wildcats were the biggest names in college basketball.

To get the Lakers ready for the season, we would take them to Lexington, Kentucky, for a few days to practice against the Wildcats. Rupp would run the practices. There were no NCAA rules governing these type of practice sessions at that time.

One day, Rupp did not think George Mikan was working hard enough, and he threw him out of practice. Can you imagine a college coach throwing Michael Jordan out of practice? That was the equivalent of Rupp tossing out Mikan at that time.

Rupp was the funniest guy who ever lived. You could sit around for hours, and he would never run out of stories to tell.

When North Carolina's Dean Smith passed Rupp's record for coaching victories in 1997, there were a lot of stories looking back at Rupp and branding him as a racist.

Rupp was a product of when he lived and where he grew up more than anything. There has been a lot said about the 1966 NCAA title game being a historic moment in college basketball, when Texas Western's all-black lineup beat Kentucky's all-white team—Rupp's Runts. Rupp wasn't the only coach in the South still playing an all-white team in 1966. Smith was coaching at North Carolina, and the Tar Heels were still all-white at that time.

1997 Final Four press pass

Here is my press pass from the 1997 NCAA Final Four game in which the Gophers played the Kentucky Wildcats.

It's hard to judge someone's behavior from thirty or forty years ago by current standards. I've gone through that myself. People ask, "How could a newspaperman serve as the behind-the-scenes manager of the Lakers? Wasn't that unethical?" It would have been unethical in the sixties and later, when conflicts like that started to become a big issue. In the fifties, newspaper people were involved with every sports team and every sports promotion in town.

One reason I got along with Rupp so long is that he had this kid, Herky, who collected Coca-Cola bottle caps. There must have been a reason for this, but I don't know what it was. Rupp would call me and say, "Mr. Sid, this crazy kid of mine wants more Coke caps." Tom Moore owned the Coca-Cola franchise in the Twin Cities. I would go out there, get a couple of crates of bottle caps, and then send them to Rupp's son.

Rupp's teams won the national championship in 1948 and 1949. The stars were Alex Groza, Ralph Beard, and Wallace ("Wah-Wah") Jones. In 1950, Kentucky elected to play in the National Invitational Tournament and lost in the first round.

Kentucky went back to the NCAA tournament in 1951 and won. The star of that team was big center Bill Spivey. The tournament finals were played in Minneapolis at Williams Arena. To show what the NCAA tournament was at that time compared to what it has become, the NCAA finals drew nothing—around 7,000 people in a building that then held nearly 20,000.

It was a whole different deal then. In 1951, the NCAA had doubled the size of its tournament field from eight to sixteen. The finals was a one-day event, with two teams playing for the championship and two others for third place. Kentucky beat Kansas State for the championship, and Illinois beat Oklahoma State for third place.

Later in 1951, I was at an NBA meeting in New York. New York City District Attorney Frank Hogan had been conducting a high-profile investigation into point-shaving in college basketball. Involved were big-name players from Long Island University, City College of New York, and other schools from the East.

At that meeting, Ned Irish of the New York Knicks said that Hogan was looking into point-shaving involving Alex Groza and Ralph Beard. Groza and Beard were out of Kentucky and in the NBA at the time.

After the NBA meeting, I went to Chicago for the College All-Star Football Game. The Cleveland Browns were the NFL champions and the team playing the All-Stars. Lou Groza was an outstanding tackle and place-kicker with the Browns—they called him Lou the Toe. His brother Alex was there to see him play.

I walked into the hotel in Chicago and there was Alex Groza sitting in the lobby. I had gotten to know Groza from when the Lakers practiced against Kentucky. I felt that I should tell him about the rumors that were circulating in New York and in the NBA that Groza and Beard had been involved in point-shaving at Kentucky.

I went over to him and said, "Alex, I know you're not going to tell me if something like this is true, but I want to tell you what's going on: The NBA is starting to get information that there was point-shaving at Kentucky."

Groza said, "That's a big joke," and walked away.

Groza and Beard wound up being implicated in point-shaving, and they were banned from the NBA. Spivey also wound up being accused and was not allowed to play in the NBA. Spivey denied that he was involved in any wrong-doing until his dying day.

Kentucky was banned by the Southeastern Conference for the 1952–1953 season. Originally, Rupp's plan was to fill the schedule with nonconference games. He called and said, "Mr. Sid, I need games. I wanted you to get Hamline and Macalester and the rest of those Minnesota schools to play us." A couple of weeks later he called back and said, "I don't need those games after all, Mr. Sid. Kentucky must not be so bad, because all those Catholic schools in the East want to play us."

As it turned out, the NCAA came in after the Southeastern Conference ban and did not allow Kentucky to play a schedule that winter. It was the first school to suffer an NCAA "death penalty," even though that's not what they called it in 1952.

Rupp called me that winter and said, "Mr. Sid, we just put in a new scoreboard in our arena. There is room for three digits, so when we get in the hundreds, everyone will be able to see it. When our conference friends come to our arena next season, we're going to try to show them that all three digits work. Fifty percent of the points we score are going to be for the points we didn't get to score this year."

There were always hotbeds where college basketball was a big deal— Kentucky, Indiana, North Carolina, the New York City area—but it was hardly the national passion in the forties, fifties, or into the sixties that it has become now. The Gophers had some decent teams and would draw well for big games. Mostly, basketball was something that was played at the university between fall football and spring football.

Nationally, the popularity of college basketball started to climb with a rivalry between Lew Alcindor (now Kareem Abdul-Jabbar) at UCLA and Elvin Hayes at Houston. When Houston Astrodome owner Judge Roy Hofheinz promoted that UCLA-Houston game and sold out the dome in 1967, suddenly the colleges and television networks started to realize there were big bucks to be made in college basketball, too.

Houston beat UCLA in the Astrodome. Then the teams had a rematch in the national semifinals in Louisville, and UCLA won. That was the start of UCLA's streak of seven straight championships, and John Wooden's dynasty—ten championships in twelve NCAA tournaments from 1964 through 1975—was what really made the Final Four the enormous event that it is today.

I started going to the Final Four during that time. I had known Wooden since 1948, when he almost became the coach of the Gophers. More than once, Wooden would finish his press conferences and then say, "Sid, if you need anything more, come on back here and we can do an interview."

The Final Four has become my favorite event to cover. You don't see all the NFL general managers and coaches at the Super Bowl. You don't see many of the G.M.s or managers at the World Series. But the athletic directors and the basketball coaches—almost all of them are at the Final Four. For someone who writes a column like I do, with a lot of notes and the need for a lot of contacts, nothing can top the Final Four.

And the 1997 Final Four topped all of them, because the Minnesota Gophers were there for the first time. The three weeks of the NCAA tournament—first in Kansas City, then in San Antonio, finally in Indianapolis—were as exciting a time as I've had in Minnesota sports.

My lasting memories will be the reception at Williams Arena after the Gophers won the Midwest Regional and clinched the trip to the Final Four, and the amazing number of Minnesota people who followed the Gophers around the country. For years, representatives of college football bowl games have been saying that even if the Gophers qualified, they didn't want Minnesota at a game, because people didn't follow the Gophers. Minnesotans proved in March 1997 that if you give them an exciting team, they will follow that team as enthusiastically as any group of fans in the country.

Clem Haskins came to Minnesota from Western Kentucky in 1986. The Minnesota program was in bad shape because the administration had run off so many players. The university ran off Mitchell Lee, Kevin Smith, and George Williams after they were accused (and later acquitted) of rape in Madison. The university also ran off Todd Alexander, an outstanding guard from Texas, after he got in some trouble.

As far as the reporter-coach relationship, Clem and I have been up and down through the years. He's a control freak. He wants to control everything, including the flow of information in the media. He doesn't want you calling the players to get information. He tries to keep a lid on recruiting information. Clem and I have had a few blowouts on those issues through the years.

Personally, I think Clem is an outstanding person, and his wife, Yevette, is the greatest. I think Yevette is one of the big reasons that most of Clem's players leave Minnesota with terrific feelings about the experience they have had. While Clem is the strict father to these kids, Yevette is the loving mother with a sympathetic shoulder to lean on.

I know there were times when Clem was not sure a coach could do the job at Minnesota. The administration would not give him any help in getting kids in school. He had a lock on a center named Elmore Spencer, and I know Clem thought Spencer could be a program-turner. When he couldn't get Spencer in school, Clem was ready to quit. If the NBA had come along with any kind of job offer, Clem would have been out of here.

When Haskins arrived, there was talk about a new basketball arena. Men's Athletic Director Rick Bay thought it was ridiculous to pump money into Williams Arena, a building that had been there since 1928. Bay's idea was to build a multi-purpose arena for hockey and basketball. There was also talk about the Gophers moving downtown to play in the Target Center that Marv Wolfenson and Harvey Ratner had erected for the NBA and the Timberwolves.

Clem was in favor of anything that would get him out of Williams Arena. That was during the first two seasons, when the Gophers were outmanned and went 6-30 in the Big Ten. Then, in the winter of 1988–1989, Clem had his first competitive team. Clem started to find out what an advantage it can be to play in Williams Arena with the wild crowds, that elevated court, the whole atmosphere. The only way you could get Clem out of the beautiful Old Barn now would be kicking and screaming.

Haskins had never been one to inflate expectations. In 1996, Clem was an assistant coach with the U.S. Olympic basketball team that won a gold medal in Atlanta. When he came back from there in August, I interviewed him, and that was the first time Clem said: "We have a team that can win the Big Ten title. That is our goal."

Obviously, Haskins knew what he was talking about. The Gophers went 16-2 and won the Big Ten by four games. The key moment for the Gophers came at Indiana, against my friend Bob Knight, when they overcame a seven-point deficit in the final minute, then won in overtime.

I called Knight the next day. He was madder than hell at his team but said, "I picked Minnesota before the start of the season. I am still picking them. They have the best personnel and a coach who does a good job. I think the Gophers can be defensed—they can be beat—but they are the best team in the Big Ten."

Actually, I think Clem had a couple of teams where the personnel was comparable to the 1996–1997 team. But Clem did a masterful psychological job with these players. When they won seven out of nine at the end of the 1995–1996 team and did not get a spot in the NCAA tournament, Clem convinced those players they had received the biggest jobbing in history from the NCAA.

It inspired those kids to work harder in the offseason than any group of basketball players in Gophers history. Except for Charles

Thomas, all of them stuck around during the summer. They played basketball every day. They lifted weights. And when Clem would see them, he would remind the players of what the NCAA had done to the Gophers at the end of the last season. When practice started October 15, those players were in the best possible shape.

The other improvement was that Bobby Jackson turned out to be a better player than anyone imagined. Jackson was not healthy as a junior, after transferring from Western Nebraska Community College. He broke his foot during summer ball, then broke it again in the fall.

When the season started, Jackson said there still was pain in the foot. He did not want to play. The truth was, some people at the university were starting to think that Jackson was too soft, that he never was going to be able to play for the Gophers.

That was exactly the opposite of what happened. Jackson turned out to be as hard-nosed as any player the Gophers have had. The tougher the situation, the closer the game, the better Jackson played for the Gophers. He has to be the best six-foot-one rebounder I've ever seen.

Jackson played well for the Gophers during that 7-2 streak at the end of the Big Ten schedule in 1996. It was not until summer ball that year that the Gophers were sure they had a special player. He was so dominant in the summer leagues that Haskins and his coaches knew they had the star that any team needs to win the Big Ten and make a run in the NCAA tournament.

Clem and I had a running debate on his substitutions. Clem always has liked to talk about how his team was ten deep. More than ever, he started talking about that with this team during the 1995–1996 season. He would run players in and out like a hockey coach. A guy would make a couple of jump shots in a row, and Clem would sit him down. It drove me crazy.

We had an ongoing debate. I kept telling him, "Let me pick out my five, you take the other five, and I'll bet you any amount that I'll beat you by forty." I still think I would have won that bet, but I have to give Clem credit. By giving all those minutes to guys like Quincy Lewis, Charles Thomas, Trevor Winter, and Miles Tarver, he developed a bench, and that had a lot to do with the Gophers' 31-4 season.

The depth probably is what got the Gophers to the Final Four.

They were playing UCLA in the Midwest Regional final in San Antonio. UCLA only used six guys. The Gophers were down ten points early in the second half, but wore down UCLA and won going away.

The Gophers were matched against Kentucky in the national semifinals. That added to the drama for me, because I went all the way back to Rupp with Kentucky basketball. And it was extra special for Clem, since he grew up in Campbellsville, Kentucky. Clem was a big name in Kentucky basketball when he got out of high school in 1963. Kentucky and Rupp still were segregated at that time, so Clem went to Western Kentucky and was the first black player there, along with his friend Dwight Smith.

Lute Olson, a close friend, also had his Arizona team in the Final Four, playing North Carolina in the first round. I knew Lute when he was a standout basketball and football player at Augsburg College in Minneapolis.

In 1975, after Bill Musselman left Minnesota, I called Lute and asked him if he was interested in the Gophers job. He wasn't. He did a terrific job at Iowa, then turned Arizona—a school that had no background in basketball—into a national powerhouse. Kentucky had Olson hired as its coach at one time, but he backed out when his family said they wanted to stay in Tucson.

Arizona and Olson wound up winning their first national championship by beating Kentucky in overtime in the title game. That came after Kentucky beat the Gophers and Arizona beat North Carolina in the semifinals.

The Gophers were not healthy versus Kentucky. I think they could have won that game, if players such as Sam Jacobson, Charles Thomas, and especially Eric Harris had been healthy. But I doubt if the Gophers could have handled Arizona's quickness in the championship game, even if they had beaten Kentucky.

Clem was in his glory during the Final Four, receiving all the plaques as coach of the year. In the finals, it was fast coaching company—Lute Olson, Dean Smith, and Kentucky's Rick Pitino. Pitino is one of the most impressive coaches I've ever met. He presents himself so well, speaks so articulately about basketball and other subjects, that it's no surprise that he has won the way he has in the NBA and in college basketball.

I told Pitino after one of his news conferences, "You should run for president. You could get the whole country to follow you. If you saw a problem, you could get it fixed." Jim Bunning, the baseball pitcher and now a Republican congressman, chewed out Pitino for introducing President Clinton at a rally during the 1996 campaign. By the time Pitino got done explaining it, he made Bunning come off as a real jerk.

The best moment in the Final Four experience was that reception in Williams Arena. The Gophers were scheduled to get back from San Antonio and the victory from UCLA at 9:30 P.M. They were more than an hour late, and the people still were waiting at Williams Arena. The roar that 15,000 people let out when the Gophers walked in rivaled the roar that 50,000 people gave the Twins at the Metrodome when they came home from winning the American League pennant in 1987.

It was another unforgettable night in the Old Barn. For me, it is always special to walk into that place. It is where I started, covering Dave MacMillan, the grand old coach of the Gophers in the 1940s. After all the changes and all the years, the Old Barn is the one thing that remains unchanged on the Twin Cities sports scene. Oh, it has been remodeled, but it's still the same. It's still the Old Barn. And I love it.

Chapter 18

Halsey, Cedric, and 'CCO

Halsey Hall was the most beloved character this area has ever had. He was a terrific announcer and the most popular master of ceremonies—for sports dinners, charity dinners, college and high school athletic banquets—of all time.

Halsey covered the Millers and minor league hockey for the *Journal*. After John Cowles, Sr. took over the newspaper business in Minneapolis, Halsey did the same thing at the *Morning Tribune*—worked on the desk, covered the Millers and minor league hockey. Several times, Halsey went to hockey games, had a couple of drinks after the game, and forgot to write his story. I loved him, but Halsey was probably the worst newspaperman of all time.

Halsey started his radio career by being part of the Gophers football broadcasts. He also had a Sunday morning coach's show, sponsored by P. B. Juster's Clothing Store, with Bernie Bierman. He might write a locker room story for the *Tribune* on a Gophers football game, but mostly he was there to do radio.

Halsey would be with us on those train trips to Columbus and Madison and Ann Arbor. What went on during those trips was unbelievable. Rollie Johnson was doing the play-by-play for the Gophers, and he liked to drink as much as Hall. So did Dick Cullum, Charlie Johnson, and George Edmond from the St. Paul paper. I don't know how those guys got up the next morning to get to the football game.

Of course, the carousing on those trips did save their lives during the thirties on a trip to Seattle to play the University of Washington.

The Gophers were spending the night at a hotel in Missoula, Montana. One of the writers, Ed Shave from the St. Paul *Daily News*, was stumbling home late at night and saw that a fire had started in the hotel. He set off the alarm, and everyone got out of the hotel before it burned to the ground.

We still were taking the trains in the forties and into the early fifties. Before we played Wisconsin, the train would stop in Portage, Wisconsin, on Friday night, and we would stay in the hotel there. That was probably the favorite stop in the Big Ten for the drinkers. One night, we were in a bar, and Halsey challenged the local tough guy to a wrestling match. The guy beat the hell out of him, then the Portage cop came and was going to arrest Hall.

We were in Cedar Rapids, Iowa, before a game against the Hawkeyes on Friday night. A women's group was having a convention, and all the rooms were booked. So, they put the Minnesota media guys in a second-floor ballroom, with a bunch of fold-out beds. The usual crew was in there drinking, and Halsey decided he had to go to the bathroom. Halsey said, "Where's the toilet in this joint?" and Cullum pointed to a door. It was the main entrance door to the room, but Halsey didn't know the difference. He went stumbling toward the door. All he was wearing was a pair of BVDs—and those were torn, meaning his manhood was flapping in the breeze.

Halsey stepped outside and was standing on the mezzanine above the lobby. There were dozens of women guests around, and they started screaming when they saw Halsey.

Ten minutes later, there was a knock on the door. Cullum answered it and there was a cop, with Hall by the arm. "Mister, this man says this is his room," the cop said.

Cullum looked at Hall and said, "I've never seen the son of a bitch in my life," then slammed the door.

The cop took Hall to jail, and I had to go bail him out. The cops sent Hall back to the hotel with a towel around him. It was midnight when we got back to the hotel. When we got back to the room, Halsey grabbed Cullum, and they started wrestling.

Cullum loved to agitate Hall. Everyone did. When he was on WCCO Radio for the Gophers broadcasts, we would steal the commercials he was supposed to read. Tom Briere and I would get his keys, move his car, and Halsey would be wandering around, saying,

"Where did I leave that damn thing?"

Way back, when the Millers were a New York Giants farm club, they would pay for Hall to cover the World Series. That was his reward for writing stories about the Millers all year. One October, the Giants decided to cut back and not send Hall to the World Series. Hall was bitching at the office about the cheap Giants. I called a friend, Haskell Cohen, the public relations man for the NBA, and asked a favor: Send a phony wire from the Yankees telling Hall that the Yankees understand the Giants are not paying for his World Series trip this year, but to come to New York anyway, as a guest of the Yankees.

Hall got the wire. He was elated. He was chomping on his cigar, saying, "The Giants, those cheapskates, won't send me to the World Series, but look at the Yankees . . . there's a real organization."

We ended up getting screwed on that practical joke. Park Carroll used to work for the Millers. The Yankees had hired him to handle press credentials for the World Series. When Hall showed up unexpectedly, it immediately occurred to Carroll that we were playing a prank on Halsey. Carroll gave Halsey his press credentials and put him in the Series headquarters hotel, as a guest of the Yankees. Carroll called me a week later and said, "I'll bet it ruined everyone's fun when you guys found out I took care of Hall."

There was a big crisis at the newspaper in 1957. Charlie Johnson put me in charge of the *Morning Tribune* as the sports editor. I told Charlie that he had to let me take Halsey off baseball. He was killing us. Deadlines did not mean a thing to Halsey. When he did file a story, it would not make any sense.

I convinced Charlie to let me put Tom Briere on baseball, and to move Halsey to the *Star*. That was historic—not having Hall's baseball stories in the *Tribune*.

By then, radio was a bigger deal for Halsey anyway. He was at WCCO every night for the ten o'clock news. Cedric Adams would read the news, and then Halsey did the sports. WCCO had 70 percent of the radio audience in Minnesota then, and the ten o'clock news was the biggest thing it had going in the forties and fifties. Airplane pilots would report that, flying over the Minnesota prairie, they could tell when it was 10:30 P.M. That was when the 'CCO news was over and the lights in all the farm houses would go out.

Halsey would be working the *Tribune* copy desk for us. He would go out for his hour dinner break about 7 P.M. Most nights, he would not come back until after the ten o'clock news was over.

When the Twins started in 1961, they brought two announcers with them—Bob Wolf and Ray Scott. WCCO knew they needed a local flavor, so they added Halsey to the broadcasts. Halsey was in heaven. He loved baseball, he loved the radio, and he loved the fact he was able to drink free on the road.

Halsey would take one suit, two shirts, some underwear, and a suitcase full of booze on the road for a two-week road trip. For a shorter trip, he would bring a shaving kit and a carrying case that held three quarts of booze. A young reporter once asked Halsey why he took his own booze on Twins trips, when it was so readily available in the cities they were visiting. Halsey said, "Son, you never know when you're going to run into a local election."

Cedric Adams was the No. 1 celebrity in the state. He was bigger than sports heroes like Paul Giel and George Mikan, and he was bigger than politicians like Hubert Humphrey. Adams wrote the local column for the *Star*, and he read the news on WCCO radio.

Cedric would go on an occasional Gophers road trip and join in the drinking. When Cedric and Halsey were together on one of those trips, it was the greatest floor show of all time. It was like being on the road with Jackie Gleason and Art Carney.

Cedric was quite the ladies man. I would be in the office, writing my column, and the phone would ring. Cedric would say, "Hartman, come on back to my office. I have a surprise for you."

It was never a surprise. I would go back to the office, and a couple of ladies would be in there, drinking and dancing with Cedric.

The editors might not have liked the fact Cedric was having parties—bordering on orgies—in his office, but there was nothing they could do about it. Cedric was more important than they were. He sold more newspapers than anyone, and he was the No. 1 guy on the radio.

Cedric came from Magnolia, Minnesota, a little town in the southwest corner of the state. His columns were mostly small-town humor. On the radio, he had a voice and a delivery that made people trust him.

The power of Cedric Adams was what turned a company like Twin City Federal into a big success. Roy Larson ran TCF, and he was a sponsor for Cedric on 'CCO. Larson would tell stories about farmers coming into the savings and loan with pillowcases full of cash and asking, "Is this Cedric Adams's bank?" When the teller said yes, the farmer would dump the money on the counter for deposit.

Cedric was having heart trouble in February 1961, and the doctors told him to slow down, while they tried to figured out a way to fix him. But he had promised Don Knutson, the construction guy and Gophers booster, that he would make an appearance at a fundraiser in Austin, Minnesota. Adams had a fatal heart attack while he was there.

At the same time, Mary Wheldon, who had been Cedric's secretary, also died. Mary and I had a serious relationship. Mary could not have children and I wanted to have children. That was probably the reason we did not get married.

Mary went to Denver and was going to find a job there. She called me one night and sounded incoherent, so I said, "Mary, call me when you're able to talk."

That's the last time I heard from her. The next thing I knew, her father called me and told me she had died that same night. What her father didn't know at the time was that I had talked to her that evening, but when he got her phone bill, there was my work phone number as the last call she had made. Nobody knew for sure if Mary committed suicide or what caused her death.

There was a funeral for Mary Wheldon one morning and a funeral for Cedric Adams early the same afternoon. That was one of the toughest days of my life.

Red Williams was a former Gophers running back and a friend. He was running WLOL Radio in St. Paul. He gave me the chance to do my first radio stuff—pregame and halftime interviews on that station's Gophers football broadcasts. I was able to get the big names in the Big Ten to do those interviews. Larry Haeg was running WCCO Radio. He started having me do the same things for 'CCO that I had been doing for WLOL.

Basically, I was terrible. I didn't have a radio voice, and I didn't know how to deliver information on the radio. Cedric Adams gave me a lot of help. He would listen to my shows and tell me what I was doing wrong.

Haeg and I became the best of friends—so close, we were almost like brothers. Everything I pitched him as far as a show was concerned, Haeg went for. The *Sunday Sports Page. Sports Hero. Prep Parade.* He backed me on all of those things.

Prep Parade ran during the week. We would interview high school coaches and give publicity to the top athletes of the week. They still do a version of that show on 'CCO.

The *Sports Hero* was a five-minute interview that would run at 4:10 P.M. and then be repeated at 6:10 P.M., Monday through Friday. The idea was to get the biggest name in sports that day for an interview. It was a huge success, but that show almost drove me to the grave. I would wake up at five o'clock in the morning, worrying about how I was going to track down Jack Nicklaus or Martina Navratilova or Franco Harris or God knows who to be that day's Sports Hero.

The show ran for nine years. I gave myself a daily nervous breakdown, but every big name in American sports was on that show at one time or another. It proved my theory: It might take pleading with a P.R. person or a coach, or hollering at an operator or hotel clerk, but I can get anyone on a telephone.

Ohio State's Woody Hayes was known as the orneriest old coot in college football, but I always got along with him. The Buckeyes were at the Rose Bowl one year, and I wanted Woody as the Sports Hero for that day.

I had a recording time of between 9 A.M. and 10 A.M. at the radio station. I was always more comfortable if I could get a promise from someone beforehand that they would call. I would start calling people from home at 7:30.

I knew where Woody was staying, and I called him at 7:30. That meant it was 5:30 in the morning when the phone rang in Woody's room in California. Woody picked up the phone and immediately said, "What do you want, Sid Hartman?"

Of course, I said, "How did you know it was me?"

And Woody said, "Because you're the only son of the bitch in the world with the guts to call Woody Hayes at this time of morning."

I was able to get Pete Rose on the morning after he had his 3,000th hit. The Reds public relations people told me, "No chance." So, I called Reds manager Sparky Anderson, and he got Rose for me.

Jack Nicklaus had played at Woodhill Country Club in the Trans-Mississippi amateur tournament when he was just a kid. I didn't know anything about golf, but my friends at Woodhill said: "You better get out here and meet this guy, because he is going to be the biggest name in golf for the next twenty-five years."

I went out, followed him around, and got to know him. If I needed him, I would call the club where a tournament was being held, leave a message, and he would call.

I was talking to my friend Bob Knight before the 1991 U.S. Open was played at Hazeltine National in Chaska. Knight and Nicklaus were buddies from their days at Ohio State. I said to Knight, "If you talk to Nicklaus, tell him to give me some time when he is up here for the Open."

A few days later, I walked into the locker room at Hazeltine, and Nicklaus said: "Come here. Why are you calling Knight? You've known me for forty years and you're calling Knight? I'll always take care of you, Sid."

One of my great *Sports Hero* catches was George Allen. He was going to be named the coach of the Washington Redskins. Allen was not talking to the press, because the Redskins wanted to save the announcement for the next day. I found out the hotel where he was staying in Washington. I called the hotel, pleaded and cajoled, and the operator put me through to Allen's room. His wife said, "George is not here. He went down to get a suit pressed."

I called back to the hotel, found out the location of the nearest dry cleaner, called there and asked for George Allen. The guy behind the counter yelled, "Is there a George Allen here?"

Allen got on the phone and I said, "George, it's Sid Hartman."

I knew Allen well. He screamed, "Sid, how did you find me here?" I told him and he said, "OK, call me back in my room in fifteen minutes, and we'll do the interview."

WCCO finally did me a favor. I would have an occasional on-air conversation with Steve Cannon, the legend of afternoon drive, and management said: "That's what you should be doing, Sid . . . talking to Cannon every day."

We killed the *Sports Hero* show and replaced it with the conversation with Cannon. I enjoy it a lot more. Plus, I don't have to wake up a hot-tempered football coach at 5:30 in the morning and ask him for an interview anymore.

On Sunday mornings during the seventies, I would come into WCCO Radio and get the interviews together for the *Sunday Sports Page* show that ran at noontime. Chuck Lilligren was in there, doing a Sunday morning show. Lilligren was an on-air personality and also did some of the farm news. Lilligren was a big sports fan, and he would get me on the air for a few minutes and ask some questions. Lilligren would give me a hard time about the local teams, and I would give the needle back to him.

'CCO started to get a response from listeners, who said they enjoyed those conversations. Management found a sponsor, and we started doing fifteen minutes. Soon, it became a thirty-minute show at 10 A.M. on Sunday. The feedback from the listeners and the ratings told management that the show was huge.

Eventually, Lilligren wanted to have weekends off. In 1981, Dave Mona became my partner. Mona's father, Lute, was the longtime basketball coach at Minneapolis South. Mona was a University of Minnesota journalism school graduate who had just left the *Tribune* in '81 to start a public relations firm. He had covered the Twins for me for a couple of years at the *Tribune* and then worked as a cityside reporter.

Mona was getting a break with this Sunday morning show. His business was small and just getting started. Mona, Meyer and McGrath became one of the biggest public relations firms in the Twin Cities, and was later sold to an international company.

Dave Mona has some bucks now. He worked hard to be a success. And being on the Sunday morning show did not hurt, believe me. That opened quite a few doors for him.

The Sunday morning show now goes from 9:30 A.M. to noon. Station Manager Jim Gustafson told me in 1996 that the show had the highest percentage of audience of any Sunday radio show in the country. There are all kinds of stories of people sitting in the pews at Mass and other Sunday services with ear phones, listening to the show.

I don't hold back on my opinions on the Sunday show, and that has created a few problems for me. I was sued by Dr. Rob Hunter, the former Gophers' orthopedic surgeon, for something I said about him on that show. CBS owned WCCO by then and successfully defended the case.

The 9:30 portion of the show is question-and-answer with Twins manager Tom Kelly, Gophers basketball coach Clem Haskins, or the ever-changing Gophers football coach. When Kelly is in one of his bad moods, that half-hour can seem like it is a half-day. There have been times when I've barked at the callers, to keep the second-guessers away from Kelly, and that has gotten me in trouble.

With Clem, some days I'll be sick of hearing every call start the same way, so I will say, "OK, caller. We know you love Clem. We know you think he's doing a great job. Just ask the question."

Clem doesn't like that. He likes to hear those platitudes.

Sunday mornings is where I became famous for three terms: "geniuses," "stiffs," and "close personal friends." The geniuses are the second-guessers. The stiffs are the people who will find something to complain about on the day after the Twins have won a seventh game of the World Series.

Many people have the opinion that I'm an egomaniac. I don't see myself that way at all. I'm not a self-promoter. But the Sunday morning show . . . it does do something for my ego. It's an upset when there is a phone line open. If there is and I mention it, boom, the line lights up with a call.

With a two-and-a-half-hour show, we get a hold of a lot of people for interviews. To be able to get a guys like Bob Knight, George Steinbrenner, and Lou Holtz to do interviews on a Minneapolis radio station on a Sunday morning, to me that's amazing.

Halsey Hall and Cedric Adams were long established as WCCO radio personalities who also worked at the newspaper. When I started doing it, the *Tribune* had a policy that you had to get written permission to have a radio show.

Every time I would get a new show, Bower Hawthorne, the executive editor and the one guy in management that I didn't get along with, would threaten to fire me. I always survived at the *Star Tribune* because of this policy: I saved my scoops for the newspaper. My primary job was being a newspaperman. If I could help the radio station react to a story that was already in the news, I would do it. But if it was a scoop, it was in the newspaper first.

If the newspaper was to come to me after all these years and say, "It's us or the radio," I would have to quit the newspaper. For one simple reason: There is no comparison in work. I work my rear end seven days a week for the *Star Tribune*.

The radio—once I got out from under the daily anguish of finding a Sports Hero—is fun. Talking with Cannon. Talking with Mona. Arguing with Eric Eskola on 'CCO's morning show. Arguing with the geniuses and stiffs who call on Sunday mornings. All of that is fun.

Chapter 19

Close Personal Friends

Bob Knight

Bob Knight still was coaching at West Point when I met him for the first time. He appeared at a coaching clinic in Moorhead. I listened to him speak and then wrote a letter, telling Knight how impressed I was with his presentation.

Knight was the guy I was pushing to replace Bill Fitch as the Gophers coach in 1970. The Gophers screwed up that deal. When Knight became the Indiana coach in 1971, we developed a close relationship. Knight has never let many reporters get close to him, but he found out I was someone he could trust.

Bob let me hang around with him at the Final Fours. When his Indiana team was there, Bob Hammel from the Bloomington, Indiana, newspaper and I were given some privileges. We attended practices and would be in Knight's group for dinner.

I was there for one of many incidents where Knight wound up getting a bum rap. The Hoosiers were in the 1981 Final Four in Philadelphia. They beat Louisiana State in the semifinals. Indiana was staying in a hotel in New Jersey, and as it turned out, the main delegation of LSU fans also were there. Knight was meeting his wife, the university president, and other people for dinner at the hotel. You had to walk through the bar to get to the restaurant. Hammel and I were with Knight.

There was a drunk wearing an LSU hat sitting at the bar. He shouted, "Bob Knight, you're an asshole." He did it a couple of times, and Knight walked over and said: "Would you please not do

Basketball friend
Relaxing at my house on the St. Croix River, Bob Knight and I enjoy the view.

that? My wife is here. The school president is here. Yell at me in the arena, not here."

The drunk then screamed: "You're a bigger asshole." He did it about four times, and finally Knight gave the guy a push. He wound up in a big trashcan that was next to the bar.

The LSU guy started screaming he was assaulted. The cops were called. There was a conference with the cops. Several LSU fans came over and said the fan, not Knight, was in the wrong. When the cops were finished, they said to the drunk, "We think we'll arrest you."

It was the big story in the Philadelphia papers on Monday morning—not the fact Knight was getting ready to play North Carolina and Dean Smith in the title game. Knight was totally innocent, but the sportswriters didn't care about that. They loved to rip him.

Something happened later Monday that knocked the Knight incident out of the headlines. John Hinckley shot President Reagan.

The NCAA delayed the championship game that night, waiting to make sure the president was out of danger. Then, the Hoosiers, with Isiah Thomas, went out and took apart North Carolina.

Most coaches go to the Final Four, whether they have a team there or not. Knight doesn't go as often anymore, but when he is there, one tradition is to have a dinner with all his former assistants or players who are now head coaches. I've been invited to those things, and the conversation is fantastic.

We have a tradition when Knight brings his Indiana team to Minneapolis. On the night before the game, there is a dinner at Vescio's, the Italian restaurant on the university campus. Knight brings a few people from Indiana, and he lets me invite Minnesota people to be there. We've been doing that for over twenty years. Most of the time, Bud Grant shows up. Knight is known for his emotion on the sidelines, and Bud is known as a stoic, but the truth is, they have the same quality when it comes to coaching: common sense. When Knight and Grant start talking about how to handle athletes and prepare them for competition, it should be put on an instructional tape for all coaches.

In 1996, Knight was inducted into the NIT Hall of Fame in New York City. Knight always has remembered taking his Army teams to the Madison Square Garden when the NIT was a great tournament, so he showed up to accept the award. The Final Four was being held in the New York area a few days later. I went in early and hung out with Knight.

We spent a lot of time walking in Manhattan. The cabdrivers would honk their horns and shout greetings to Knight. When we went to the Garden for the NIT games, we sat in a section that was empty. All of a sudden, the section was full of coaches who were at the game. The media might not like him, but coaches love Knight. He's the Pied Piper to coaches.

Athletes also admire Knight. Putting in four years with Bob isn't the easiest thing in the world, but the bond between Knight and former Indiana players is the strongest of any coach-athlete relationship that I've seen.

A number of years ago, Knight was in town visiting, and I took him to a Vikings training camp in Mankato. We went in the locker room. The players were supposed to be on the field at 3 P.M. It was four o'clock before most of them made it, because they were getting Knight's autograph and talking with him.

Knight has done a lot of favors for me. There was none bigger than in 1984. He was coaching the U.S. Olympic team, with Michael Jordan, Patrick Ewing, Chris Mullin—many great players. Many cities were trying to get the Olympic team to play in its arena against a collection of NBA All-Stars that included Magic Johnson, Larry Bird, and Kevin McHale. I asked Bob to play that NBA team at the Metrodome. It was the first time the Dome was used for basketball, and we drew a huge crowd. Knight was introduced and received a standing ovation from the Minnesota crowd.

After the game, Knight brought the Olympic team to my house on the St. Croix River for dinner. Jordan was on the other side of the room. Knight looked over at Jordan and said to me, "He is going to be the greatest basketball player who ever lived." Knight was right, of course.

One big mistake Knight did make was agreeing to give writer John Feinstein full access to himself and to his basketball team. I warned Knight ahead of time: "Don't let him in your practices and team meetings. It will be twisted around, and you will come off looking bad. If a guy has a chance to make a million bucks, he's not going to give a damn what he writes about you."

Feinstein wrote all the stuff that was supposed to be off the record and wound up getting rich. Knight did not make a dime from it.

Knight has a passion for hunting and fishing. A friend of mine, Tom Swanson from Minot, North Dakota, hunts game birds with Knight out by the Missouri River. He tells me that Knight is the most relentless hunter he has seen.

One of Knight's athletic heroes was Ted Williams. Knight was fascinated by Williams's ability and devotion to fishing. He wanted to meet Williams to talk fishing. I made a call to Ted's Florida home and learned that he was attending a Sears Roebuck meeting in Chicago, as Williams endorsed some of the firm's products. I was able to contact Williams in Chicago. We wound up on a three-way conversation—Williams, Knight, and myself.

Williams said: "I'm going to ask your man one question. If he answers it correctly, then we'll talk." Ted asked Knight what kind of a

Olympic medal, 1984
Bob Knight presented me with this Olympic gold medal for my contributions to the 1984 team. Knight's team that year included Michael Jordan, Patrick Ewing, Chris Mullin, and many other great players.

lure he would use to catch a certain fish in a certain situation. Knight answered it correctly, they had a long talk, and became friends. They went fishing together in Russia. Williams gave Knight's 1987 Indiana team a pregame talk before it won the national championship.

Knight had called me to ask a favor: David Halberstam, the famous author, and Knight are friends. Halberstam was planning to write a baseball book based on the American League pennant race of 1949. He was trying to get an interview with Williams. Knight called and said, "Halberstam is a good guy. Can you help him out with Williams?" I contacted Williams and he did the interview.

One of my prized possessions is an autographed copy of the book, *Summer of '49*, with a note reading, "For Sid H., who unlocked the door which led to a great interview. With gratitude, D. H."

For Sid Hartman –
Who unlocked the door
which unlocked the door
which led to a great
interview. With
gratitude

Dave Halberstam
May 24, 1989
P292
see

David Halberstam's autographed note
Here is David Halberstam's autographed note to me in a copy of his book Summer of '49, *thanking me for setting up an interview with Ted Williams.*

Knight and Williams are two identical personalities: men's men, fierce competitors, demanding of themselves.

George Steinbrenner

George Steinbrenner's main sports interest originally was football. He was an assistant coach at Northwestern and Purdue. Steinbrenner would come in to scout a Minnesota game, and he would show up at the press party on Friday night. That is how I first met him.

After that, Steinbrenner owned the Cleveland team in the American Basketball League. That was the league that tried to compete with the NBA several years before the American Basketball Association. I was in the NBA at the time and helped George get a few players who were marginal players for us.

Steinbrenner bought the New York Yankees in 1973. He would come to town with the Yankees, and we would spend the day together, before going to the ballpark.

Steinbrenner has done so many amazing things for people. He made a commitment to pay for the medical studies of Ron Karnaugh, the 1992 Olympic swimmer whose father had a heart attack and died during the opening ceremonies in Barcelona. He gave a job to Al Ferrera, the old Dodgers outfielder, so Ferrera could have medical insurance for a kidney problem.

I was sitting with him a number of years ago in his Yankee Stadium office, and he was chewing out the Yankees' farm director. He grabbed one of the newspapers and screamed, "Don't tell me about your problems. You don't have problems. See this story . . . this kid has problems. He needs $19,000 per month in medicine or he's going to die." Then, Steinbrenner told his secretary to get the kid and his family to come to the stadium. The family came the next day and had dinner with George. He gave the family a check for $19,000 before dinner and another check for $19,000 after dinner.

Admittedly, George would not be the easiest guy to work for. He is The Boss. He brings a football mentality to baseball, which normally has a lower-key, less-emotional atmosphere. He thinks baseball players should approach a game in the same manner as football players approach a game.

In a football locker room, you can hear a pin drop before a game. In a baseball clubhouse, the players are screwing around. That's one of the things that gets him upset and causes him to go off on players at times during a season.

I was caught in the middle when Steinbrenner and Billy Martin were going through their continual melodrama. They were both close personal friends of mine.

One of Martin's famous episodes occurred at the Radisson South in Bloomington. I had seen Billy earlier in the evening, and he was not drinking. He was with his friend Howard Wong in the hotel bar, and this marshmallow salesman from Illinois started giving Billy a hard time. Martin was trying to be on his good behavior. He left the bar. The guy followed him into the lobby and kept after Billy. That's when Billy hit him. The St. Paul newspaper had a story a couple of days later that made Billy look like the bad guy.

Steinbrenner called Martin and said, "Billy, did you hit that guy?" Martin said no. That was a lie.

George fired Billy five times. He always brought him back, for two reasons: First, because he loved Billy; and second, because Billy was a great manager. George would tell me, "Billy is his own worst enemy, but the little S.O.B. is the best manager I've had. No matter who I put in there, I can't find a guy who can manage a ballclub as well as Billy Martin."

George was heartbroken when Martin died. He arranged to have a memorial service for Martin at St. Patrick's Cathedral in New York. A New York columnist ripped Steinbrenner for that, saying the memorial service was George's ego trip. That was B.S.

George felt that New Yorkers loved Billy—going back to his days as the second baseman for the Yankees—and that there should be a meaningful tribute in the city. And if you're going to have a memorial service for a Catholic man in New York, St. Patrick's is the place to have it.

Jerry Burns

I met Burnsie in 1952, when he was hired as the offensive coach for Forrest Evashevski at Iowa. The Hawkeyes had the horses in those days, but Evashevski always gave a lot of credit to Burns for the innovative offenses they would use.

Evashevski quit coaching to become the Iowa athletic director after the 1960 season, and Burns was his replacement. The Hawkeyes were supposed to be loaded again, but the injuries they suffered right away were almost the story of Burnsie's head coaching career there. He lost an All-American quarterback, Wilburn Hollis, and an All-American running back, Larry Ferguson, in the first two games of his first season.

A couple of years later, Burnsie had a great running back, and he needed to get him eligible in summer school. There was a geography professor named Bill Peterson, and the running back needed a passing grade in that class to play football the next fall. Burnsie called the professor "Steamboat" Bill Peterson. He called me up and said, "I'm bringing Steamboat Bill to the Twin Cities this weekend. We have to show him a good time, so he'll pass my running back. He's a Mississippi River nut. We have to take your boat out on the river and let him explore."

I let Steamboat Bill drive the boat, and he puttered around, in and out of these nooks of the rivers, for hours. It was driving me crazy, but Burnsie kept signaling me to shut up, that he needed the running back.

Burns also arranged with Calvin Griffith for Steamboat Bill to go a Twins game at Met Stadium and sit in the owners' box, right next to the home dugout. The professor got to meet Sam Mele, Harmon Killebrew, Bob Allison, Earl Battey, all the big-name players.

Burnsie also was going to Winnipeg to see Bud Grant, who was coaching the Blue Bombers at the time. Burnsie took Steamboat Bill on that trip, too. Grant gave the professor a couple of beautiful Hudson Bay blankets as a gift from the Blue Bombers.

And then, when the summer session was all over, Steamboat Bill came to Burnsie and said: "Coach, I really appreciate what you have done for me, but I cannot pass this young man. His work in my class has been too poor."

Burnsie laughed, shook Steamboat Bill's hand, and said: "You know, professor, I have to admire you. I did all that stuff for you, and you still won't prostitute yourself."

I would go to the NCAA convention every year. The coaches meetings were held at the same time, and it was a chance to maintain contacts. I would hang out with Evashevski, Burns, and the Iowa guys at those meetings. Burnsie would get a couple of beers in him—that's all it took with him—and give me nothing but crap. The meetings were in Philadelphia one time, and we were having dinner. Burnsie went to the men's room, came reeling back to the table, and said, "Hey, Sid, why is your picture in there? People are using it for toilet paper."

Bump Elliott was the Michigan football coach at the time. He was having dinner with us and said, "I know you love the guy, Sid, but don't you ever get sick of the crap he gives you?"

I said, "You're right, Bump. It's time for me to get even."

When we got back to the hotel, Burns went straight to his room and collapsed into bed. A couple of hours later, I went down and saw the bellman. I gave him twenty-five bucks and said: "Get me a bucket of ice, then we're going up to a room, and you're going to let me in."

I went in the room and threw the whole bucket of ice on Burnsie's head. He didn't move a muscle. I saw him the next morning, and he said: "I must have had a fever last night. My whole bed was soaked when I woke up this morning."

Burnsie became the victim of circumstances at Iowa. The Hawkeyes were maneuvering around the NCAA rules pretty good with Evashevski as coach. Then, when Evy became the athletic director, he got religion as far as what could be done in recruiting players. The boosters were not allowed to do the same things for Burnsie that they had done for him.

Iowa's talent went way downhill. Burnsie was 3-6 in 1964 and 1-9 in 1965. The fans and the alumni were all over Burnsie. It was a tough thing for Evashevski to do, but he had to fire Burnsie. Iowa found out it was not the coach's fault. The Hawkeyes went twenty years without a winning season, until they found Hayden Fry, another guy who can be creative in recruiting.

After Burns was fired at Iowa, Vince Lombardi hired him as his defensive backfield coach in Green Bay. Burnsie was there for two seasons. Grant had come down from Winnipeg to the Vikings in 1967. He ran the offense himself the first season, then decided he needed some help. Grant wanted Burnsie, but with Pete Rozelle as commissioner, the NFL had tampering rules that prevented one coach from hiring assistants away from another. So, I did the tampering. I called up Burnsie and said, "Bud wants you to come over here and run the offense for him."

Burnsie went to Lombardi and asked permission to talk to the Vikings, then came to work for Grant. Bud and Burnsie were a great team for the next sixteen years.

A couple of years after Burnsie left Green Bay, Lombardi said to me: "Sid, I thought we were supposed to be friends. I know you were the son of a bitch who lined up Burns for the Vikings."

When Bud quit the first time, Mike Lynn passed on Burnsie and gave the job to Les Steckel. Everyone thought Steckel was an outstanding young coach. Burnsie was devastated. I thought he was going to drive over to the Mendota Bridge and jump.

Marty Schottenheimer called from Cleveland and wanted to bring in Burnsie as his offensive coach. Burnsie was going to take the job, but Lynn and Grant both begged him to stay—said this young coach was going to need him. Steckel promised Burnsie that he would have complete autonomy to run the offense.

That turned out to be a lie, of course. Steckel brought in a bunch of yahoos who were friends of his. He paid no attention to Bud's guys—Burnsie, John Michels, Bob Hollway. That had a lot to do with Bud coming back in 1985, seeing Burnsie, Michels, and Hollway get treated that way by Steckel.

After the Steckel disaster (3-13), Bud came back for big money, then quit after one season. This time, Lynn did not outsmart himself. He gave the job to Burns, the guy who should have been the head coach two years earlier.

In my opinion, Burnsie did a fantastic job. He turned the Vikings into contenders again. He had an excellent working relationship with his boss, Lynn. The players were willing to go to the wall for him. Burnsie is a guy who never has had an enemy.

After the 1987 season, his team put together an amazing stretch of football. The Vikings went to New Orleans to play the strong team that Jim Finks had put together and just manhandled the Saints. Then, they went to San Francisco, the lopsided favorite to win another Super Bowl. The Vikings defense did such a number on Joe Montana that day that the fans in Candlestick Park booed Montana off the field.

I had one of my infamous press box episodes that day. Cornerback Reggie Rutland intercepted a Montana pass and was running for a touchdown. I got up and started hurrying down the press box, saying, "Go, baby. Go, baby, go."

The other sportswriters got all over me for that. What can I say? I wanted Burnsie to go to the Super Bowl.

The Vikings had to play one more outstanding team on the road: the Washington Redskins. The game was decided on a fourth-down play from near the goal line. Darren Nelson always has taken the heat for letting the pass get away that cost a touchdown and prevented the Vikings from taking the Redskins in overtime.

The fact is, Anthony Carter ran the wrong pass route and took his man—cornerback Darrell Green—right into Nelson. If Carter would have done what he was supposed to do, Nelson would have walked into the end zone.

If they had beaten Washington, the Vikings were a cinch to win the Super Bowl. The Redskins killed Denver in that game. The real losers in that 17-10 defeat in Washington were not the Vikings but the nation's sports media. Why? The coaches for both Super Bowl teams have long press conferences every day from Tuesday through Friday. Jerry Burns would have had the greatest B.S.'ing, story-telling, shoot-from-the-hip sessions in the history of press conferences. The national media would have found out Burnsie was one of the all-time characters.

I've been close to Burnsie and his family for forty years. His wife, Marlyn, is a saint. Years ago, she was having a hip operation at Mayo Clinic in Rochester. Burnsie called me and said, "She'll be out of surgery early in the afternoon. I'll see you there."

I drove to Rochester. When I got to the hospital, there was a call from Burnsie. He said, "I'm playing golf in Cedar Rapids, Iowa. Hold her hand until I get there."

Forrest Evashevski

I would get to the NCAA meetings, check into the hotel, and get a key to my room. I would open the door, and Forrest Evashevski's suitcase already would be there. He never got a room. He always stayed with me.

Evashevski took Iowa to the Rose Bowl in 1956. When he did that, the Green Bay Packers tried to hire him as general manager and coach. Evy was going to be in Minneapolis on a Monday, to appear at Dick Cullum's Quarterback Club. Every year, the club would have a Rose Bowl meeting, and they would try to get the coach of the Big Ten team to come in for it.

Evashevski had access to a private plane when he was at Iowa. He flew into Green Bay before coming to Minneapolis for the Quarterback Club. Jerry Burns wanted Evy to take the Green Bay job in the worst way. Burnsie wanted to get into pro football.

On Sunday night, Evashevski was staying at the downtown Radisson in Minneapolis. I was there with him. The Packers were calling every fifteen minutes, trying to get him to say yes. Finally, at 1 A.M., Evashevski turned down the job. So, the Packers went to their second choice—Vince Lombardi.

I went to Pasadena to cover the Hawkeyes in the Rose Bowl. We were staying at the Huntington Sheraton Hotel. Evashevski and Burns kept going to the front desk and changing my room. I must have gone through five rooms. Finally, they put me in with Al Grady, a sportswriter and a guy I didn't get along with. Evy and Burnsie thought that was hilarious.

I became close friends with the Evashevski family. His wife, Ruth, made the world's greatest lasagna. When covering a game in Iowa City, I would eat dinner at the Evashevskis' on Friday night, and Ruth always made lasagna.

When we went to Iowa with the Gophers later in the fifties, we would fly on the team plane. Evashevski would be at the airport to pick me up. That drove Minnesota Athletic Director Ike Armstrong crazy. Armstrong was always telling Murray Warmath, "Sid is giving Evashevski our plays."

To which Murray would say, "Sid doesn't know our plays."

Evy's son, Frosty, was a football star in Iowa City. He wound up playing at Michigan. I was there one Friday night, and we all went to Frosty's high school football game. It must have been ten below. I was Frosty Hartman that night.

Evashevski would use that private plane to fly into Minneapolis on occasion, to have dinner at his favorite restaurant—Charlie's Cafe Exceptionale. Evashevski came in one night and called my number. It was changed. He called information. There was no listing for S. Hartman.

I was married then, and my wife had gotten us an unlisted number. Evashevski was back in Iowa City the next day. He called me at the office and said, "Hey, Sid Hartman. I was in Minneapolis last night, but I couldn't get ahold of you. You're too important. You're more important than the Iowa football coach is in Iowa City. You can look in the Iowa City phone book and find a listing for Forrest Evashevski."

That was it. The S. Hartman listing went back in the Minneapolis book.

Vince Lombardi

Vince Lombardi and I always had an outstanding relationship. When the teams came out for the early warmups, I would go down on the field and talk to the coaches. When the Packers were playing the Vikings, I would always have a good conversation with Lombardi.

In 1967, I was on the sidelines at Met Stadium, and Lombardi said: "I have to get out of this thing. They don't want you to win in this league. They want to punish you for success."

Lombardi was upset that the NFL was changing its rules for the draft. The rule had been that a team could draft a redshirt player after his junior season in college. "Redshirt" means the player either had been injured or held out of competition for a season, and thus could come back to play in his fifth year of college.

Lombardi had great success using that rule. That is how he was able to keep the talent flowing into Green Bay, even with the Packers winning all the time and drafting at the bottom of the heap. I wrote about how upset Lombardi was about that rule change and that he would quit. It turned out that he won the Super Bowl, making him two for two in the first two years of the Super Bowl, and then he did quit.

The College All-Star Game—between the NFL champions and the College All Stars—still was being played in Chicago. I was the secretary for the college football writers. We would have our annual luncheon in Chicago, and it was my job to get the speaker. I called Lombardi and asked him to be the speaker. He agreed. We talked for awhile. I asked Lombardi if he missed coaching, and he said, "I don't miss the calls at home at night by some of the jerk sportswriters."

Lombardi came to Chicago and gave his usual speech. The college writers had not heard it as often as the NFL writers. Vince received clippings of columns from sportswriters all over the country—praising him and saying how much football missed him.

In Green Bay, they were naming the street next to the field Lombardi Avenue. Max Winter and I went down for the ceremony. Lombardi told me about all the clippings he had received after his speech in Chicago and said, "Maybe there aren't as many jerks in your business as I thought. Maybe I miss coaching more than I thought. I think I'm going to go with the Washington Redskins."

Lombardi became the general manager and coach in Washington. He would have won big there, I'm sure, but cancer got him.

Louie Jacobs

Louie Jacobs owned a company called Sports Service in Buffalo, New York. Louie had the concessions contracts at many of the arenas and stadiums across the country.

I first met Louie when I was ten years old. I had won an award for selling the most popcorn among the kids working as vendors for Millers games at Nicollet Park. Sports Service had the contract. Louie was in town on business, and he gave us the awards. I was the smallest kid getting an award. Louie remembered me and would say hello when I ran into him at the ballpark.

When I got into the newspaper business and the NBA, we became extremely close friends. Every Sunday night, starting in 1944 and for nearly the next forty years until his death, I would get a call from Louie Jacobs. He knew everything that was going on in sports. He had the concessions contracts, so if teams were being sold or being moved or if a new guy was coming in to run a football, baseball, or basketball team, Louie knew about it.

Louie was never identified as the source, but he gave me more stories than anyone over the years. For instance, Louie told me a couple of weeks ahead of time that it was set, the Boston Braves were moving to Milwaukee.

Until television started to get big in the sixties, there was a thin line between success and bankruptcy for many sports operators. Louie bailed out many, many owners with loans through the years. He wanted to make sure they kept operating, so he could keep selling peanuts, popcorn, and hot dogs.

Jacobs owned the Cincinnati Royals in the NBA at one time. He also had a deal to buy the Yankees—along with Yankee Stadium and three minor league ballparks—for $2.6 million in the fifties. He tried to get Arthur Wirtz in Chicago and Jim Norris in Detroit, the guys who basically ran the NHL, to go in with him. Wirtz and Norris would not go for it. Louie was sick, because he thought it was the greatest deal of all time, and he would have been right.

Bud Wilkinson

Charles ("Bud") Wilkinson played football for Bernie Bierman's Gophers from 1934 through 1936. He was a Minneapolis kid—handsome, clean cut, Minnesota's version of Jack Armstrong.

The Gophers had a chance to hire him away from Oklahoma after Bierman was ousted following the 1950 season. The downtown guys were willing to give Wilkinson all the money in the world. University President Lew Morrill and new Athletic Director Ike Armstrong screwed it up. Basically, they did not want a football coach as powerful as Wilkinson would have been.

Wilkinson stayed in Oklahoma and continued his dynasty. Wilkinson remained such a popular figure in the Twin Cities that, several times, I went to the Orange Bowl to cover Oklahoma. Minnesotans still were interested in Wilkinson.

Bud had gotten the job after Jim Tatum quit at Oklahoma and went to Maryland. Oklahoma was playing Maryland in the Orange Bowl, and it was a huge game.

Stanley Woodward, the former sports editor at the New York *Herald-Tribune*, was writing in a Miami newspaper at the time. Wilkinson would let me sit in on his team meetings. Woodward wanted to do a special piece on Wilkinson, and he convinced Bud to let him sit in on the team meeting, too. The agreement always had been that what Bud said in these meetings was off the record.

I saw Woodward taking notes. Gomer Jones was Wilkinson's No. 1 assistant. I said, "Gomer, what's the deal? Is Woodward going to write this stuff?"

Gomer said, "He knows better than that. He won't write it."

The next morning, the phone rang in my hotel room at seven o'clock. It was Jones and he was in a panic. He said, "Sid, that son of a bitch wrote everything. Our whole game plan is outlined in the Miami paper. Come on down here. We have to buy up all these newspapers and get rid of them, before Bud sees one. He'll have a nervous breakdown if he sees this."

We collected all the papers in the hotel and in the pay boxes out in front. Bud saw the article anyway. Then, Oklahoma went out and beat Maryland. Bud said, "I think Woodward confused Maryland more than he helped."

Bud was a big Republican. He quit at Oklahoma to run for the U.S. Senate. When he lost, he went to work for ABC, doing college games with Chris Schenkel. Wilkinson was an outstanding broadcaster.

The one mistake he made was giving that up to come back as coach of the St. Louis Cardinals. Bud had never been in pro football and he was sixty-two. His rapport with the players was great, but the front office B.S., with a screwed-up organization like Bill Bidwill's Cardinals, drove him nuts.

Wilkinson was close to Richard Nixon. When Bud still was doing television, the Gophers were playing Missouri, and he was there to do the game. We were talking before the game, and I remember clearly as could be, Wilkinson predicting exactly what was going to happen to Nixon. He said, "Nixon is paranoid, and he has guys around him like Haldeman and Ehrlichmann who feed that paranoia. Nixon's political career is going to come to a sad end."

Yours truly
Here I am in 1997, armed with my trusty tape recorder. (Photo © Brian Peterson)

Chapter 20

The Private Side of Life

I joined Oak Ridge, the Jewish country club in Hopkins, in the mid-fifties. Max Winter was the guy who got me in. I did not play a lot of golf, but the laughs you could get at the annual meeting were worth the membership fee and the monthly charges.

Ben Berger, the co-owner of the Lakers, was the worst golfer in history. At Oak Ridge, there is a pond in front of the first tee. You have to hit the ball maybe seventy-five yards to carry the pond. Berger would scull two or three shots into the water every time he played the hole.

Berger would get up at the membership meeting and in his thickest Jewish accent say: "Vat do ve need that lake on the first hole for? Der are more balls in der than Vilson's got."

That was Wilson—as in the sporting goods company.

I played on Sunday mornings with Max Winter's group for a number of years. I shot in the nineties most of the time, clearing the pond in front of the first tee with regularity.

The other players in Max's foursome were Si Meshbesher and Sam Rubinstein, who was almost as terrible on the golf course as Berger. Winter and Meshbesher had standing bets with Rubinstein. They would give him two strokes a hole and still take all of Rubinstein's money.

One winter, Rubinstein went to Hawaii and did nothing but take golf lessons for two months. He did not tell anyone where he had been or what he had been doing. When the next golf season started at Oak Ridge, Rubinstein made the same bet with Winter and Meshbesher—two strokes a hole, a standing bet for the whole summer. They played the first match of the season, and Rubinstein was hitting every shot straight. He didn't hit the ball far—maybe 100 yards—but when you're getting two strokes a hole, all you have to do is hit it straight. He became known around the club as Fearless Rubinstein. As long as he had his two strokes a hole, he would play Winter and Meshbesher for any amount of money.

Winter owned The 620 Club in downtown Minneapolis, and Meshbesher was a lawyer. The first few rounds that year, they figured Rubinstein's improvement was a fluke. When it got to be the Fourth of July and he still was hitting the ball straight, Winter and Meshbesher started to whine. "We have to change the game, Sam," Max would say. Fearless would hear nothing of it. After all those years of humiliation and, worse, losing money, Fearless was getting his revenge. He almost owned The 620 Club and the law firm by the time the summer was over.

The big event in the forties and early fifties at Oak Ridge was the pro-am on the Monday before the St. Paul Open—a regular tour event at Keller Golf Course in Maplewood. The player who won the pro-am at Oak Ridge would make more money than did the winner at Keller.

The members would pay to be a pro's partner. Then, on Sunday night, there would be a dinner at the club, followed by a huge auction, called a Calcutta in golf. The bidding for players such as Sam Snead, Julius Boros, and Cary Middlecoff would go crazy. The players would get a guarantee, plus a cut of the Calcutta. In the early fifties, the winning golfer could leave Oak Ridge with ten grand.

One year, Snead was paired with Ben Berger. They were starting on the tenth tee. Berger lined up for his drive, took his swing, whiffed, and then hit the ball on his back swing. The ball went flying backwards and hit a tree next to the tee box. There was a big crowd around the tee to watch Snead. Berger's ball came caroming off the tree and almost killed four people.

In addition to being the worst golfer in the world, Berger was nervous about playing with Snead. He kept hitting shots that were unbelievably bad, even for him.

I knew Snead a little bit. After watching Berger play two holes, Snead called me over and said, "This is a put-on, right? Someone is

Grandchildren
Here I am with two of my grandchildren, Justin and Kally.

paying this guy to do this, in order to screw up my game."

There was another mostly Jewish course in Golden Valley called Superior. Later, it became Brookview, and is now a public course. As much gambling as there was at Oak Ridge, there was more at Superior. That's the only reason people were members there—to gamble on the golf course.

Guys like Red Anderson and Marty Falk played for huge stakes. It got so bad that they started playing flashlight golf at night. The only time you could use the flashlight was to find your ball. You had to hit shots to the green without the benefit of light.

I stopped at Superior to have dinner. The dining room looked out over the course. You could see the flashlights out there. There was a character named Abie the Agent who was at Superior all the time. Abie came over all excited and said: "Sid, vat do you think? Peetch black and they are playing golf. I don't understand."

I never did catch the golf addiction. My son, Chad, came up with it instead. He plays to about a five-handicap at Oak Ridge. Me? I was undefeated as a golfer—against Ben Berger.

Al Rubinger and I were maybe eight years old when we first met. Al's dad, Sam, had a little furniture store on Washington Avenue in Minneapolis. My dad drove a delivery truck and made some deliveries for Sam Rubinger. Al and I met at the Milwaukee Road depot, when we were there with our fathers, waiting for furniture to come in on the train.

Al's mother died when he was nine, and he was in the Jewish orphanage in north Minneapolis for a year, before his father remarried. Al got started in business the same way I did: delivering newspapers as a young kid.

We also played together in the Working Boys Band, a band for grade school boys from poor families that was started by Allen Abbott, the band director at South High. Rubinger and I rode the street car to Whittier Grade School on Twenty-sixth and Blaisdell to practice with the band. I played the trumpet. Louie Armstrong was never in danger of losing any gigs to me.

When John Cowles, Sr. came in from Des Moines in 1935 and bought the *Star*, he promoted like crazy and had an army of kids going door to door, selling subscriptions. Al sold more new subscriptions than anyone. Al wound up having a news run for the *Star* at the same time I had my news run for the *Tribune*. Those were good jobs.

There was a recreation room with three pool tables and a lunch counter right across the street from 425 Portland Avenue South—still the address of the *Star Tribune*. In 1940, Al and I came up with $500 and bought the place from a gambler named Petey Cohen. Al was nineteen and I was twenty. It was called the Press Row Recreation Room. The whole crowd in there was newspaper people—mailers, press men, the advertising salesmen. The guys from the sports department and the copy desk would come in for lunch, too. We didn't get rich, but for a couple of young men running a business, we did OK. Al and I sold it after eighteen months, and had about $300 to split.

Al's wife, Dorothy, and my sister, Bernice, were good friends. I've always been proud of how I worked growing up. My sister and brothers were the same way. Bernice was selling subscriptions to *Liberty Magazine* when she was five years old.

Once I got a car and a news run, I was making good money, but I wasn't bringing much home to help my mother, Celia. I was spending it on the car, on clothes, and losing it in craps games at Charlie Banks's joint on Plymouth Avenue. We got busted in there one night, and the cops took me away in the paddy wagon.

While I was doing that, Bernice was going to high school and working to help pay the bills for my mother and her two younger brothers. Bernice was bright and wanted to go to college, but she could not do that right away. She was working for a wholesale drug company, and the family needed her paycheck.

After a couple of years of working, Bernice was able to start at the University of Minnesota. She met Dorothy there, and they would study together at my mother's house on Irving Avenue. I introduced Al Rubinger to Dorothy. They started dating, got married, and have had a great life together. Dorothy died in spring 1997. She was a great companion to Al and a fine friend to my family.

Al started a business college called Humboldt Institute. The biggest part of the business was training young people for jobs in the airline industry. We have remained the best of friends through the years.

In 1959, Al was getting into the real estate business. He was going to build a twenty-six–unit apartment building on Blaisdell. I told him I would be interested in getting involved in something like that. There were several investors, and we came up with $5,000 apiece.

The first building was a success, and we expanded—not rapidly but cautiously. Roy Larson from Twin Cities Federal and some of the

Family

My family gathered for this portrait in 1997. On the left are my grandchildren Kally and Justin, with their mother, Chris Schmitt, standing behind them. Chad and his wife, Kathleen, are next to Chris, and Chad is holding Hunter. I am in the foreground holding Griffen. (Photo © Brian Peterson) other bankers in town had confidence in us and gave us the mortgages. A friend named Harry Goldman was our builder. He would put up the buildings at cost, then make his money as a partner in the apartments.

We have always pumped the money back into the apartment buildings, so the property would maintain its value. Al has spoken at seminars on how to operate a rental property business.

Al built this thing, I didn't. Al's son Bruce has been running the business for us for quite a few years. Bruce is a terrific person and a sharp kid.

Corporate Report, the business magazine in the Twin Cities, did a story on our real estate holdings a couple of years ago. They came up with some outrageous figure—$25 million—for the value of my holdings. The article was complimentary to our operation, but Al had the most accurate reaction when he said: "Wouldn't it be great, Sid, if the business was worth as much as they said it was worth?"

Al and I have done pretty well for a couple of paper boys from north Minneapolis. It's not the business success that has been most important to me. For almost seventy years, I've had a friendship with Al Rubinger that comes from Heaven.

I have been married once, to Barbara Balfour. She had been married previously and had a daughter named Chris. I never formally adopted Chris, but she is my daughter, and her kids, Justin and Kally, are my grandkids.

Barbara and I were married in 1964. The divorce became official in 1972. There were times during the marriage when we were split. Put it this way: If you were going to pick out the easiest people in the world to live with, Barbara and I would not finish ahead of June and Ward Cleaver on the list.

Chris was five when we were married. Her father had moved to California, so I raised her. Chad was born on May 29, 1965. That was the happiest day of my life.

After the divorce, I had joint custody of Chad but not Chris. There were times when Chris became a pawn in the disagreements between Barbara and me. I would pick up Chad for a weekend, and sometimes, Chris was not allowed to come along.

I would go see her at school and bring a gift to her. It was always important to me to keep Chris as a part of my life. Later, Barbara moved to Monterey, California, and both Chris and Chad lived with me in Golden Valley. Chris always has introduced me as her father. Justin and Kally introduce me as grandpa. I walked Chris down the aisle for her wedding.

Chris and Chad have a good time telling stories about me as the world's biggest klutz. I have no chance with mechanical things. I proved that one day when Chris was eighteen and had moved into an apartment in St. Paul. Chad and I were visiting her. She had bought a moped. They convinced me to drive it around the parking lot of the apartment building. I took off, going maybe ten miles per hour. One problem: I had no idea how to stop it. I started dragging my feet. The soles on my shoes started rubbing off on the asphalt. My shoes were actually smoking. The kids thought it was the funniest thing they had ever seen.

Another time, at the house on the St. Croix River, Chris had prepared a nice dinner. There was a light out in the chandelier above the table. I climbed up on a chair to put in a bulb, and wound up pulling the whole chandelier down on her dinner.

There you have it: Sid Hartman, the guy who can't change a lightbulb.

Chad was running around Met Stadium, Met Center, and Williams Arena by the time he was three years old. He knew more sports personalities as a grade schooler than most media people knew after years in their jobs.

I've always been a football, baseball, and basketball guy—with hockey as a necessary fourth in Minnesota. Chad's interest went beyond that. He could rivet himself in front of the television to watch Bjorn Borg and John McEnroe play tennis. He loved golf, and his No. 1 sports hero is Jack Nicklaus.

With that level of interest, it's not a surprise Chad wanted a career in sports. He went to Arizona State and majored in broadcast journalism. I gave him a hard time about choosing a party school—with year-round golf—as a college.

"Party school?" Chad would say. "Not Arizona State. It's the Harvard of the West."

Chad was the play-by-play announcer for the Arizona State games on the college station. He came out of college with experience—to go with talent. Fortunately for him, Chad was not blessed with his old man's radio voice.

I could have helped advance his career as soon as he got out of Arizona State. I know George Steinbrenner would have taken care of him with a broadcasting job in the Yankees organization. My theory was this: If you can help somebody get something, he still has to produce, or he's not going to keep that job.

I never was able to get Chad to buy that theory. He has been absolutely, 100 percent set on getting everything he gets in broadcasting with no help from me. Almost any father in the world is allowed to use his connections to help a son. I'm banned from doing anything for my son. The ban comes from my son.

Chad beat around the bushes before coming back to the Twin Cities as a broadcaster. He did play-by-play for Double A baseball with Orlando in the Southern League. He did Continental Basketball Association games in Rochester, Minnesota, and La Crosse, Wisconsin.

A low-rated Twin Cities station, WDGY, switched to an all-sports format in 1989, as a tie-in to being the station for Timberwolves broadcasts. Later, the station became KFAN. Chad was hired to host a sports talk show and to do some of the Timberwolves play-by-play on radio—when Kevin Harlan was doing TV or was not available—and on the cable telecasts.

Former *Star Tribune* sports columnist Dan Barreiro and Chad were partners for a three-hour, afternoon drivetime sports talk show on KFAN. Chad now has his own daily show on KFAN, where he discusses a wide range of topics, both sports and non-sports related.

For years Chad did play-by-play and analysis on the Timberwolves broadcasts and telecasts. In my opinion, he is outstanding on play-by-play and as a color commentator.

As it turned out, Chad was right: He could make it in sports broadcasting without me.

May 29 has turned out to be my lucky date. That was the date Chad was born in 1965, and that was the date he was married to his beautiful wife, Kathleen, in 1993. The wedding was held at my home on the river. The ceremony took place in the front yard, overlooking the St. Croix, and the reception was held under a huge tent in the backyard.

Chad and Kathleen have two sons—Hunter, who was born in April 1995, and Griffin, who is twenty months younger. That gives me four grandkids, along with my daughter, Chris Schmitt's, two children, Justin and Kally.

I've been threatening to retire from the *Star Tribune* for a few years. Who knows? Now that those four grandkids have become the most important part of my life, I could actually go through with it.

I reached my fifty-third anniversary as a newspaper reporter in 1997. Another five, six years, maybe that ink will stop running through my veins. [*Editor's note: Ten years later, and still going strong.*]

Chapter 21

Jottings

Throughout my newspaper career, at the Minneapolis *Times*, *Tribune*, and *Star Tribune*, a Sid Hartman column generally has consisted of two or three main items, and then a long, notes portion called "Jottings." Now that I've gone ahead with that book I've been threatening to write for the past twenty years, it would not be complete without such a section.

Bob Knight did me a lot of favors. One of the best was when he agreed to patch up things with former Gophers coach Bill Musselman. Knight and Musselman came into the Big Ten at the same time in 1971. They had been high school rivals as athletes in Ohio. There was not much love there from the start, then the Gophers had the brawl with Ohio State in January 1972. Knight felt Musselman had created the atmosphere for that brawl and blamed him for the demise of the coaching career of Fred Taylor, who had been Knight's college coach.

When Indiana played at Williams Arena, I would go to the Hoosiers' morning shootarounds. Knight and Musselman had not talked since the brawl, and it was 1975, which turned out to be Musselman's last season. I said to Knight, "You're always saying you'll do anything for me, so here's what I want. I want you to shake hands with Musselman tonight."

Knight said, "Bullshit. None of that."

I got to the game that night and, beforehand, was sitting on the steps that lead from the arena to the locker rooms, talking with Knight. He said, "OK, go get him."

I went to the Gophers locker room, grabbed Musselman, and he shook hands with Knight, and they have gotten along since. Musselman accepted an invitation from Knight to bring his South Alabama team to play in Indiana's Hoosier Classic in December 1997. Restoring this relationship was important to me because Knight is a close personal friend, and I've always liked Musselman, despite the Brawl and other problems he has had.

Ohio State football coach Woody Hayes was supposed to be the tyrant of all time, but I had a great relationship with him. I would call Woody's home. His wife, Ann, would say, "I don't know if he came home last night. I'll check." She would look at the kitchen table. If the lunch bag he had taken to the office the day before was on the table, it meant Woody had made it home. If the bag wasn't there, it meant he had been up all night, getting ready for a game, and had fallen asleep on his office couch.

One day I called, and Ann said, "Sid, my son passed the bar exam. I finally can afford a lawyer to get a divorce." She made a lot of use of that line, but she loved Woody, the tough old goat . . .

Minnesota coach Murray Warmath and Woody had tremendous respect for one another. If Minnesota was playing an opponent that Ohio State had just played, Murray would call Woody on Sunday morning and get a scouting report. Then, at the Gophers coaches meeting, the scout Minnesota had at the game would get up and start giving his report on how Ohio State won the game. Murray would say: "You're wrong. This is how Ohio State won the game. Woody told me."

Howard Cosell came to Minneapolis to speak at the B'Nai B'Rith dinner honoring Dr. John Najarian, the wonderful surgeon at the University of Minnesota. I picked up Cosell at the airport. We had to stop at the bar before the dinner. He had four bourbons, straight with a splash of water on the side, at the bar. We went into the ballroom where the dinner was being held, and Howard went to the front table. He started giving me the finger—not an obscene gesture, but the finger to get my attention and signal that he wanted two more drinks. I got him two more bourbons. He gave me the finger again, and I

Sportscasters
Howard Cosell and I shared many a pressbox during the years.

shook my head: No more drinks from me. A couple of minutes later, I saw the waitress bring Cosell two more. That was eight bourbons, not counting what he had on the plane coming in. And then Cosell got up and made one of the greatest speeches I've ever heard, about the love and marriage between a Jewish man and a Christian woman, and how bringing together two upbringings such as that is the kind of understanding and commitment the world needs.

Cosell was also here after his biggest flap. On a *Monday Night Football* broadcast in 1983, Cosell had referred to Washington Redskins receiver Alvin Garrett as a "little monkey." There was an uproar that this was a racist remark. ABC was doing a Thursday night telecast from Minnesota, and Cosell came into the Twin Cities from Washington. Cosell was in Mike Lynn's office at Vikings headquarters, calling people such as Jesse Jackson. Cosell wanted black leaders to come out in support of him and assure everyone that he was a champion of equal rights, not a racist. Cosell really wanted to get O. J. Simpson, who was his colleague on *Monday Night Football*, to make an impassioned plea in his defense. O. J. was coming to the Vikings' offices when he got in from Washington. I went to the lobby at Winter Park and waited. When O. J. arrived, I took him into another office and had him call Cosell. When Howard got on the phone, O. J. said, "My plane was delayed. I'm still in Washington. What's up?" Cosell told him about all the heat he was getting and that he needed O. J.'s support more than anything in the world.

Simpson said, "Support? It's about time they caught on to you, Howard. I've always known you were a racist S.O.B." Then, O. J. hung up.

I went back to Lynn's office, and Howard was going crazy. He said, "That's it. If Simpson doesn't back me, I'm finished."

O. J. let Cosell sweat for about five minutes, then walked in, and everyone had an enormous laugh.

Minnesota was choosing a men's athletic director to replace Rick Bay in 1988. I was supporting former Minnesota tennis coach Jerry Noyce. Noyce was running the Northwest Health Clubs for Marv Wolfenson and Harvey Ratner. Noyce was an outstanding administrator and fund-raiser. He had the support of the Minneapolis business community. University President Nils Hasselmo called Noyce on a Sunday and said, "The job is yours."

Noyce said, "We have to sit down and talk about a contract." They were going to do that on a Tuesday.

Then, Women's Athletic Director Chris Voelz and some St. Paul boosters started complaining. They thought Noyce was tied in too closely with Minneapolis. Hasselmo was intimidated, as was his custom, and changed his mind. He decided to hire McKinley Boston, who was the athletic director at Rhode Island. Not only did I think Noyce was the man for the job, but Hasselmo had treated him shabbily.

Mac Boston had been a lineman for Warmath's last championship team in 1967. When he came to town for the announcement, we had a meeting. I said, "Mac, I remember you as a football player, but I don't think you were the man for this job."

I was wrong. Boston was a fantastic athletic director for the Gophers before becoming a university vice-president in 1995, overseeing men's and women's athletics and student affairs. I'm probably as

Sportscasters
Brent Musburger and I have covered many of the same events over the years.

close to Mac Boston, socially and personally, as any athletic director we have had at the university, including Paul Giel.

The New York Giants were playing the New York Jets in the Yale Bowl in New Haven, Connecticut, in 1967. It was a big deal because it was the first time the Giants' new quarterback, Fran Tarkenton, was playing against the Jets' Joe Namath. I had gotten to know Namath through Clive Rush, who had coached at Ohio State and then with the Jets. I was doing *Sports Hero,* the interview show on WCCO Radio, and Rush had lined me up with Namath several times. I walked into the Jets locker room after the game, went over to Namath's locker, and he said, "Hey, Sid, how are you doing? Looking for Clive. He's over there."

I said, "No, Joe, I want to talk to you."

He said, "I'm not talking to the New York newspapers these days, so I'm not doing an interview at my locker. I'm about to take a shower. If you want to stick your microphone in there, I'll give you a couple of minutes."

Namath went into the shower, and I followed him.

That story circulated around the country. I received twenty clippings from newspapers across the United States, about how this guy Sid Hartman followed Namath into the shower with his tape recorder. Everyone had a good laugh, but I was also the only writer in the country who had quotes from Namath on his first game against Tarkenton.

Verne Gagne was a solid end in football and an outstanding wrestler at Minnesota. He won an NCAA wrestling title in 1949. Tony Stecher was the boxing and pro wrestling promoter in Minneapolis. He was taking care of the guys in the Minnesota wrestling program—slipping them a few bucks under the table. After Gagne won his NCAA title, he wanted to turn pro. He only weighed 190 pounds. Stecher did not think he could promote Gagne as a winning wrestler at that weight. I said, "Tony, do me a favor? Give Gagne a chance. The kid is dying to be a pro wrestler, and he needs the money." Stecher put him in against Abe Kashey, the ultimate villain. Gagne did well and went on to become one of the biggest sports names we ever had in Minnesota.

Those old television pro-wrestling shows at the Calhoun Beach Hotel—with Marty O'Neil doing the interviews—made Gagne a big hero to everyone, including my father, Jack Hartman. My old man knew nothing about sports, but he always wanted to go to the wrestling matches. I would get him tickets. I could not have convinced him in 100 years that it was fake.

Minnesota's all-time football legend, Bronko Nagurski, also got into wrestling. He was playing for the Chicago Bears in the 1930s and was wrestling in the offseason. He hated it . . . hated the fake part of it. He did it strictly for the money. I got to know Nagurski through the wrestling at the Minneapolis Auditorium. We had a great relationship. Al Rubinger, my business partner, and some of his buddies would take a fishing trip to Rainy Lake every summer. Nagurski would come over from International Falls and join them.

Charles Kuralt was doing his *On the Road* series for CBS, and he had been trying to get Nagurski—who ran a gas station in the Falls—to

Dugout interview
Armed with my trusty tape recorder, here I am interviewing Reggie Jackson during his days with the New York Yankees.

be on the show. Bronko was a private man and wanted no part of it. Steve Isaacs was the managing editor at the Minneapolis *Star*. He was a friend of Kuralt's and asked me if I could help get Bronko. I called and explained the situation to Bronko. "CBS? I don't want to be on CBS," he said, but he did it as a favor to me.

A few years later, the NFL brought Bronko to the Super Bowl in Tampa to honor him. His eyes had gone bad by that time. The NFL had a reception for Bronko. I went over to say hello to him at the reception. Ira Berkow wrote about our meeting in the *New York Times*. I reached out to shake his hand and said, "Bronko, Sid Hartman." And Bronko looked at me through his thick glasses and said, "You're not Sid Hartman. I know Sid Hartman."

Bronko Nagurski, Jr. was an outstanding football player at

Home run king
Here I am interviewing the reigning home run king of baseball, the Atlanta Braves' Hank Aaron.

International Falls in the 1950s. I tried to help the Gophers recruit him. I was calling all the time, telling Bronko he had to send the kid to Minnesota. Finally, he said, "My wife is a very Catholic woman, Sid. I can't do anything with her. She wants her son to go to Notre Dame."

Next to a Gophers football game, the biggest thing going after World War II and through the fifties was the state basketball tournament. There were eight regions around the state. When teams from places like Edgerton, Lynd, and Walnut Grove made it to Williams Arena, people went crazy. You could not get a ticket except for the consolation games on Friday afternoon. Well into the sixties, the *Tribune* would send reporters to the eight regional finals. Early in the week of the tournament, we would send a reporter and a photographer to the towns of the high schools that were coming to Minneapolis.

I was the sports editor of the *Tribune* for twelve years, but even then, I would get in the car with *Tribune* sports photographer John Croft and drive 300 miles to a regional game or to a town that was coming to the tournament. I did it because of the excitement you would see and feel in those small towns.

Richie Olson was a twenty-three-year-old coach when he brought Edgerton to the tournament in 1960. He had a bunch of Dutch kids who didn't look like basketball players at all, but, man, could they play the game. Dean Veenhof. Dean Verdoes. Darrell Kruen. Le Roy Graphenteen. And Bob Wiarda, the one Edgerton starter who did not make the all-tournament team. Olson would yell at his players or the referees. The whole crowd would be roaring, but Olson's voice was so high-pitched you could hear him all the way to the top row of that old Barn. In the finals, Edgerton beat Austin, a big town and a perennial powerhouse, and the whole state went crazy.

Ted Peterson covered the high schools—and also state amateur baseball—for the *Tribune*. Ted would be in the office on Friday night, and he would leap over the desk to take phone calls on the high school games from outstate Minnesota. We would run a huge wrapup with as many games and highlights as possible in the outstate editions. The *Tribune* went to the entire state in the forties, fifties, and sixties. Ted Peterson let people in every little town in Minnesota know what was happening with their high school team. He wrote a gigantic notes column on Sunday that was called "No Can Pick 'Em." Bob Sorenson, our sports makeup editor at the *Tribune* who died way too young of cancer, used to ask Peterson, "We have to move that 'No Can Read 'Em' copy, Ted. Is it finished yet?"

Whenever people would tease Ted about his high school coverage, he would lecture them on the importance of outstate readers. Ted was the most indispensable person we ever had in the sports department at the *Tribune*. These days, we don't push outstate circulation—the advertisers are not interested in it—like we used to. And the state basketball tournament? The high school superintendents, athletic directors, and coaches succeeded in turning it into a non-event. They lobbied for a multi-class tournament, finally got it starting in 1971, and it has been downhill ever since.

Chicago Tribune Sports Editor Arch Ward started two great events: baseball's All-Star Game and the College All-Star Football Game. That college game was the first football game of the season, pitting the top college seniors from the previous season against the reigning NFL champion. The game was played annually from 1934 through 1976. Eventually, two things did it in: The NFL champions became more and more dominant, and the NFL Players Association did not like the idea that rookies could blow out a knee in the game and get robbed of an NFL career. The College All-Star Game was a wonderful event during its heyday. They used to announce crowds of 100,000 in Chicago's Soldier Field. I would cover it every year. The best game ever might have been in 1950, when the College All-Stars beat the great Otto Graham and the Cleveland Browns. Clayton Tonnemaker, the tremendous Minnesota linemen, had a magnificent game for the All-Stars that day.

Al Kaline had his 3,000th hit for the Detroit Tigers, and I called him the next morning. Later, when other reporters called, Kaline said: "I'm not taking any more calls this morning. I talked to two people this morning—the President and Sid Hartman."

Rod and Marilynn Carew have been close friends. I admired Rod as much as any athlete we've had in the Twin Cities. Marilynn is one of the great ladies of all time. When Rod and Marilynn brought their nineteen-year-old daughter, Michelle, back here from California to be buried after she died of leukemia in 1996, that was the saddest service I've ever attended. But Rod, Marilynn, and Michelle will save a lot of lives because of the attention they brought to the national bone-marrow donor program (1-800-MARROW-2).

When the Yankees were in town playing the Twins in the early sixties, Roger Maris's father Rudy would come down from Fargo, North Dakota, and we would have breakfast at the downtown Radisson Hotel.

Breaking Babe Ruth's home run record in 1961 almost ruined Roger's health. Fans booed him unmercifully, simply for having the guts to hit sixty-one home runs. Maris was being booed at Met Stadium, and he made an obscene gesture. After the game, I went into the visiting clubhouse and walked over to Maris's locker and all of the New York writers came running. He told them to get lost, then said to me, "Sid, quote me as saying whatever you think I should say." I thought he should apologize to the fans, so that's what Maris did the next day in my column.

When Maris died of cancer, I went to the funeral in Fargo. I've never seen as many important sports people gathered together as there were for the Maris funeral. Maris was a good guy who was bum-rapped by a bunch of sportswriters who wanted to rip him and then get an interview. That doesn't work with many athletes, and it didn't work with Maris.

I used to hear what was going on around town and would give news tips to the *Tribune*'s city side and business department. They did not always act. Sometimes, the story would come out in another media outlet, and I would say to the editors, "I told you that was going to happen. Why didn't you do something about it?" Bill Steven was the executive editor of the *Star* and the *Tribune* and he said: "When you get stuff like that, start putting it in your column. We'll call it 'Off the Sports Beat.'" They would bold face the type and put it in the middle of the column. The first public mention in 1957 that Bill Norris was leaving Sperry Univac and heading a group that would start a new technology company—Control Data—appeared in my column. Steven left and was replaced by Bower Hawthorne as executive editor. Hawthorne killed "Off the Sports Beat." The other departments were tired of the sports section beating them on their stories.

I had more trouble with Bower Hawthorne than any editor. He had a neighbor, Paul Foss, who hated me and told Hawthorne a million lies about me. Foss convinced Hawthorne to let him write a column called "Monday Morning Quarterback." Foss's column was a joke. The day we got permission to permanently dump Foss's "MMQ" was one of the finest days in the history of Twin Cities print journalism.

I sent a note to former NFL Commissioner Pete Rozelle in the spring of 1996, wishing him the best and saying how much I appreciated our friendship through the years. Both Pete and his wife, Carrie,

Close personal friends

From left: Minnesota Twins star center fielder and sports announcer Kirby Puckett, Bo Jackson, myself, and Bob Costas.

had been diagnosed with brain tumors, a sad, amazing coincidence. I suggested to Pete that they come to the Mayo Clinic—the greatest hospital in the world—to see if the doctors there had any ideas. Pete wrote me a note that included this: "I cherish our relationship over the years and have always had the greatest respect for the pro-football oracle of the Midwest." Pete died a few months later.

Colonel Earl Blaik was the most powerful man in college football when he coached at West Point. His sister, Mabel, lived in Minneapolis and was married to a fellow named Dewey Newcombe. I met Blaik when he was in town visiting the Newcombes. Later, I was covering my first Army-Navy game, which was the biggest game of the season in the forties and fifties. I was at the press conference after the game, and Blaik shouted out, "You in the brown coat, with the black hair, come up here." He took me in the back room and introduced me to several generals.

Blaik always had stood for discipline and the highest ideals. When Army had the cribbing scandal in which numerous Army football players were found to have violated the West Point honor code by cheating in the classroom, it really hurt him. Blaik's son, Bob, had been the quarterback on that team. Later, Bob was an assistant coach at Minnesota and wanted to get a job with Bud Wilkinson at Oklahoma. I called Wilkinson in Bob Blaik's behalf. When I saw Wilkinson at the NCAA meetings in Cincinnati, he said, "I have a spot for him on my staff, but the problem is we play Army next year. I won't hire him unless his father says it is OK."

So, I called Colonel Blaik, and he said, "Sid, I thought I told you I wanted you to get Bob out of coaching so he can go to work with our oil company, not further into coaching." Blaik gave Wilkinson the go-ahead to hire his son. What he didn't tell anyone was that he was going to quit coaching at West Point before the next season started.

Blaik still was around West Point when Bob Knight was there coaching basketball. When Knight and I would be together and had some time, we would call up Colonel Blaik. He was one of the grandest men that I've ever met.

Edina was a new high school in the fifties. There was a superintendent named Milt Kuhlman, and he used to call me all the time to recommend coaches. John Mariucci and I gave him the recommendations to hire Willard Ikola as Edina's hockey coach. Ikola had been a star goaltender at Eveleth High and then Michigan. He was in the Air Force at the time. Kuhlman hired Ikola without ever meeting him. When Ikola reported to Edina to start work, Kuhlman called me and said, "Who is this little guy you got me to hire? Are you sure the kids are going to listen to him?" Ikola, of course, turned out to be one of the best high school coaches Minnesota has ever had. I had tried to recruit Ikola and John Matchefs for Minnesota out of high school. It was a blow to Minnesota hockey when both those guys went to Michigan.

Kuhlman was also looking for a football coach. I recommended former Gophers quarterback Jim Malosky who was at Morris High School. Malosky had success at Edina before taking the job at Minnesota-Duluth.

I was always tight with the people at Edina High, which won everything in high school sports for years. Everyone called Edina the "Cake

Eaters," but those Cake Eaters had great sports programs.

My great failure with Edina was not convincing Bob Zender to go to the University of Minnesota. Zender was the Edina center on three state championship basketball teams from 1966 through 1968. I tried like crazy to get him to play for the Gophers, but he wound up going to Kansas State to play for Cotton Fitzsimmons. The good news was that I was always calling Fitzsimmons to get updates on Zender, and we became good friends. Cotton has been a good contact for me in the NBA.

The celebration in 1997 of the fiftieth anniversary of Jackie Robinson's breaking into the major leagues of baseball reminded me of an early scoop I could have had. When I first broke into the business, I was kind of an apprentice to Branch Rickey who ran the Dodgers and often visited St. Paul where the Saints were a Dodgers farm club. Rickey kind of adopted me: He would call me when he was coming to St. Paul, and I would pick him up at the hotel, take him to Lexington Park, sit with him during the day, and take him back to the hotel after the game. I'll never forget him talking in 1946 about this player by the name of Jackie Robinson that at the time was playing for Montreal, the Dodgers' other minor league team. Rickey talked about someday breaking the color barrier with Robinson if Robinson proved he could play in the big leagues. I got excited when Rickey mentioned a couple times that before he sent Robinson to the big leagues he might have him play a season in St. Paul, in 1947. In those days, the Dodgers shuffled a lot of players between their two minor league teams.

I remember mentioning this news to Louie Green, who was in the slot, running the sports desk for the *Tribune* at the time. I told Green that I thought I would write something about Rickey mentioning he might break the color barrier in bringing up a black player to the major leagues. Green said, "You're nuts. That's never going to happen." I could have had a big scoop because in the next year, 1947, Robinson was playing for the Dodgers—major league baseball's first black player.

Speaking of breaking the color barrier, I was at the NBA draft meeting in 1950 when Walter Brown of the Boston Celtics shocked everybody by drafting the first black player in the history of the basketball league, Charles Cooper of Duquesne University. There was silence in the room. One reason for the shock was that most of the teams were earning a lot of their revenue at the time from the income derived of doubleheaders with the Harlem Globetrotters. The Globetrotters would play the first game of the doubleheader against their opponent, then the NBA teams would play the second game. In those days the Globetrotters were the big draw and would sell out every building. The other NBA owners knew that the minute that Cooper was drafted, Globetrotters owner Abe Saperstein would cancel all of the NBA doubleheaders. Sure enough, Saperstein canceled the games, and it was a long time before peace was made and the Globetrotters began playing on NBA bills again.

I decided to stop in Las Vegas for a few days on my way to the Rose Bowl one year. My old friends—the one-time gamblers from the second floor of Jack Doyle's joint on Hennepin Avenue—lined me up with a room at the Sands. The manager was a guy named Jack Friedman, and the Minneapolis guys told me to look him up. So, I did that, and Friedman said, "Frank Sinatra is singing here tonight. Find me later, and we'll go to Frank's show."

When he sat down later at the show, I saw there was a handgun in the pocket of Friedman's jacket. Sinatra started singing. He had gone on for about an hour, and Friedman was getting nervous. He didn't want these high rollers sitting in the showroom all night. He wanted them outside in the casino, losing money. Sinatra sang a couple more songs, and Friedman said, "If that S.O.B. sings one more song, I'm going to shoot him," and then he patted the handgun. I wasn't 100 percent certain that this guy was joking . . .

Later, Sinatra was having dinner with his entourage, and Friedman and I joined them. Friedman introduced me to Sinatra as being a guy from Minnesota.

At the Rose Bowl, Sinatra saw me and yelled, "Hey, Minnesota."

Roast

The Spectator's Club held a roast for me a couple years back. Here I am with, from left, WCCO Radio personality Roger Erickson, then–Minnesota Twins owner Calvin Griffith, then–Minneapolis Star and Tribune *Sports Editor Charlie Johnson, University Athletic Director Paul Giel, and Bud Grant.*

Chapter 22

They Say

For many years, my column would end with a quote from people involved in the daily sports news. The small headline above this section of the column would read "They Say." The tradition continues here with anecdotes and observations from a collection of my close personal friends, family members, and colleagues in the newspaper and radio business.

Harvey Mackay, Minneapolis businessman and best-selling author: "In 1996, I was in the process of writing my fourth book, *Dig Your Well Before You're Thirsty*. The marketing approach for this book is that this is the only networking book you will ever need. For the book, I interviewed the five or six people who have the best Rolodexes that can be found.

"My family and I spent three weeks in Atlanta for the Olympics. We were sitting there at the opening ceremonies when Muhammad Ali, fighting Parkinson's disease, appeared in the spotlight to light the torch. There was the most amazing cheer and outpouring of love I have ever heard in an arena.

"Several times in Atlanta, I was at events when Ali showed up, and the reception was remarkable each time. He showed up to see the Dream Team, and the ovation was deafening. The players dropped everything they were doing to come over to shake hands with and to embrace Ali. It was the same everywhere he went.

"I started thinking, 'This man has to have the greatest network of any person in the world. I can't finish this book without talking to Muhammad Ali.'

"I spent the next six weeks trying to get an introduction to Ali. I racked my brain, contacted everyone I knew, trying to find someone who knew someone who could get me a meeting with Ali. Finally, I found Howard Bingham, a writer and photographer who has been one of Ali's best friends for the past twenty years.

"Bingham made a few calls and arranged for us to have a meeting on Ali's eighty-eight-acre estate in Barrien Springs, Michigan, a small town outside of Chicago. We arrived and went through the gate and were greeted at the door by Ali's wife.

"We went to his office, and Ali walked in and said, 'Hello. My name is Joe Frazier.' We laughed at that and then Bingham introduced me as being from Minneapolis. Ali nodded in recognition of Minneapolis, then pointed at me and said, 'Sid Hartman.'

"And I thought, 'Harvey, you dummy. You spent six weeks calling everyone you knew around the country, trying to find someone who could get you in contact with Muhammad Ali. And you failed to ask the most obvious guy—Sid.'"

Chris Schmitt, daughter: "Did you ever try taking a walk with Sid? We'll go to a movie, to dinner, or shopping. We'll get out of the car. I'll be getting the two kids organized. I will look up. He is two blocks away. I'll start screaming, 'Sid, Sid. Come back, Sid.' Even now, in his seventies, Sid is the fastest walker in the world."

Tom Swanson, car dealer, Minot, North Dakota: "Sid and I became friends through Jon Roe, a longtime buddy of mine and a longtime colleague of Sid's at the *Star Tribune*. I have sold Sid a number of Cadillacs in recent times. Sid and automobiles are not compatible.

"Sid's cars must have all the latest equipment and technology. Within two years of getting a splendid, new vehicle, Sid is ready to trade it in. Not long ago, Sid was ready to trade. Over the phone, I asked him the condition of his vehicle, and he said, 'Perfect.'

"When we sold him that Cadillac, the outside rearview mirrors had power and they were heated. The car was dark blue. When this 'perfect' Cadillac arrived for trade-in, the mirrors were primer gray and held in place entirely by duct tape. They neither moved nor were heated as originally designed. We must assume the rearview mirrors wound up in this condition as the result of being backed out of Sid's garage.

"With an earlier Cadillac, it was an absolute must that Sid have a compact-disc player—again, the newest technology. My son, Joey, was taking a ride with Sid. There was a Frank Sinatra CD sitting on the seat, still in its package. Although his intentions were good in buying a CD of his favorite singer, Sid confided to Joey that he did not know how to use the CD part of the car's stereo system—and he couldn't begin to figure out how to get those damn discs out of the package in which they are sold.

"If you have ridden in a car driven by Sid, you know that his many years of navigating in Twin Cities traffic with moderate success is proof positive of the existence of guardian angels."

Lou Holtz, football coach: "I was at the Mayo Clinic in Rochester for neck surgery during the 1996 Notre Dame football season. Sid and Harvey Mackay, two dear friends from my time coaching in Minnesota, helped me to get into Mayo on comparatively short notice. Sid came down to visit on the same day I had gotten out of surgery. I did not feel much like talking with anybody, but Sid had come for a visit, so we talked.

"Sid always had told me about the close personal friends he had at Mayo Clinic. I knew Sid had an unbelievable number of friends and contacts in the world of sports, but I wondered if all his claims about Mayo might be exaggerated. I found out differently. Once the healthcare workers at Mayo discovered I was a friend of Sid Hartman's, you could not believe the service I started to get.

"Sid's visit that day proved three things to me: 1) He is kind and considerate; 2) he is going to talk no matter how you feel; and 3) everybody is his close personal friend."

Dave Mona, public relations executive and Sid's WCCO radio partner on Sunday mornings: "I knew Sid from the time I was six because my dad, Lute, was the basketball coach at South High in Minneapolis. I was the editor of the *Minnesota Daily* at the University of Minnesota. I went to work at the Minneapolis *Tribune* and actually covered the Twins for two years when Sid was running the sports department.

"In 1981, I quit to start a public relations firm. I figured a side job might be a necessity, so I dropped off an audition tape at WCCO Radio. Three weeks later, I received a call from the station, asking if I listened to *Sports Huddle,* the Sunday morning show. I said yes, and they offered me a tryout on the show. I thought Sid would be the guy I was replacing, but it was Chuck Lilligren—Sid's foil—who was leaving.

"I went to the station the next Sunday for my radio debut. The air time was 10:05. It was 10:03 and I still had not seen Sid. The show was being introduced and in walked Sid. He looked at me and asked, 'Do you know how to turn the mikes on?' The engineer said, 'Don't worry, Sid. I'll get you both on the air.'

"Ten seconds before we were to be on the air, Sid said, 'No offense to you, but this isn't going to work. I'm going to ask them to cancel the show.'

"We're still on."

Bernice Shafer, sister: "I was divorced. I was working full time, and I had young children. Sid would come over and play with the kids and help me out around the house whenever possible. It has been wonderful to see Sid with four grandchildren in recent years, because he loves kids so much.

"There's only one thing that drives me crazy about him. His whole life, Sid has told me something and then said, 'Don't tell anybody. This is private. This is just within the family.' And then he will go on his Sunday radio show and tell the whole world about 'Bernice over in St. Paul, my sister who smokes.'

"Sid bought a beautiful home on the St. Croix River a number of years ago. He is always adding on to it—an enclosed porch, a crow's nest, extra rooms here and there. That comes directly from our father. When we were living in a house on Humboldt Avenue, our father put on two back porches, and he built two big garages. Meantime, all of the kids—my brothers and myself—were in one bedroom. Finally, I took over one of the porches and turned it into a bedroom.

"Sid can't stop adding on. In that respect, he is his father's child."

Jon Roe, *Star Tribune* sportswriter: "Sid and anything mechanical or electronic are not close personal friends. In the newspaper business, typewriters started to be phased out around 1977 and replaced by computers. Reporters going on the road were issued an oversized, portable computer called the Teleram. Once the story was written on the computer, you would go through several steps to prepare the machine, then place your phone in a cradle inserted in the top of the machine, and send your story to the computer in the office.

"Sid was going to take a Teleram on the road for the first time, and he was desperately concerned. He asked me to prepare him for this Mount Everest–like challenge. I typed up a list of the 'Ten Commandments for the Teleram.' The Ten Commandments started with the most basic step, turning the machine on and off, to typing in the proper coding, to getting the proper end of the telephone into the proper end of the cradle.

"We had numerous practice runs in the office, and Sid succeeded in sending test copy to the office computer. He went off to his assignment in Florida. The next day, at dinner time, the phone rang at my home. It was Sid. 'Jon, the machine doesn't work,' he said.

"We went through it. Sid was doing everything properly. All I could say was, 'Sid, it has to work.' He called several more times. Same story. Machine doesn't work.

"Finally, I received a call at midnight. It was Sid. He said, 'Something you told me was wrong, Jon. It didn't work. I had to dictate my whole column to a copy boy in the office.'

"We went through it step-by-step again. 'Yes, I did that,' Sid said. 'Yes. Yes. Yes.' Finally, he said, 'Everything worked great until I called the number. Then, all I would get was this squeal on the other end of the phone.'

"To which I screamed, 'That's what you were supposed to get, Sid . . . a squeal. That was the computer in the office, saying go ahead and send your story.'

"'Oh,' said Sid, and hung up."

Bud Grant, lifelong friend and Hall of Fame football coach: "I was playing football for the Gophers in the late forties. We played a game on a Saturday afternoon at Memorial Stadium, then we were going to drive to western Minnesota, to go duck hunting on a Sunday morning. Sid decided that he wanted to come along and go duck hunting for the first time.

"We took Sid's car. The others in the group were Otis Dypwick, the sports information director, my teammate Gordie Soltau, and myself.

"Sid was driving through Litchfield, and the local cop stopped him for speeding. Sid introduced himself as the sportswriter from the Minneapolis *Tribune* and said to the cop, 'Do you follow Gophers football? Look who I have in the back seat—Gordie Soltau and Bud Grant.'

"The cop was a fan. He congratulated us on the victory and talked about what an exciting game it had been, even listening on the radio. Sid said, 'Would you like to go to next week's game in person?' The fellow said, 'That would be great. I love the Gophers.'

"Otis had some tickets for the next week's game, and he gave Sid two of them. Sid gave the tickets to the cop, who said, 'Thank you very much. And here's your ticket for speeding, Mr. Hartman.'

"Sid cussed about that cop for the rest of the trip."

George Brophy, former sportswriting colleague and longtime baseball executive: "In the thirties and forties, Sid's nickname was 'Blackie.' There are a couple of versions as to how he received that moniker, but this is the first one that I heard:

"During the Depression, there was something called a Six-Day Bicycle Race—same thing as dance marathons, only these were people riding their bikes until they dropped. There was a bike race at the Minneapolis Auditorium.

"Sid was a young kid and wanted to get in to see it. He did not have the money for a ticket. Being filled with ingenuity, he climbed through the air ducts that heated the building. When he came out the other side, he was covered with soot. Some of his buddies, already inside the Auditorium, started laughing and calling him 'Blackie.'

"That's my version of how Sid got his nickname, and I'm sticking with it."

Al Rubinger, lifelong friend and business partner: "I took an annual summer fishing trip with friends to Rainy Lake. Bronko Nagurski, the great Gopher, came over from International Falls to join us several times. Sid was not an outdoorsman, but he also did not want to miss anything. So, he decided to meet our party at Rainy Lake.

"We drove up. Sid flew in on North Central Airlines. He got off the plane wearing a suit, white shirt, tie, and dress shoes. Those were the clothes he had brought to go fishing. When you fish Rainy Lake, there is camping, portages, the whole deal.

"We found him some boots and an old shirt. One fellow had an extra pair of denim pants that he allowed Sid to use. The only problem was this guy weighed about 300 pounds. Sid cinched his belt around those pants and was ready to fish.

"We got to a portage, and we loaded down Sid with equipment. He was struggling along, ducking under branches, and the pants came loose and fell down to his ankles. He was in the mud, stepping on those pants, trying to hold on to that equipment, slipping, sliding, tripping. His fishing partners were having a laugh, to say the least."

Joe Soucheray, former colleague and now *St. Paul Pioneer Press* news columnist: "Larry Batson hired me to come to work in the *Tribune* sports department in 1975. I was told to report to work on a Sunday afternoon. I arrived early, wearing a suit and a tie, and feeling extreme anxiety. I proceeded to the sports department and there was no one there. I stood around, not knowing what to do.

"After about thirty minutes, I saw this man marching rapidly through the newsroom and toward the sports department. He was clutching an arm full of newspapers and other pieces of paper on which he had made notes. Soon, I recognized that this was Sid Hartman, the legend I wanted to meet more than anyone else in the employ of the *Tribune*.

"I was trying to decide what to say in way of greeting, when Sid blew past, papers fluttering in his breeze, without acknowledging my presence. He sat down at a desk twenty feet away. The desk was covered with a mound of newspapers, media guides, and other publications. He tore through this pile of debris, then started typing frantically.

"After several minutes, he looked up, saw me and bellowed, 'Hey, you.'

"I stepped toward him, in anticipation of this first exchange of two colleagues. Sid bellowed again: 'You, genius. How do you spell "music"?'

"Sid and I wound up traveling to many major events together. We were in Miami for a Super Bowl. On Saturday night before the game, I had arranged to have dinner with several sportswriting friends, including Jim Hawkins from the *Detroit Free Press*.

"Our group ran into Sid in the hotel lobby, and he decided to join us. We crowded into a cab, with Sid in the front seat, with the driver. We were chatting in the back of the cab, but Sid seemed oblivious to the conversation, which was unusual for him.

"We were riding down Collins Avenue, toward Joe's Stone Crab Restaurant. Sid kept peering to his left, past the driver and between the condominium towers. This went on for several minutes. I nudged Hawkins, squeezed into the back of the car next to me and said, 'I think Sid is about to astound us with an observation. Be ready.'

"Sid peered for a few more blocks, then blurted, 'Boy, this town would be in big trouble if that damn ocean dried up.'"

George Mikan, basketball legend: "When my team in Chicago, the American Gears, folded in 1947, the Minneapolis Lakers—a new team—had my rights in the National Basketball League. My agent, Stacey Osgood, and I flew to Minneapolis to meet with Max Winter and Sid Hartman.

"The four of us met for three hours in the Lakers' office, and I wasn't sold. My salary with the Gears had been $12,000, and I didn't see a reason to take less. Osgood and I decided to head back to Chicago.

"Sid was going to give us a ride to the airport. Max Winter said something to him in Hebrew. Hartman took us on the longest, slowest tour of Minneapolis and St. Paul that I've ever experienced. He drove us leisurely around, talking about the virtues of the Twin Cities, pointing to the parks, the lakes, the golf course, and all the time going away from the airport.

"By the time he got headed in the right direction and made it to the airport, we had missed the last plane to Chicago. Stacey and I were stranded for the night in Minneapolis. We saw through the charade. We realized that Max's message in Hebrew to Sid was to make sure we missed that plane.

"Rather than get mad, Stacey and I had a good laugh. We figured, if Sid had gone to all that trouble, the Lakers must be getting ready to meet my asking price. And that's what happened. The next morning, the four of us met again, and the Lakers agreed to give me the $12,000.

"Sid and I have been friends since that first meeting. I think he is still the best sportswriter in the Twin Cities."

Dennis Brackin, *Star Tribune* sportswriter: "One of Sid's endearing qualities is gullibility. If he hears something positive about a local sports team, he desperately wants to believe it. Through the years, we've tried to take advantage of that gullibility and boosterism to play practical jokes on Sid around the office.

"My favorite came in 1985, after Lou Holtz had directed the football Gophers to a 6-5 record and Independence Bowl bid. Less than a week after the Gophers received this bowl bid, Holtz left for Notre Dame. Sid's colleagues in the sports department were of the opinion that not much enthusiasm existed for a 6-5 team going to a bowl game in Shreveport, Louisiana.

"We were teasing Sid about the public's apathy toward this event. He was insisting that Minnesotans were panting with excitement over this meeting with Clemson, another 6-5 team.

"I decided to organize a Sid call-in among my neighbors. I gave them the number to Sid's office at the newspaper and a schedule as to when to call—every five minutes, starting at 6 P.M. It went like this:

"6 P.M.: 'Hi, Sid. Can you tell me if any tickets are available for the Independence Bowl?' 6:05 P.M.: 'Hello, Sid. Could you provide me with information about chartered planes for fans going to the Independence Bowl?' 6:10 P.M.: 'Sid, can you tell me anything about hotel accommodations in Shreveport?'

"After a couple more calls, Sid bolted from his office, charged over to the naysayers in the sports department and shouted, 'I can't believe the interest in this Independence Bowl. I've been taking call after call.'

"When we all laughed, Sid knew he had been had again. He cussed and returned to his office."

Kevin McHale, former basketball star and vice-president of the Minnesota Timberwolves: "Everyone thinks Sid is such a gruff person. Not really. We had a situation where a good friend of my family had a serious health problem. Sid heard about it and was on the phone saying, 'What can I do? I know people at the Mayo Clinic. I know people at the University Hospitals. We'll get this thing done.' That's the side of Sid people don't see, the side where he will do anything for his friends. That's why I love him so much.

"Sid has acted up and screamed at press conferences. There have been times when I've had to say, 'Sid, please relax and be quiet.' But then you have a real problem, and you see how Sid really is—how he steps to the plate for you. That's what makes him special."

Dark Star, WCCO-AM Radio personality: "The power of Sid's personality never ceases to amaze me. Mike Max and I came up with the idea of having a TV show based in the Twin Cities that would have a format similar to *The Sportswriters* show out of Chicago. We first tried to sell this in 1995. Sid Hartman was not available, and we couldn't come up with any advertisers.

"A year later, we were able to get Sid to agree to be on such a program. We went back out looking for advertisers—including some of the same people who had turned us down—and told them we had Sid. We sold out the show in twenty-four hours. Amazing!"

Chad Hartman, sports broadcaster and son: "I moved in with Sid at twelve. Before then, my mother, Barbara, and Sid were separated, and I was living with her. When the following event occurred, I was about eight. I would be with Sid on Wednesdays and every other weekend. Sid was always looking to do something to make those Wednesdays special.

"One time, he took me to a putt-putt golf course in Bloomington. I enjoyed it. I didn't want to leave. Sid said we had to go and I threw a tantrum. We were walking to the car and I'm resisting. Sid was pulling on my arm. I lost my balance, went into a car fender, knocked out a front tooth, and chipped another.

"I was bloody and crying, but Sid was worse. He was borderline hysterical. He took me to a dentist's office and ran through the waiting room, into the back, screaming for the dentist. The dentist took me into another room. He calmed me down, cleaned off the blood, and said, 'How are you doing?' I was OK.

"The dentist, a guy with a sense of humor, said, 'Your Dad is very worried. You want to play a joke?' I was all for it. He told me to start screaming. I did and Sid came charging through the door, saying, 'What's wrong?' Even dentists liked to pull practical jokes on Sid.

"A couple of years ago, I was having trouble with my teeth. The dentist said I needed a root canal. He asked, 'Have you ever had a blow to your front teeth?'

"I called my father and said, 'Thanks a lot, Sid. Now, I need a root canal.' He started to apologize for the putt-putt golf incident.

I said, 'Sid, it's OK. It was twenty-three years ago.'

"A clear vision of Sid's love of family came after I decided the University of Minnesota was not the place for me. I was there a year, but I didn't like it. I decided on Arizona State.

"This was the first time I was going to be away from him for any length of time. Sid drove me to the airport and saw me off. When I looked back, he was crying. I thought, 'He really does love me and loves his family.'

"A couple of years later, I came back for Thanksgiving. I saw Sid and he looked terrible—almost as upset as that first day his only son left for Arizona State. I said, 'Sid, what's wrong? You look terrible.'

"Sid shook his head forlornly and said, 'It's a bad day, Chad. Lou Holtz has quit at the university. He's going to Notre Dame.'"

Tim McGuire, *Star Tribune* editor: "Kirby Puckett's retirement from the Twins in 1996 due to glaucoma-induced blindness in his right eye saddened all Minnesotans. While everyone else was commenting with melancholy over the premature end to a marvelous career, I was not surprised to read and hear from Sid that there was a chance that one morning Kirby would wake up, would be able to see clearly again, and would be able to resume a Hall of Fame career.

"I'm sure there was ridicule toward Sid over writing something like that, but to me, it was an example of the cornerstone of his belief system. Sid believes that if you are a good person, if you work hard, if you do whatever you can do for friends and family, that in the end everything is going to turn out just fine.

"Our son Jason has Down's syndrome. He is the source of both great joy and great frustration in our lives. Sid has known our son for Jason's entire life. Sid always tell us, 'Jason is going to be just fine.' He says, 'I know a kid who had the same thing as Jason, and now he is running his father's company. The Mayo Clinic took care of him.'

"Of course, this boy did not have the same thing as Jason. In his head, Sid knows this, but not in his heart. If he would admit Jason's life will always be what it is, it would go against Sid's belief in the power of goodness, hard work, love, loyalty—and, of course, the Mayo Clinic."

Epilogue

Randy Moss. Red McCombs. Zygi Wilf. Joe Mauer. Justin Morneau. Johan Santana. Ron Gardenhire. Jac Sperling. Jacques Lemaire. Marian Gaborik. Doug Risebrough. Don Lucia. Latrell Sprewell. Sam Cassell. Lindsay Whalen. Hilary Lunke. Laurence Maroney. Greg Eslinger. Tim Brewster. Dan Monson. And Jan Gangelhoff.

These were all names that had little or no meaning to Minnesota sports fans when my autobiography, *Sid!*, was first released in 1997. A decade later, all these names carry great significance in a sports market that is more crowded and more nonstop than at any time in my long tenure at the Minneapolis newspaper and WCCO Radio.

The drama of these past ten years started in April 1998. The Vikings had finished 9-7 the previous season and won their first playoff game for coach Dennis Green. It came in almost miraculous fashion, as they recovered an onside kick and then scored a touchdown to beat the New York Giants 23-22 in Giants Stadium.

Still, there were empty seats at the Metrodome during the 1997 season. There was a definite sense that people were bored with the Purple.

Then, the Vikings were sitting with the twenty-first pick in the 1998 NFL Draft. Every team in the league knew that Randy Moss, the receiver from Marshall University, had amazing talent.

Lou Holtz had tried to get Moss to Notre Dame. He told me that Moss was the best high school football player he had ever seen on film. Holtz actually had Moss set to go to Notre Dame, but then Moss had a problem in high school, and the powers that be made Holtz pull the scholarship offer.

It was a risky move by Green and the Vikings to draft Moss, but it wound up being the best gamble they had ever taken. Moss brought interest in the team to an all-time high. I've never seen so many people wear a player's jersey—Moss' No. 84—to games as Vikings fans did during his heyday here.

It was amazing how quickly Moss captured the town's attention. It happened on October 5, 1998, a Monday night game in Green Bay. The Vikings and the Packers were both 4-0, but the Packers were solid favorites. Green Bay had gone to two straight Super Bowls, and Brett Favre was the hottest property in the league.

But the Packers were no match for Moss and the Vikings that night. The Vikings won 37-24, and they went on to finish the regular season 15-1. The only loss came in the season's eighth game, when they lost 27-24 to my friend Tony Dungy's Buccaneers in Tampa Bay.

It's my opinion that Moss falls in the same category as Bobby Knight: everything he does gets blown out of proportion.

The cameras were always on Moss on the sidelines. Squirting water in the direction of an official, walking off the field in Washington with a couple of seconds left in the game—if it wasn't Moss, no one would've noticed. But any controversy involving him became a national story.

Usually, you can't point to a single player in a team sport, especially in football, and say, "He sells tickets." But Moss sold tickets.

He's done some goofy things, yes. And when he gave me an interview and made the statement, "I play when I want to play"—well, that follows him to this day. If you read the whole interview, it wasn't that bad, but people pounced on those seven words.

Despite all the controversy and the crazy things Moss did, it was a huge mistake to trade him. He was the greatest receiver the Vikings have ever had. He was the greatest offensive player they've ever had. He also did a lot of good things without getting publicity, such as raising tons of money for St. Joseph's Children's Home.

I also think Moss made Daunte Culpepper what he was as a quarterback for a few years. Once he didn't have Moss, Culpepper was a much different player.

There's no doubt that owner Red McCombs forced the Moss trade on coach Mike Tice and the front office after the 2004 season. Moss wasn't traded because of his conduct, but because Red was so cheap.

The Vikings wanted to sign three or four free agents, and McCombs told the front office that if they wanted to spend that money, they would have to balance it by trading Moss.

The franchise hasn't been the same since the Moss trade. It hasn't been the same for Randy, either, stuck in Oakland with a lousy team.

McCombs was here for one reason: to make a killing financially. He did that, but in the process, he did a lot of damage to the Vikings with his frugality. Coach Tice never had a chance to make the Vikings a serious contender, because Red wouldn't spend anywhere near the salary cap, and he wouldn't pay the going rate for assistant coaches.

Red was the champion BS'er of all-time. He paid $220 million for the entire Vikings operation in 1998. He later sold the Vikings catering service for $28 million, received $30-40 million in expansion checks from Cleveland and Houston, and then sold the club to Zygi Wilf for $640 million.

Add that up. Before taxes, Red walked out of Minnesota, after seven years, with a profit of nearly a half-billion dollars.

He also walked right into the Vikings' 15-1 season. He had nothing to do with putting that team together.

I still believe that, of all the disappointments we've had in my time in Minnesota sports, losing the NFC title game to Atlanta following that '98 season was the worst ever. The only thing close was in 1967, when a great Twins team went into Boston needing to win one of two games to get to the World Series, and they lost two games that they had chances to win.

But the Vikings' loss to Atlanta—that was probably the worst, because everybody in town was absolutely convinced that the team was headed to the Super Bowl for the first time in more than two decades. The fact that they lost because of a missed field goal by the usually sure-footed kicker Gary Anderson (he hadn't missed one all season) only made it that much more difficult to swallow. The Vikings lost, 30-27, in overtime.

I remember walking to my car in a parking ramp later that night, and people were screaming at me. I was afraid I was going to get beat up because the Vikings weren't going to the Super Bowl.

The team returned to the NFC championship game two years later, but were embarrassed, 41-0, by an ordinary Giants team. That was the beginning of a real falloff for the franchise. Red's cheapness was finally taking its toll.

Coach Denny Green left with one game left in the 2001 season. People continue to say he was fired, but he wanted to be let go. He told me during that season, "This organization is done. Cris Carter is coming to the end of his career. Randall McDaniel is gone. We had the tragic situation with Korey Stringer. And Red won't spend any money to fill the holes."

Denny practically told me was quitting. It worked perfectly for him when Red let him go. Green got to leave, and Red still had to pay him.

Fortunately, Red finally sold the team in 2005. New owner Zygi Wilf stood back that season, but then he fired Tice and brought in his own coach in Brad Childress. It was a rough first season—6-10 in 2006—but I think Childress is going to do well, eventually.

For sure, the Vikings are a lot better off with Wilf as owner than they were with McCombs.

What makes sports great is that you never know. The situation with the Twins is Exhibit A. Back in 1997, things looked absolutely hopeless. The franchise was in the midst of eight straight losing seasons.

A decade later, they had the American League's Most Valuable Player (Justin Morneau), the Cy Young Award winner for the second time in three years (Johan Santana), and the only catcher in history to win an American League batting title (Joe Mauer).

Twins owner Carl Pohlad has been remarkably loyal to the main people running the organization. He shook things up after the 1986 season, and since then, he's had two team presidents (Jerry Bell and Dave St. Peter), two general managers (Andy MacPhail and Terry Ryan), and two managers (Tom Kelly and Ron Gardenhire).

For a brief period in 2000, the Pohlads brought in Chris Clouser, a family friend and former Northwest Airlines executive, to be the CEO. That didn't work out for the Twins or for Clouser. He received a lot of ridicule for trying to set up a temporary outdoor stadium in Bloomington and play a series to generate momentum for a new ballpark.

Clouser also floated the idea of firing Tom Kelly to the Pohlads. That was never going to happen. Carl wasn't going to fire a manager who had done as much for him—a man he was as close to—as Kelly.

The Twins don't fire anybody. They are loyal. And when Carl gives somebody authority, that person is allowed to make decisions. It was Dave St. Peter's call, and his alone, to leave WCCO Radio after forty-six years and sign a radio contract with Stan Hubbard and KSTP.

As someone who knows how much CCO has done for the Twins over the years, I think it's a decision the Twins will live to regret, but Carl let St. Peter make the call.

The Pohlads have changed the way they operate a lot in recent years. When the Twins weren't drawing fans in the 1990s, and the league had very little revenue sharing, the payroll went to rock bottom. The team also wasn't doing a great job of developing players. When revenue sharing came in, Carl didn't put that money away in the bank; he spent it on payroll.

Back in the 1990s, I wrote in my column that Carl should spend money for a certain player. He sent me a bottle of red ink, with a note attached that said, "If the Twins did what you want them to do, they would be out of business."

Mr. Commissioner
Greeting NFL commissioner Paul Tagliabue at a press conference.

299

The Twins have been both good and lucky in recent years. For instance, in 2001, the Twins had the first choice in the amateur draft, and they went with Mauer, the catcher from Cretin-Derham Hall. I was one of the few media guys who said the Twins should take Mauer. Most everyone else got on them for not taking Mark Prior, a pitcher from Southern Cal who was being lauded as big-league ready.

Prior signed with the Cubs and was in the majors in 2002. The Twins could have used another starter like him, and they got a lot of heat for taking Mauer instead of Prior.

Now, a few years later, Prior has been laid up much of the time with injuries. Mauer was an all-star and league batting champion in 2006, at age 23.

It's a contest between Mauer and Dave Winfield as to who is the greatest all-around high school athlete we've had in Minnesota. Mauer was the best football player in the state, the best baseball player, and an outstanding basketball player. Winfield was a great pitcher, a great hitter, and a big-time college basketball player, and he was chosen in the NFL draft, even though he didn't play the sport.

Beyond Mauer, the Twins were both lucky and good in getting Justin Morneau. He was the team's third-round pick in 1999, behind outfielder B. J. Garbe and catcher Rob Bowen. Garbe was a complete bust. Bowen never did anything for the Twins. And Morneau, a kid from British Columbia, is the league MVP at age 25.

As I said, you never know.

The Twins' longest battle over the past decade was for the new stadium. The bill finally passed, at four o'clock in the morning on the last day of the 2006 legislative session. Months later, they were still waiting to start digging the site for the new stadium. But when the ballpark does get done, it will be a great boon for downtown Minneapolis, which really needs something.

Dean Johnson, the leader of the Senate at the time, and Steve Sviggum, then the Speaker of the House, deserve a lot of credit for being able to steer the ballpark bill through the legislature. It's a shame that Johnson was defeated in the next election—not because he was pro-stadium, but because the anti–gay rights people did everything they could to beat him.

I got grief for years for the way I pushed for a Twins stadium. When my grandkids were in school, other kids would say to them:

"My daddy doesn't like your grandpa. He doesn't want to pay taxes for a stadium."

Then, in January 2007, Hennepin County started collecting the tax—0.15 percent, or three cents on $20—and I don't think anyone who is paying the tax has noticed.

One great guy the Twins have had who carried over from the worst days and helped lead them to the division title was Torii Hunter. Kirby Puckett took Hunter under his wing, and as a leader and a good guy, Torii became another Kirby.

If I were to name the top five Twins who you'd like as a person and a player, Torii and Kirby would both be on the list. Kirby's death in the spring of 2006 hit Torii hard; it hit every Minnesotan who followed the Twins hard.

I don't think Kirby was ever the same emotionally after he lost the sight in his right eye and was forced to retire in 1996. He put up the good front, and he certainly was thrilled to get into the Hall of Fame, but to love the game as much as he did and have it taken away so abruptly, it hurt him a lot.

If you look at Twins history, who would be Mr. Baseball? There have been a lot of great players, a lot of great people, but there's no doubt that the number one Twins player of all-time was Kirby Puckett.

Glen Taylor, the owner of the Timberwolves, is a lot like Carl Pohlad. If you're one of his guys, you're going to get every chance to be successful. Glen stuck with Kevin McHale as the boss of his basketball operation when a lot of people—the public, the local press, even the national media—called for him to be fired.

I go back with McHale to when he was a senior at Hibbing High School and playing in the state tournament. He's one of the all-time great Gophers, a great NBA player, and a guy with a wonderful personality.

All the criticism has been tough on him. He's made some mistakes, and the biggest came in the 2003 NBA Draft. The Timberwolves had the twenty-eighth pick, and they got a big break when Josh Howard from Wake Forest, the ACC player of the year, was still available.

Some experts thought he was undersized for an NBA forward, but at the twenty-eighth spot, when you looked at the available players, everyone seemed to agree: Howard was a no-brainer.

For some reason, McHale took Ndudi Ebi, a skinny high school player out of Houston. As it turned out, Ebi couldn't play a lick, and Howard turned into an all-star for the Dallas Mavericks.

The Timberwolves received a bad blow when Commissioner David Stern took away five first-round draft choices after it was discovered that the team had made an illegal, under-the-table deal with forward Joe Smith. Then, Stern gave them back one first-round pick, in 2003, and they messed it up by taking Ebi.

That can't happen. A team can't go five seasons, from 2000 to 2004, with one just first-rounder—and screw that up—and hope to recover.

The Wolves did have the great playoff run in 2004, after bringing in Latrell Sprewell and Sam Cassell during the off-season, but that team came apart in a hurry. The Timberwolves are hurting, and it's hard to see how they are going to get back into contention.

I know one thing: The answer is not trading Kevin Garnett. He's one of the greatest athletes in all my time covering Minnesota sports—certainly, the greatest basketball player, along with George Mikan.

Another mistake, along with drafting Ebi, was firing coach Flip Saunders with thirty games left in the 2004–05 season. A coach takes you to the Western Conference Finals one spring, and you fire him before the end of the next season?

It's been proven, obviously, that Flip wasn't the problem. I felt sorry for Dwane Casey, too, when he was fired just twenty games into the 2006–07 season. If Casey had a fault, it was that he was too nice a guy.

The Wolves have made bad decisions, and they've also had terrible luck. Malik Sealy was killed by a drunken driver in May 2000. Other careers have been cut short by injuries. And they had the Joe Smith disaster—which I'm still convinced was a Taylor deal, not McHale's.

Hopefully, they can get a break in the next couple of years and make another playoff run with Garnett. Because they often have not had the right players surrounding Garnett, I don't think people in Minnesota have fully appreciated his greatness.

He's a good guy, too. With all the money he's made, he still competes hard every night.

Norm Coleman, then the mayor of St. Paul, gets a lot of credit for getting an NHL expansion team and a new arena. He worked at it, obviously, but Governor Arne Carlson had more to do with it.

There are always legislators with pet projects. During the 1998 session, Carlson told every one of those people, "If you want your project, vote for the hockey arena in St. Paul."

They wound up with a terrific building, the Xcel Energy Center. It was sort of like Baltimore's Camden Yards was for baseball, the first of the new-style ballparks that have been built all over the country. The Xcel was the first of the new-style hockey arenas, with big, roomy concourses that are open to the action below. People waiting in line for a beer can see into the arena.

The Wild draws a different crowd than the hockey cult the North Stars had in Bloomington. This is a younger crowd, including young families from the suburbs, and even after a half-dozen seasons, people seem to have a good time every night.

Eventually, the Wild will have to win at a higher rate, but for now, the team still is enjoying a honeymoon period with the fans.

The guy who put everything together for the Wild was Jac Sperling. He's as sharp at marketing an organization as anyone you can find. Sperling made a good move in hiring Doug Risebrough as general manager, and then Risebrough made the perfect hire for the team's coach: Jacques Lemaire.

Lemaire came with a reputation as the best coach in the league, and he gave the Wild instant credibility. He led the Wild to the Western Conference Finals in 2003 with a team that probably didn't even belong in the playoffs.

Jacques, in his own way, is a great salesman. He starts talking about hockey, and he knows so much more than his audience that he just gets them in his pocket.

The Wild can get beat 5-1, and you come out of a Jacques press conference convinced that the only problem was a couple of bad breaks. He's the master—and there hasn't been a coach this secure in his job in Minnesota since Bud Grant.

The Wild could lose ten in a row, and nobody would say a word criticizing Jacques.

Testimonial dinner
With my close personal friend George Steinbrenner at the testimonial dinner honoring my fifty years with WCCO, in 2005.

Ten years ago we were celebrating Clem Haskins leading the Gopher men's basketball team to the NCAA Final Four for the first time. The mob of folks that followed the Gophers and Bobby Jackson to San Antonio for the Midwest Regional was amazing. It was like a home game when they beat Clemson and then UCLA in the Alamodome.

I liked Clem, both as a coach and as a man I considered a friend. And the public loved him. He kept Williams Arena full for Big Ten games and any other important games.

People scream at me, tell me I'm crazy when I say that I don't think Clem knew everything that was going on with Jan Gangelhoff writing papers for players. Clem told me exactly that in private conversations: He didn't know she was writing papers for the players.

I do know that Clem put a lot of pressure to make sure his players stayed eligible, and some people took it from there.

Then, there was the incident in Champagne, Illinois, that caused the accusations of academic fraud to come out in the St. Paul newspaper.

Players Eric Harris and Russ Archambault had gone out the night before a game. They had a couple of beers and stayed out past curfew. Clem benched Harris, a starter, for the first half of one game, and he threw Archambault off the team.

Archambault had had other problems, and Harris hadn't, but Archambault's family felt he had been wronged. His mother knew Gangelhoff, and she helped put Gangelhoff in touch with George Dohrman from the St. Paul newspaper.

All hell broke loose. The story broke the day before the Gophers were going to play Gonzaga in the first round of the 1999 NCAA tournament. The Gophers played the game shorthanded and lost. A few months later, Clem was bought out and the Gonzaga coach, Dan Monson, was hired here.

There was such fallout from the academic-fraud scandal that Monson had a hard time getting even marginal players to come to the university. Clem went to the Final Four because he was able to recruit Bobby Jackson from a junior college. Monson didn't have a chance to get a player with that background, and those guys are often the difference-makers.

In March 2006, as the Gophers were getting ready for an NIT tournament game in Cincinnati, our newspaper, the *Star Tribune*, reported that Monson was going to be fired at season's end.

I wasn't involved in that story. As it turned out, Monson wasn't fired. Athletic Director Joel Maturi announced the next day that Monson was coming back, but that story killed any chance of recruiting for Monson. He was fired seven games into the 2006–07 season.

The atmosphere in "The Barn" really has gone downhill. There are rows of empty seats, even for Big Ten games. There's one guy who could have filled Williams Arena right away—Bobby Knight—but the Gophers didn't have the guts to take a run at him.

I was as surprised as anyone when Maturi and the university president, Robert Bruininks, decided to fire Glen Mason as the football coach on the last day of 2006.

I've said time and again, there must be some reason that the Gophers haven't had even a piece of the Big Ten title since 1967, long before Mason came on the scene. The administration's lack of adequate support for the football program has had a lot more to do with the Gophers being a second-division program than having inadequate coaches.

Mason was here for ten years and proved he was a good coach. He beat Penn State regularly. He beat Ohio State. He beat Michigan once, and had a couple of other chances. He won some bowl games.

Mason's biggest problem was the press. He shouldn't have read newspapers. Every time he saw something that was negative, he would get angry.

He would tell me, "That clipping is going to be in every coach's hands, and they are going to pass it on to recruits." He really let it bother him, especially in 2006, when the *Star Tribune* ran a story on running back Gary Russell's academic situation. That's another story that was overblown by us, in my opinion.

The public's reaction to Mason's replacement, Tim Brewster, was very positive. Brewster is an outgoing guy, a real salesman. But if the administration doesn't get on board, and he doesn't win, the new stadium on campus will be only seventy percent full within a few years, and things will be like they have been for the last forty years: mediocre, at best.

One area where the Gophers have no worries is men's hockey. Coach Don Lucia has the best college hockey job in the country, and he takes full advantage.

Doug Woog won a lot of games as coach, and he is a wonderful person. But Woog didn't run the same tight ship as does Lucia.

Hockey parents can drive coaches crazy, even at the highest collegiate level, but not Lucia. The parents don't run Lucia. He runs them. He tells the parents he'll talk about anything with them, except hockey.

Minnesota has never had an athlete who meant more to a sport than Lindsay Whalen did to women's basketball. When she arrived at the University of Minnesota as a freshman in the fall of 2000, the Gopher women's team was playing at the Sports Pavilion and not drawing enough fans to pay the electric bill.

They were terrible, and completely off the radar of the Minnesota sports scene.

Four years later, they were filling Williams Arena for NCAA tournament games, and it was as loud in there as it has ever been for a men's game.

Brenda Oldfield (now Frese) had something to do with the turnaround when she came in as coach in 2001–02, and so did Janel McCarville when she arrived that same year. But Whalen, the young woman from Hutchinson, was the phenomenon, the drawing card.

The thing about Whalen was, when people came to watch her, they were never disappointed. She always delivered.

There's never been a dumber move than the Lynx, Minnesota's WNBA team, not making a deal with the Connecticut Sun to get Whalen. If they had to give up the whole franchise for Whalen, it would be a good deal.

I'll say it again: Nobody—not Kirby, not Garnett, not Moss—has had as great an impact on a sport in Minnesota than Whalen had with women's basketball. It was nothing, and she made it something special in 2004 when she led the Gophers to the Final Four.

Speaking of phenomenons, Tiger Woods was here for the 2002 PGA Championship at Hazeltine National—and he didn't disappoint.

It was great when we had Jack Nicklaus and Arnold Palmer here for big tournaments in years gone by, but the galleries that followed Woods around were unbelievable. He's the Pied Piper out there.

He birdied the last three holes at Hazeltine on the final day. My son, Chad, the golfer, tells me that's as tough as any three-hole stretch. You can't make three birdies, but Tiger did, and nearly pulled out a dramatic, come-from-behind victory.

The crowds will be bigger, and chasing Tiger as enthusiastically as ever, when he comes back to Hazeltine for the 2009 PGA tournament.

I received two big honors in recent years. In 2003, I was given the Curt Gowdy Award as the print media representative at the Basketball Hall of Fame in Springfield, Massachusetts.

For me, it was totally unexpected. It also had special meaning, since I went way back with Gowdy. I was close with Bud Wilkinson when he was coaching Oklahoma to national championships, and I would go to a game or two a year. Gowdy was the Sooners' play-by-play man, and we got to be good friends.

To get an award named after a man I respected as much as Curt Gowdy was a tremendous feeling.

In 2005, a testimonial dinner was held to celebrate my fifty years on WCCO Radio. To have all those people show up—Bud Selig, Bobby Knight, Lou Holtz, George Steinbrenner, and all the top local people—was very moving for me.

Some people felt that the fact that the money was going to the University of Minnesota's athletic department was a conflict of interest. We raised over $500,000, and the money was put in an account for scholarships for minority football players. They are going to use it after I pass away.

I can't figure out how that's a bad thing.

Bud Grant was the local sports figure who spoke to the crowd. He got a little choked up talking about our friendship, which goes back to 1946. And I got choked up listening to him.

Of all the people I've met in sports through the years, my relationship with Bud is unique. He's my best friend.

Index

Aaron, Hank, *92, 274*
Abbott, Allen, *260*
Abdul-Jabbar, Kareem, *223*
Adams, Cedric, *231, 232–233, 234, 237*
Alcindor, Lew, *see* Abdul-Jabbar, Kareem
Alderman, Grady, *142*
Alderman, Willie, *45*
Alexander, Todd, *224*
Ali, Muhammad, *283–284*
Alioto, Joe, *141*
Allen, Bernie, *99*
Allen, George, *235*
Allison, Bob, *99, 100, 102–103, 247*
All-Star Game,
    baseball, *85, 101, 132, 276*
    college football, *53, 210, 252, 276*
Alpert, Mike, *67*
Alpert, Mikey, *105*
American Association (baseball), *79, 93*
American Basketball Association (ABA), *215, 245*
American Basketball League (ABL), *245*
American Football League (AFL), *89, 90*
American League (baseball), *79, 85, 97, 298*
Anderson, Gary, *297*
Anderson, Red, *260*
Anderson, Sparky, *235*
Archambault, Russ, *305*
Arizona State University, *33, 264–265, 293*
Armstrong, Ike, *61, 63, 189, 192, 251, 254*
Army (football), *241, 278–279*
Aschenbrenner, Frank, *56*
Ashland College, *209*
Atkins, Doug, *114*
Auerbach, Red, *72, 75, 76*
Baer, Maxie, *105*
Baldwin, Howard, *199*
Balfour, Barbara, *263–264*
Baltimore Bullets, *205*
Baltimore Colts, *35*
Baltimore Orioles, *132*
Banks, Tommy, *42, 44*
Barnhill, Dave, *81, 93*
Barreiro, Dan, *265*
Basketball Association of America (BAA), *68, 72*
Baston, Bert, *56, 59*
Battey, Earl, *99, 247*
Bay, Rick, *225, 270*
Beard, Ralph, *221–222*
Behagen, Ron, *209, 210–211*
Bell, Bert, *89*

Bell, Bobby Lee, *134*
Bell, Jerry, *298*
Bellamy, Walter, *204–205*
Bengtson, Phil, *34*
Berger, Ben, *67, 68, 77, 88, 192, 257, 260*
Berkow, Ira, *24–25, 273*
Berman, Chickie, *42, 44, 45*
Berman, Dave, *45*
Bidwill, Bill, *255*
Bidwill, Vi, *88*
Bierman, Bernie, *13, 50, 51, 55, 56, 59, 118, 119–120, 137, 229, 254*
Bingham, Howard, *284*
Bird, Larry, *215, 242*
Bjorklund, Bob, *62*
Blackmun, Harry, *149*
Blaik, Bob, *279*
Blaik, Colonel Earl, *63, 278–279*
Blair, Wren, *192–193, 196*
Blaska, Duane, *134*
Bloedel, Bill, *62*
Blumenfeld, Isadore, *42, 44*
Boivin, Bill, *121*
Boni, Bill, *125*
Boros, Julius, *258*
Bostock, Lyman, *150*
Boston Braves, *81, 253*
Boston Bruins, *192*
Boston Celtics, *73, 75, 77, 281*
Boston Red Sox, *79–80, 85, 88*
Boston, McKinley, *270–271*
Boswell, Dave, *132*
Boyer, Bill, *83, 86, 89, 108, 145, 180*
Boyer, Clete, *81*
Brackin, Dennis, *291*
Braman, Norman, *179, 180*
Brandt, Gil, *158*
Brawl, The, *210*
Breuer, Randy, *213*
Brewer, Jim, *167, 207, 209, 211*
Brewster, Tim, *295, 306*
Briere, Tom, *94, 230, 231*
Brody, Sam, *43*
Brokaw, Tom, *1*
Brooklyn Dodgers, *83*
Brooks, Dave, *202*
Brooks, Herb, *189, 196–198, 200, 202, 216–217*
Brooks, Patti, *197*
Brophy, George, *94, 97, 172, 288*
Broten, Neal, *194*
Brown, Paul, *13, 57, 90, 117*
Brown, Tom, *66*
Brown, Walter, *77, 204, 281*
Broyles, Frank, *65, 158*
Bruininks, Robert, *305*

313

For more stories and insight from the Upper Midwest's number one sports journalist:

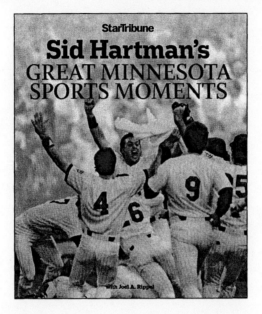

Sid Hartman's Great Minnesota Sports Moments

Get the inside history of Minnesota sports as only Sid Hartman can tell it!

From the glory years of the original Millers, Saints, Lakers, and North Stars to today's Gophers, Twins, Vikings, Wolves, and Wild, Hartman recounts the top sports stories that have given Minnesotans something to cheer about, from "Killer" and Kirby to KG.

Legendary *Star Tribune* sportswriter Sid Hartman has been on the front lines of Minnesota sports for more than six decades. Now, Sid collects the big stories and locker-room scoops to chronicle the state's sporting highs—and lows.

More than 200 action-packed photographs from the *Star Tribune*'s award-winning photographers bring the legends to life, making this an attractive book for every Minnesotan's coffee table.

Hardcover, 176 pages, 100 color and 140 black-and-white photos, $29.95
ISBN-13: 978-0-7603-2656-5; ISBN-10: 0-7603-2656-8

Visit **voyageurpress.com** or call **1.800-826-6600**